ACTIVITY THEORY

Studies in Critical Social Sciences Book Series

Haymarket Books is proud to be working with Brill Academic Publishers (www.brill.nl) to republish the *Studies in Critical Social Sciences* book series in paperback editions. This peer-reviewed book series offers insights into our current reality by exploring the content and consequences of power relationships under capitalism, and by considering the spaces of opposition and resistance to these changes that have been defining our new age. Our full catalog of *SCSS* volumes can be viewed at https://www.haymarketbooks .org/series_collections/4-studies-in-critical-social-sciences.

ACTIVITY THEORY

A Critical Overview

ANDY BLUNDEN

Haymarket Books
Chicago, IL

First published in 2023 by Brill Academic Publishers, The Netherlands
© 2023 Koninklijke Brill NV, Leiden, The Netherlands

Published in paperback in 2024 by
Haymarket Books
P.O. Box 180165
Chicago, IL 60618
773-583-7884
www.haymarketbooks.org

ISBN: 979-8-88890-240-0

Distributed to the trade in the US through Consortium Book Sales and
Distribution (www.cbsd.com) and internationally through Ingram Publisher
Services International (www.ingramcontent.com).

This book was published with the generous support of Lannan Foundation,
Wallace Action Fund, and the Marguerite Casey Foundation.

Special discounts are available for bulk purchases by organizations and
institutions. Please call 773-583-7884 or email info@haymarketbooks.org for more
information.

Cover design by Jamie Kerry and Ragina Johnson.

Printed in the United States.

Library of Congress Cataloging-in-Publication data is available.

Contents

PART 1
Basic Principles of Activity Theory

PART 2
Diverse Research in Activity Theory

Preface

Activity Theory is a powerful theory for the transformation of human life in pursuit of social justice and emancipation. Its origins lie in the aftermath of the Russian Revolution of 1917, but its journey over the following century has been long and difficult. The insights of its founders, which had the potential to transform the human sciences, are still to be fully realised. Activity theorists have innovated and improvised on the foundations laid by its founders and have implemented many brilliant projects. However, there has not been sufficient reflection on the fundamental concepts of the theory to ensure that these innovations are integrated within the theory, generalised and taken into broader fields of research and intervention. That is my aim here.

I shall use the term "Activity Theory" to refer to that whole family of practices variously know as "CHAT – Cultural Historical Activity Theory," "Sociocultural theory" or "Cultural Psychology," all having their origins in the work of Lev Vygotsky (1896–1934). I emphasise that I regard Activity Theory, in this sense, as a *family* of practices sharing grandparents but which over the years, like any family, has diverged in interests and characteristics. The work I did with *An Interdisciplinary Theory of Activity* (Blunden, 2010), was to trace the thread connecting the members of this family and how they have diverged, by following the use and interpretation of Vygotsky's epoch making idea of "unit of analysis." This is the concept which established Activity Theory's heritage in Hegel and Marx. It is the concept from which Hegel opened each of the sciences outlined in his *Encyclopaedia*, and the key which opened Marx's *Capital*, Vygotsky's magnum opus, *Thinking and Speech* and Leontyev's theory of activity. Now my aim is to critically review the work which has been subsequently done by activity theorists, notwithstanding some theoretical limitations, and assert the concepts from which this current of thinking set out. My aim is to see that a clear, consistent theoretical framework for Activity Theory comes into view. I do not limit myself to domains where activity theorists have been active, but also venture into territory which has hitherto lain outside the scope of our work.

Vygotsky founded a general theory of psychology. But because of its orientation to the socio-cultural determination of the mind, the context of its founding in the wake of the October Revolution, and its roots in Hegel and Marx, Activity Theory is by its very nature an interdisciplinary theory of human life. Activity theorists see that human beings are what they are in the context of the activities they participate in and are committed to. Human beings isolated from the activities that animate and sustain them (and have done so in the past) are not fully human beings at all. Activity Theory could be called a "non-psychological" theory of the mind, inasmuch as it sees subjectivity as located *between* people rather than inside them. The history of human culture, carried forward in the artefacts we have created and passed on to later generations and the activities we have invented, has a pervasive influence on everything we are. To be a human being is to acquire this culture, use it, modify it and pass it on to the next generation. These artefacts include spoken words, signs, tools, the land on which we live and the air we breathe. Regrettably, human activity is threatening to destroy the capacity of our natural inheritance to any longer provide the conditions for human life. The task of modifying human activities so as to guarantee not only social justice but the very conditions for human life is pressing.

Activity Theory sees "activity" as an aggregate of activities, each oriented to some ideal, the maintenance and perfection of some aspect of human life, and each characterised by its own norms and rules, its own tools and techniques, organised around the achievement of its central motivation. That ideal could be restoring people to health, providing them with food, raising them from childhood or selling them cigarettes. Nonetheless, in what is to follow I shall deal with the fact that the activity's ideal, its object-concept, is not always or even usually clear, stable or fully developed, and people participate in such activities for their own reasons and not necessarily through commitment to the object-concept.

We understand that it is the experiences through which people pass in the course of following through on the commitments they have made that their personalities are formed. We use the Russian word *perezhivaniya* for those experiences which from time to time dramatically reshape a person's life as they confront sometimes impossible situations and deal with them. But we understand that in general, if someone is suffering then the best thing we can do is to help them change their situation rather than medicate them or apply a talking cure. The crisis of humanity will not be solved by pharmacology or surgery.

In what follows I shall draw extensively on interventions carried out by fellow activity theorists around the world. In addition to sharing these inspiring projects I shall show how they demonstrate the need to further develop the concepts first devised in the early days of the USSR. This broadening of Activity Theory is necessary to facilitate its application to a wider field of phenomena than those which have been its main focus to date.

A first glance, the notion of "an activity" may seem to limit the scope of the theory. But this is not the case. "Activity" is a particular lens which can be applied to any of the human sciences. It is a lens which generates insights into human life, in particular exactly *how* social and cultural situations constrain and form the human personality and how these processes can be changed. It gives insight into people's motivation and how, from being products of their circumstances, people can learn to control their own behaviour and change their situations, including the transformation of the institutions and projects in which they participate. But there is no particular boundary around the domain in which Activity Theory can provide insights.

Insofar as Activity Theory has focused on particular types of problem – namely, psychology, education, disability, child and youth development and organisational change – this is an historical accident. It originates from its origins in Stalin's USSR, under conditions where social theory was forbidden as a topic for scientific discussion, as any deviation from official orthodoxy risked being seen as treasonous. Then later in the United States, any variety of Marxism was taboo in scientific circles and not understood by the general public. This context no longer exists, as Activity Theory has taken root on every continent, and while Marxism is still marginalised it is not taboo. Further, the most pressing problems confronting humanity are those manifest on the plane of social theory, rather than the restricted plane of psychology. We need to change institutions and practices, not fix individual victims.

My own view of Activity Theory draws on the well-known Russian figures: Lev Vygotsky, Alexander Luria, A.N. Leontyev, Evald Ilyenkov, Vasily Davydov et al., as well as contemporary figures like Mike Cole and Yrjö Engeström. However, I read all these through the lens of Marx and Hegel. For example, all activity theorists claim to use the concept of "unit of analysis," but because they lack a background in Hegel and Marx, *all* of the present generation of activity theorists use garbled versions of the idea in their work. No one of these figures is absolutely authoritative, but as a current of practice which continuously clarifies and corrects itself, all its principal ideas can be grasped without ambiguity if seen in the context of the entire current of theory from Hegel and Marx onwards.

My close reading of Hegel and Marx over decades gives me the confidence to stand by the explanations I give of the foundational principles of Activity Theory even if other activity theorists have written differently. Activity Theory is not "what activity theorists think." It is what follows with necessity from the foundations laid by Hegel, Marx and Vygotsky and a commitment to social justice and human emancipation.

Acknowledgements

It was conversations with Tim Dornan which gave me the impetus to write this book and the frequent reference below to medical institutions and professions and the application of Activity Theory in these contexts is owed in large measure to Tim's advice and the work of his younger colleagues in the UK's NHS. Tim also gave me invaluable advice on the technique of writing. All errors and misunderstandings of course are mine and my responsibility and no one else's.

In addition, I owe a particular debt to Morten Nissen whose work with social workers in Copenhagen helped me clarify my ideas in relation to the concept of an "activity." I also owe a great debt to John Cripps Clark, Nick Hopwood, Megan Anakin and Ivana Guarrasi in particular for their critical feedback on my work over the past couple of years. Bridget Leach and Julian Williams both read my manuscript for style and clarity. Laya Hooshyari has given invaluable advice based on her experience as a clinical psychologist by challenging and encouraging my work in a number of areas. Fernanda Liberali, Monica Lemos, Aydin Bal, Paul Ernest, Brecht de Smet, Eduardo Vianna and Helena Worthen kindly contributed copious insights acquired in their exemplary interventions using Activity Theory. It was the innovative work of Tim Dornan and these other practitioners which encouraged me to complete this work. I also thank Sohrab Rezvani, Laya Hooshyari, Julian Williams and Beth Ferholt for their productive discussions on *perezhivanie* in movies. For whatever I have achieved over the past 20 years I owe an inestimable debt to Mike Cole at UCSD and to David Fasenfest for recognising my work as worthy of publication.

Figures and Tables

Figures

Tables

PART 1

Basic Principles of Activity Theory

∴

CHAPTER 1

Introduction

Activity Theory is the science which takes social life to be an aggregate of *activities*. This is what it means to say that it takes activities as "units of analysis." When introduced in 1934 by Vygotsky it was an historic innovation in the human sciences. Later on, in the body of this work, you will find ample examples and illustrations of the basic concepts of Activity Theory which I am about to outline. The examples are needed to help you grasp the concepts securely and integrate them into your research and the practical programs you plan to implement.

But first, I will briefly outline the foundations which underlie Activity Theory. It will not be hard for you to find statements by well-known activity theorists or even declarations by Marx himself, which contradict what I say. The concepts of Activity Theory cannot easily be read off the pages of books written in this current of thinking, because, unfortunately, not everyone uses the relevant terms in the same way. Were we to require general agreement on our terminology and concepts, at this point, we would have nothing to work with at all. My explanation of the concepts and terms is based on following the entire development of concepts from Hegel and Marx, through Vygotsky and the Soviet Activity Theorists, observing when from time to time important aspects of concepts have been lost or become mixed up with other concepts. Equally, some concepts introduced by the earliest and most esteemed of our founding writers have not withstood the test of time and have necessarily been abandoned or modified and later writers have indeed creatively developed the concepts of Activity Theory. Reading current Activity Theory as an historically elaborated whole like this makes it possible to separate error from truth.

In the end, what I am offering in this introduction is a more or less consistent set of foundational concepts for Activity Theory research and intervention. Following the introduction, I will critically review a range of projects conducted by Activity Theorists in the light of the fundamental concepts of Activity Theory.

1   Behaviour, Consciousness and Activity

Science must have as its subject matter a substance which is *objective*, that is to say, objects or processes which can be experienced from differing points of view and yet despite differing appearances *be the same thing*. The need for an objective subject matter was the first great stumbling block which psychology faced in the nineteenth century. Human behaviour could be observed, but the inner workings of the minds of the actors could not. And yet everything that human beings do passes through their consciousness; how could we understand human behaviour unless we understood what was going on in the consciousness of the human actors?

Introspection did not provide such an objective subject matter for psychology because (1) unmediated observation is restricted to only one point of view, that of the subject themself, (2) the subject's observing of their own consciousness essentially modifies what is observed, and (3) people are not reliable reporters of their own state of mind. So it is not sufficient to ask what someone is thinking and presume that you have thereby a record of their consciousness. Further, putting one's state of mind into spoken words is itself a demanding task which inevitably *transforms* what is being described. In general, asking someone what they are thinking is just one clue as to their consciousness, but one would be a fool to think that what you are told is necessarily the unvarnished truth.

As a result, in the nineteenth century two currents of psychology emerged. The first was *Cultural Psychology*, whose subject matter was the vast and rich field of cultural production – art, literature, institutions, and so on – objective manifestations of the mind in real human life (e.g., Wundt's *Völkerpsychologie* or Dilthey's *Geisteswissenschaften*). The second was *Physiological* or "brass instrument" *Psychology* (e.g., Helmholtz, Pavlov et al.), which could, for example, measure the time taken for a stimulus on the tip of a finger to reach the brain, or detect changes in the heartbeat betraying a lie.

However, Cultural Psychology could *describe* the activity of consciousness in vivid colours, but it could not *explain* consciousness at all, while on the other hand, Physiological Psychology could *explain* psychological phenomena but its scope was limited to the *trivia* of human life.

Lev Vygotsky (1896–1938), the founder of Activity Theory (in the broad definition which I am using here), was successful in uniting the *rich content* of Cultural Psychology with the *objectivity* of experimental science hitherto limited to the trivial domain of Physiological Psychology. Looking back at his work from the present, we can say that he did this by means of the concept of *activity*, and in particular, by means of the concept of *an artefact mediated action* – in which an individual uses a product of the wider culture, be it a spoken word, a tool or a sign – to do something.

People using an artefact to solve some task, such as using an alarm clock to wake up on time, or using a label to remember what is in a jar, or a word to comfort a friend, are activities which can be observed in the laboratory. By varying the task and the means provided for solving the task a researcher can observe how culture forms human activity before their very eyes.

Hitherto, science had tried to understand the relationship between human beings and the world through the model of the philosopher contemplating a natural object. We could say that an observer looking at a natural object was the unit of analysis for epistemology.

What this conception missed was (1) that the relation of the mind to the world is an *active* one; we must look in order to see, (2) the object and the observer are not foreign to one another, but are generally both part of the same culture, and (3) when we do something we always *use* something handed down to us by our forebears to do so. So long as we think of perception as if we were a bit of photographic paper on which an object leaves an imprint, we can never understand human action. Our ideas are not just reactions to external stimuli. The cultural products we incorporate into our activity are *part* of our activity. In that sense, the products – land, tools, words, signs – of the activity of other people far away and long ago, are introduced into our actions from an early age and become part of our activity. This enculturation is accomplished thanks to collaborators who have helped form us as members of a certain community at a certain time and place by providing us with these artefacts and setting the problems we have to solve with them. This is how we come to act more or less like others in the same community and know about the objects to be found in our environment.

"Activity" differs from "behaviour" in that behaviour is what is observable in what people do, *abstracted from* their reasons for doing it, their conscious-ness. Behaviour is the subject matter of Behaviourism. If consistently carried out, Behaviourism could lay claim to being an objective science, but as with Physiological Psychology, its domain of explanation is extremely limited. Behaviourism and Physiological Psychology together constitute "Objective Psychology." But everything that people *do* – apart from physiological reac-tions such as producing goose bumps or sneezing – passes through the mind and can only be understood to the extent that we can understand the reasons people have for what they do. Two different people can do the same thing for different reasons or do different things in response to the same stimuli, so it is impossible to explain anything but the most trivial of responses so long as one ignores consciousness as an explanatory principle.

For Activity Theory, "consciousness" refers to the *totality* of psychic processes mediating between physiology and behaviour as such (See Figure 1). That is, for us "consciousness" includes not only conscious awareness (sometimes referred to as "mental processes") but also psychological processes of which the subject is *not* aware at the given moment. That is, consciousness *includes* the sub-conscious as well as thoughts we are aware of. A moment's reflection tells us that there are numerous degrees of awareness – some things are almost inaccessible to us while other thoughts slip into and out of our awareness as our attention moves from one thing to another. "The subconscious is the potential conscious" (Vygotsky, 1930a).

Further, consciousness has no separate existence apart from nervous processes mediating between physiology and behaviour. However, both consciousness and the physiological processes accompanying it are part of a more complex process – *activity*, in which people incorporate words, tools and signs in their activity as they collaborate with others. Neither behaviour nor consciousness will make any sense abstracted from this social activity. Activity Theory therefore includes the subject matters of Behaviourism and Physiological Psychology as parts of the whole which is activity.

Direct responses to stimuli – such as withdrawing your hand from a flame – which are not mediated by consciousness are the subject matter of Objective Psychology. All the rich fabric of human life however lies outside the purview of Objective Psychology but is part of the subject matter of Activity Theory.

"Activity" here includes both behavioural acts and the consciousness which makes those acts intelligible. We prefer not to say: "Activity is a *unity* of behaviour and consciousness," but rather: "Consciousness and behaviour can be *abstracted from* activity." That is, "activity" is the primary, most basic concept, the concept which is comprehensive and self-explanatory; consciousness and behaviour are abstracted from the study of activity, and can only be explained and understood by reference to activity. That is, both "behaviour" and "consciousness" are abstractions; they represent only one side of the whole, and can only be understood insofar as they can be placed back into the context of that whole – activity. Understanding one or the other on its own is like trying to follow an argument while hearing only one side.

This appears to pose a fatal contradiction: consciousness is not observable, so it would seem that actions are not fully observable either! But this is not the case. Vygotsky showed us how it was possible to develop methods of observation and experiment which allow us to systematically study consciousness. Properly understood, *activity reveals consciousness* even more surely than physiology, though Activity Theory is not blind to physiology either. In observing behaviour we notice numerous aspects of physiology which are manifest, and under laboratory conditions observation of physiological changes can be significant for research. However, because human activity is so tied up with the culture and the activity of others, Activity Theory is almost invariably at work with people active in their cultural environment, and laboratory work can only answer specialised questions subordinate to the study of activity as a part of the social context in which it occurs. Nevertheless, when asked at the conclusion of an interview what her message to fellow Vygotskyists was, Natalia Gajdamaschko (2020) replied: "We need more experimental support for our argument ... not just to theorise, but to see if anything has changed since Vygotsky created his psychology."

When I say that consciousness is all those psychic processes which mediate between physiology and behaviour, this tell us *what* consciousness is and how it is manifested, but it does not in any way at all *explain* the development of consciousness. For that we must turn to the artefacts and other people who are involved in our activity – all of which are *outside the skin* – to explain consciousness. More on this presently.

Activity Theory is motivated by its emancipatory interest, and it is neither possible nor useful to carry around MRI machines and lie detectors while participating in the lives of the subjects of our research and interventions. Consequently, physiological investigations do not play a significant role in the practice of Activity Theorists. Further, activity theorists have found that to a very large measure the difficulties people face in life originate from the situations they are in, not in physiological problems. Consequently, most of our work is directed at helping people change their situation. This is not to deny that there are psychological issues which have their origins in physiology, but these issues are not generally the focus of Activity Theory. The scalpel and the hypodermic have their place, but on the whole they cannot solve the problems facing humanity.

The inaccessibility of consciousness to immediate observation is not a problem unique to Activity Theory. Geology, Historiography or any other science faces the same problem of having only mediated access to its subject matter. Geologists study the strata and mineral composition of the earth and *deduce* its means of formation millions of years ago. Historians have only the traces left by historical events and from these traces (especially documents) they reconstruct and explain events now far in the past. Particle Physics sets up elaborate experimental equipment to observe traces left by invisible subatomic particles, from which they are able to deduce the properties of the particles. In fact, every moment any of us interacts with other people we are engaged in observing activity and deducing the consciousness behind the behaviour. These observations and this calculation are in turn part of the consciousness which makes our own behaviour intelligible.

At this point, the reader might still insist that if consciousness is deduced from the observation of behaviour, surely that means that *behaviour* is what is fundamental. The reason that we nevertheless take activity as fundamental lies in the problem of knowing what is *an* activity or *an* action. It turns out that making sense of behaviour entails the segmentation of activity into *discrete actions* and *discrete activities* each with their own goals and motives, and this is only possible in the light of the associated *motivations*. In fact, we cannot make sense of activity at all other than by recognising within the mass of activity discrete activities and discrete actions, each with their own motivation. We will return to this issue presently.

2   Substance, Monism and Dualism

We could summarise the above reflections by saying that the substance of Activity Theory is activity. In philosophy, "substance" refers to the most basic concept of what exists for the given philosophy. Every philosophy has substances. For the earliest Hellenic thinkers the substances were earth, fire, water and air; for the Atomists, everything was made up of identical, discrete atoms. Modern Philosophy (and Psychology) was initiated with René Descartes' observation that while everything outside the mind was of one substance: matter, our ideas of what existed were of a fundamentally different substance: consciousness. Descartes' view is what is known as mind-body dualism.

This is, in itself, an undeniable truth: your idea of a $1 coin is categorically different from the $1 coin itself, and anyone who does not know the difference is literally insane. However, this ontological *dualism* provides a very poor epistemological foundation for science. If we set out from mind and matter as our fundamental categories, then we very soon discover that all the mind knows about the world is the sensations in our sense organs; what lies beyond these sensations is inaccessible. A hundred years of development of European philosophy after Descartes arrived at Kant's philosophy: everything in the mind is an appearance and we can have no knowledge of things-in-themselves beyond sensation.

In general, any science which says of its field of study: "There are fundamentally two kinds of things here," is to be forever embroiled in contradictions and puzzles. There may indeed be two, or more, kinds of thing within the field of study, but just so long as that variety of entities cannot be grasped as forms or aspects or products of a *single substance*, then so long is that science working in the dark, unable to *understand* its own subject matter. For example, if we tell a school pupil that everything in the world is either a solid, a liquid or a gas, this provides little *understanding* of the world, merely a description. But when the child learns how solids melt into liquids and liquids evaporate into gases, and that solid, liquid and gas are merely *states* of the same underlying matter, then they have begun to learn some Physics. Likewise, it was only when chemists were first able to arrange all the elements known to Chemistry into a periodic table that Chemistry started to become a true science. This representation was true even though it was some time (1869 to 1914) before the Periodic Table was explained in terms of the number of protons in the nucleus of a molecule. And it was only when the cell was identified as the basis of all living organisms and natural selection the principle uniting all organisms into a single process that Biology became a true science. Particle Physics will become a true science only when the 17 types of particle currently known to Physics are understood in some way as products, phases or aspects of the same process.

So when we say that activity is the (only) substance of Activity Theory we are indicating a commitment to *monism* – understanding the whole field of human activity as a single coherent whole. Of course, Medicine, Chemistry, even Mechanics, offer insights into human life which are not usefully topics for Activity Theory, but all those aspects of human life which are normally the subject matter of the "human sciences" – Psychology, Political Science, Sociology, Linguistics, Anthropology, etc. – are within the scope of Activity Theory. Even then, we will find that Activity Theory has much to offer the natural sciences insofar as they touch on human activity, such as in the conduct of experiments or in matters of human health.

Activity Theory does not deny the existence of individual difference derived from each person's biological inheritance and the effects of these differences on the personality. That such differences exist is an obvious fact. However, (1) these differences are given and we cannot retrospectively change our parents or the genetic accidents which formed us, and (2) in any case, to an overwhelming degree what we are is *what we have made of* our biological inheritance, and *that* is formed in activity, not biology, and *that* is the bit we can do something about.

Of course, surgical and pharmacological interventions affect our bodies and impact in turn our minds and our activity. These are not topics on which I am qualified to speak. Activity Theory has a long involvement in disability and the education of people with disabilities, but Activity Theory does not deal in surgical and pharmacological interventions. Surgical or biochemical interventions may impact on the basic underlying neurological organs, but the higher psychological functions which characterise human life are formed by complex *systems* of the basic neurological organs, and it is only in activity that these systems underlying the higher psychological functions are formed and restructured.

Nor does Activity Theory deny the existence of material objects within its field of study. On the contrary! But insofar as material objects are involved in human life, we see them as *artefacts* – material entities which are produced or singled out by and used in and therefore defined, given meaning and understood by means of human activity; they are *part of* activity. More on this presently.

The concept of "activity" is more or less synonymous with "practice," even though the use of one or other of these words tends to be a marker for the theory in which they appear. However, when activity theorists talk about activities or practices they take it that the relevant consciousness is *part of* the activity or practice; we don't say "putting theory into practice" or "theory *and* practice" because theory is itself a practice, every practice includes a theory. The only difference between the words is their connotations – on the one hand of consciousness and on the other of behaviour. Likewise, I use "project" synonymously with "activity," emphasising that a discrete activity is meant.

Thus Activity Theory is a *monist* theory, having only one substance, and as such, Activity Theory owes its origins to the philosophy of G.W.F. Hegel (1770–1831).

3   Continuity and Discontinuity

It was a discovery of Hegel's, though one for which he is rarely credited, that to understand a phenomenon concretely, to be able to grasp it securely and clearly, you have to know it first of all as a single, *discrete* instance.

Initially, we think of some phenomenon in terms of an abstraction like "space," or "art" or "knowledge." But when we try to clarify the meaning of these abstract terms we come across difficulties. We grasp them well enough for everyday use, but when we try to define them it often happens that we find ourselves tied up in an infinite regression of terms defined by other terms. This problem of "where to begin" has dogged philosophy and science for centuries. It was Hegel's solution to this problem which created the current of science of which Activity Theory is a part.

We can think of the whole phenomenon as a large number of instances rather than a continuous substance or process. Essentially, then, we can build up a coherent understanding of the Many by first grasping the One, and the idea of a *continuous* substance is merely an abstraction from the Many based on what holds the ones together. Hegel demonstrated this over and over again, unfolding in outline each of the sciences covered in his *Encyclopaedia* from a One. The One could be an individual event, action, thing or any discrete being.

The method of beginning from the One is *not* individualism. It is *holism*. It turns out that it is only the forming of a *concept* of the One which allows us to form a *concept* of the whole, which in turn allows the whole to be grasped concretely and integrally, *as a whole*. For example: if you claimed that the clouds, the rivers and icebergs were all "water," everyday observation could never resolve this claim. The observation of one changing into the other would be convincing, but does not yet *explain* it. But with a knowledge of natural science you would insist that all these forms of water are made up of the same water molecules in different combinations. With the concept of "water" founded on a water molecule with an 105° angle between the two H-O bonds, you have a scientific concept of water which unites clouds, rain, rivers, oceans and icebergs in a single process in which the bonds between identical water molecules vary according to temperature.

This insight is central to the entire development and identity of Activity Theory and I will further explain the idea presently. But it is central to Activity Theory that we do *not* see activity as a *continuous* substance; rather, we see activity as made up of so many *activities*, each of which is made up of discrete *actions*. Crucial to understanding human life, as Activity Theory sees it, is to grasp and explore single actions, single activities and how single actions and single activities cohere and relate to one another, and constitute definite social formations. This corresponds to the essential insight of the ancient Atomist, Democritus, and the same insight lies at the basis of the periodic table of chemistry and the foundations of biology in cells, organisms and species. Likewise, the human sciences have had to discover their own "units."

But hasn't it been said that we must understand the world as so many *processes* rather than as being made up of discrete *things*? May be. But the problem of understanding processes is the same as that of understanding *any* continuous substance. A single snapshot of a process or even a series of snapshots, as in a movie, cannot capture *movement*, merely its appearance. It was Hegel again who showed us that movement can only be grasped and represented by discovering the *contradiction* in a single, discrete moment. Once we grasp the contradiction inhering in a single, momentary instance of a process or phenomenon, then we understand the *law* of its movement and development, its motive force.

For example, a pundit might say "house prices are rising," but unless you know the contradiction which is driving the rising cost of housing (e.g. low interest rates or shortage of land) then you have no reason to be certain that next month house prices might not start going down. Mere patterns of observation mean very little. The ground of any difference we see has to be found in the underlying contradictions.

So we must supplement the requirement to make some *unit* the starting point for a scientific understanding of a phenomenon with the requirement that we must grasp that unit in such a way as to exhibit the *internal contradiction* which is the source of its movement and development.

If activities are to be the single substance of Activity Theory, then it means that we see everything as an activity or a part or phase or kind or composite or a product of activities. It is not that everything is an activity, or that some things are activities and some are not; rather it is *as* and *through activities* that we understand *everything* in human life. Activities are not a special kind of thing alongside other things which are not activities.

4   Actions, Goals and Motives

The basic substance of human life, as we have said, is activity, but "an activity" is an *aggregate of actions*. (See Figure 1) So before we can determine what constitutes *an* activity, we must first clarify exactly what is meant by "an action."

In the words of A.N. Leontyev, the Soviet-era psychologist who coined the term "Activity Theory," an action is a *"process, the goal and motive of which do not coincide with one another."* This is the contradiction at the heart of every action, which determines its development and makes it intelligible.

Although this definition has the merit of brevity, it makes the meaning of "an action" dependent on two other concepts: "goal" and "motive." In short, the goal is the immediate outcome intended of the action, and the motive is the reason for doing it, the more remote situation which is ultimately intended.

However, we can only properly understand the meaning of goal and motive from within the concepts of action and activity from which they are abstracted (See Figure 1). The concepts of activity, goal and motive must be developed together as essential aspects of the concept of "an action." This Leontyev did by means of a genetic development tracing the evolution of human life from more primitive organisms, but I will try to achieve the same result more economically and less speculatively.

When we ask: "Why did the chicken cross the road?" the answer: "To get to the other side" is funny because we have imagined that the chicken must have had a *reason* to cross the road. In fact, the chicken did not have a reason; it is not a rational being. The goal of crossing the road had no other motive than to cross the road. If we were to ask a *person*: "Why did you cross the road?" then we would rightly expect them to give a *reason*. That is, the action of crossing the road would be part of a collection of actions (an activity), perhaps carried out by the person themself (for example, to catch the bus into the city to buy a new jacket), perhaps carried out by a number of different people collaborating with one another (for example, to form a picket line to ensure the success of

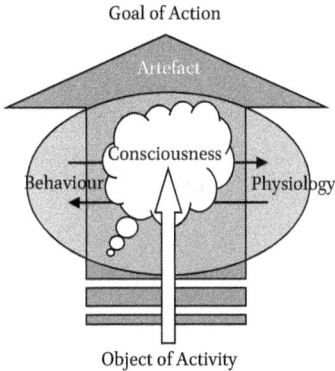

FIGURE 1   Elements of an action

a strike). That is, the immediate intended outcome of the action (to get to the other side) *differs from* the reason for doing it (to catch a bus or form a picket line). Actions are oriented to intermediate goals towards fulfilling the situation which is the motive of the action. While the higher animals are capable of carrying out activities which require a whole series of actions to satisfy their motive, humans commonly carry out actions which are intelligible only on condition that their motive is achieved thanks to the *foreseeable collaborative actions of others*, even *strangers*. That is, that the action is part of a (collaborative) *activity*, which generally includes some social division of labour.

That is, an action fulfils intermediate *goals* for the achievement of a different, more remote goal which provides the *motive* of the action.

The *goal* of an action can be determined simply by observing the action (including whether it evidently fulfils the intention of the actor). The *motive* of the action requires us to observe the foreseeable consequences of the action (insofar they evidently fulfil the intention of the actor) including the actions of others (such that the outcome evidently fulfils the intention of the actor).

"Action" and "activity" are not mutually exclusive categories, they are relational concepts. If a trade union carries out an action to stop work at some enterprise, then that action (goal: to stop work, motive: to get a pay rise) is itself an activity made up of a thousand different actions by different members of the union – putting a picket line in place, distributing leaflets, etc. Thus, actions can be collaborative just as, conversely, an activity could be carried out by a single person. The point is the difference between the intermediate goal, on one hand, and the remote outcome which makes the action and its goal intelligible, on the other hand. Some activities however do not have a motive outside of themselves, and these are the archetypal activities. For example, a public hospital makes sick people well – no other justification is needed for that activity – it fulfils a normative expectation of the whole community.

Further, one and the same action can be part of different activities, serving more than one motive. For example, I go to work to earn a wage, but perhaps also to build up my CV, irrespective of whether I am motivated that my employer earns a profit or our customers receive a satisfactory product.

4.1   *Operations*

To complete this definition, Leontyev also defined *operations* which are "portable" actions controlled by their conditions rather than being *consciously* controlled towards the goal of the action. For example, an operation would be taking a step as part of the action of walking across the road, unconsciously matching your balance and stride to the shape of the ground. If you miss the kerb and stumble, your movement automatically springs back into conscious control until you regain your balance (momentarily reverting to the status of an action). Actions are made up of an aggregate of operations. Many of the actions of an institution may be "collective operations" inasmuch as the operation is so routine for that institution or project that no special control or supervision is needed on the part of the executive. But in what follows below I shall have very little to say about operations, so the reader need not trouble themselves too much with this concept.

In clarifying the meaning of "an action," I have made reference to intentions, and not just outcomes. Activity Theory is not indifferent to the intentions of the actor since intentions are crucial to make sense of someone's actions. While we have recourse to the observation of physiological reactions or simply asking a person about their intentions, as well as observing the activities of which the action is a part, in the end, intentions must be deduced from a comprehensive observation of activity. Actions must always be interpreted *in their context*, and their context is above all *other actions*. Thus, everything needed to understand an action is available for objective, scientific observation.

In short, an action is doing something for a reason. The motive is the reason for doing something and the goal is what is done, an intermediate step towards fulfilling the motive of the action. What characterises human activity is not so much *what* we do but the *reasons* we have for doing them. But in Activity Theory we do not conceive of these reasons as verbal explanations, but simply in terms of the activities to which an action contributes. Goal and motive are both situations in the world.

Unforeseeable consequences and interference by the independent action of others raise further questions which will be dealt with much later.

5   Artefacts

I mentioned above that while activities are the only substance for Activity Theory, the material world plays an ineliminable role in activity. By "material" I mean anything that exists outside of and independently of your consciousness. It exists objectively, but its *meaning* is dependent on human activity.

The concept of "Nature," on the other hand, is everything which exists independently of human activity. Activity Theory is not Natural Science. That is, we do not speculate about the nature of a world beyond and outside of human activity. We leave that to others. But Activity Theory *is* concerned with the scope and limits of human activity and human activity is both constrained and enabled by the necessary inclusion of material objects and processes in our actions. The concept of "material" includes both the natural processes and objects which existed before human beings existed, continue to exist outside of our activity *and* the artefacts which constitute our "second nature." Human activity is itself a *material* process. The concept of "matter" expresses the interconnectedness of everything outside of our consciousness and through this concept we are able to learn about natural processes outside of human activity as such, through our activity. But human activity is not a *natural* process, because it is mediated by consciousness. We do things for *reasons*, imagined future situations, not simply in response to stimuli.

The material world is included in activity by means of *artefacts* – what we know of the world beyond human activity we know thanks to those material products of human activity which are included as mediating elements in our activity. The various measurements physicists take from the material world are products of specific forms of activity, and are meaningful in the context of the relevant actions.

We are not capable of telekinesis. We can do nothing without the mediation of material objects. Just as all our activity is done in and through the use of material objects and processes, all our knowledge, including our knowledge of Nature, is derived from activity. Among the material objects we use are included our own body, itself a product of human activity over millions of years, as well as all the domesticated plants and animals and the land which we have cultivated over many generations. All these artefacts are what constitute our material culture.

Consequently, in Activity Theory actions are always conceived of as *artefact mediated actions*. An artefact is defined as a material object or process which is produced by or used in human actions. So strictly speaking, the words "artefact mediated" are redundant because all actions are essentially artefact-mediated.

The accumulated mass of the artefacts of a society is both the residue of its past activity, available for future archaeologists to reconstruct how we lived, and the material basis for our present day activity. On our own in Nature, without the support of our "second nature," most human beings would survive hardly more than a few days. (Equally, we would not last long without the help of other people.) The most pressing problem of our times is that human activity is undermining the natural conditions for human life. On the whole, the impact of human activity is now well understood. What patently remains to be understood is how human activity can be changed so as to reverse this unsustainable, destructive process.

5.1   *Words, Tools and Signs*

There are three kinds of artefact which mediate human actions – words, tools and signs – which are connected with one another developmentally and distinguished from one another functionally, that is, by the specific role they play in a human action. All artefacts are material objects or processes, produced by and/or used in human activity.

The first *tool* was the human hand. With our hands we plucked things from their natural setting, carried them home and used them for our own purposes. Our own anatomy developed through our facility with our hands. All the tools subsequently invented by human beings had their beginning with the human hand, extending its powers and combining them with products of their labour.

The first *words* arose alongside and in close connection with tool-use; as our forebears plucked things from Nature and used them they formed concepts of them. Their use of these artefacts was accompanied by gestures and words (signed or spoken) and these words gave objective form to our concepts and communicated them to our collaborators and helped us build communities. Speech is essentially *doing something with words* in the presence of the listener, but word-use has been enhanced by telecommunication and recording, blurring the distinction between word and sign. "Word" in Activity Theory generally indicates a spoken or signed word, rather than a written word. Further, "word" is interpreted as a sign (symbol) for a concept, so it may include a *phrase* with a semantic content, as well as a single word.

It may seem odd to refer to a spoken word as an *artefact*, since it is produced in the very act of speech and has only a transient existence. In this they are clearly something very different from tools and signs, which endure beyond the situation in which they are created. Although a given individual instance of a word has only a transient existence, the word (i.e., the universal which each individual word realises) is ever present in the subject's social environment, repeatedly appearing in specific contexts. A word is sustained as an artefact of a culture by its repeated use over a period of time in a variety of contexts.

The first *signs* arose as extensions of our technical activity (i.e., tool-use). Written words or word-like symbols appeared only in the past 10,000 years. Written words are enduring and are interpreted in the absence of the writer, and thereby formed the basis for building large, class-based communities. Literacy did not arise naturally from the conditions of early humans but arose a few thousand years ago in a handful of civilisations and spread across the globe from there. All normally developing children acquire speech, but writing is generally acquired only in literate communities through deliberate instruction.

Vygotsky introduced the term *"psychological tools,"* functionally distinguished from "technical tools" to include "language, different forms of numeration and counting, mnemotechnic techniques, algebraic symbolism, works of art, writing, schemes, diagrams, maps, blueprints, all sorts of conventional signs, etc." (Vygotsky, 1930). Psychological tools differ from technical tools in that they are directed at controlling the *mind* – one's own or that of another. Technical tools, on the other hand, are directed at controlling the processes of *Nature*. But *all* tools are material artefacts. A tool is a tool, but tools can be psychological tools (such as a book) or a technical tool (such as a hammer), depending on whether it is being used to influence the mind or to intervene in a natural process: to convey an idea, or prop open the door, for example.

Nowadays, there is a manner of speech in which people use the word "tool" to refer to any *means* – concepts, actions, methods, etc. This expression is well-meaning, indicating that a person does not lack ability but simply needs the "right tools." We do not use this manner of speech in Activity Theory, because it is always important to know exactly which *material objects and processes* mediate the relevant actions and this should not be conflated with the vague concept of a "means." If someone used such and such a method, it is still important to know which book or spoken advice or instrument was used.

Vygotsky was hostile to the use of the term "artefact" to lump together words, tools and signs because the role of each in human development is different. Writing in the early 1930s, Vygotsky feared that his insights into the origins of the intellect in word-use would be obscured by subsuming word-use and sign-use under the abstract general heading of "artefact mediation" understood in terms of orthodox Marxist conceptions of labour, i.e., tool-use. Tools play a completely different role in expanding the scope of human activity and developing practical intelligence than do words and signs. "Artefact" is only adequate as a general heading and to indicate the universality of mediation, but in every specific instance it is important whether the given action is mediated by speech, tools or signs (all of which are material objects or processes).

Apart from the political implications of subsuming the use of tools, words and signs under artefacts, the use of the term "artefact" obscures Vygotsky's dialectical method. "Artefact" is one of those general terms whose meaning is only made clear by the determination of a unit. But the relevant units are at least three quite different entities (word, tool or sign), each of which arises at a different point in human development, both phylogenesis and ontogenesis. In that specific sense, "artefact" is an *abstract* concept, and should be avoided, other than, as Vygotsky said, as a general heading or to indicate the universality of mediation in human activity.

6   Activities

But what is *an* activity? According to the Soviet-era founder of Activity Theory, A.N. Leontyev, an activity is characterised by the *object* which provides its motive. For Leontyev, the object is the externally existing situation which orients the activity.

> Thus the concept of activity is necessarily connected with the concept of motive. Activity does not exist without a motive; "non-motivated" activity is not activity without a motive but activity with a subjectively and objectively hidden motive.
>
> LEONTYEV, 1978

"Society produces the activity of the individuals forming it" (*op. cit.*), but not in an immediate way, as if by a stimulus → response reaction. Participation in activities is mediated by psychic reflection, which in turn has been shaped by prior participation of individuals in the life of their society and the complex web of relations between the various activities. The object of an activity is a societal product which exists independently of any person and generally meets the needs of individuals in a socially mediated way, typically either by consumption of the object or by providing an income. But, to use a Hegelian expression, *the object differs from its concept in some way*; for example, it is a useful product which, having been consumed, must be *reproduced* before it can be consumed again, or it is a person's health which is defective and needs to be *rectified* by medical treatment. Yrjö Engeström has called the object "'the raw material' or 'problem space'" (Engeström, n.d.). In fact, it would be better to say the object is "the raw material *and* problem space."

Although Leontyev's definition is intuitively compelling and remains the main foundation of Activity Theory to this day, it is rife with contradictions. I have examined some of the contradictions in Leontyev's theory at length in my article "Leontyev's Activity Theory and Social Theory" (Blunden, 2015), and I will only briefly review these contradictions here, insofar as they are relevant to *all* versions of Activity Theory, including Yrjö Engeström's theory and modern European and American versions of Leontyev's theory. What I have come to realise more recently however is that this definition is *too restrictive*, from the point of view of representing human life, from the point of view of using Activity Theory as a means for research and from the point of view of intervening in order to foster social change.

If clarified and purged of a number of contradictions, Leontyev's definition of an activity indicates an *ideal-typical* activity, within the entire field of activities for which the connection between the constituent actions and the activity as a whole is problematic or less well defined.

The topic I am about to introduce here – what is *an* activity? – is the central topic for this entire work. After giving an initial answer to the question, I will review the genealogy of Activity Theory and then complete the review of the concepts generally well known to activity theorists and then, in the main body of this work, illustrate the problematic character of this question and its varying answers through research done by colleagues around the world.

6.1   *What Is an Activity?*

Actions are the *micro* units of analysis for Activity Theory and activities, which are the *macro* units of Activity Theory, are nothing more than aggregates of actions. The question is: *how* do the mass of actions segment themselves into coherent aggregates of actions to constitute activities?

An activity is not a mental entity, such as my desire or my image of a better world, nor is an activity an aggregate of people, such as an organisation or institution, or an aggregate of behaviours such as is generally to subject matter of "social psychology." It is an aggregate of *actions*. Further, Leontyev observes that activities are "non-additive" units of activity because any action may be part of more than one activity at the same time; activities can "overlap" and subsume one another. The issue is: how do we know *which* actions aggregate together as *an* activity? What is it about all the actions which mean that they are all part of the same activity?

In its original conception by A.N. Leontyev, an activity is an aggregate of actions, each in general executed by a different person for a specific goal, and all directed towards the achievement of the same more remote object. But the concept of "an activity" does not actually exclude a series of collaborative actions, all of which are actions by the *same person* and which constitutes the life of that person or even an *episode* in the life of a person – their "life project."

The concept of "object" in Leontyev represents both the thing acted upon and the final state of that thing which the activity tends to bring about – the process of its (re)production, its maintenance. The "object" here is not strictly a psychological concept, because it does not necessarily function in the mind of the actors *as* a motive. It is more correctly a societal entity, and a product of societal processes. Nonetheless, the "object" is evident in the collaborative tendency of all the actions towards the realisation of a certain condition of the object and the participants will generally all be aware of it. For Leontyev, societal norms or policy determine what is required of the object – if it is auto-mobiles, it is *enough* automobiles to meet the needs of the community, if it is a patient in a hospital, it is a good state of health for the patient. The activity is regulated by business owners, government officials, administrators, and so on to see that the object is achieved. In general, it is *societal* processes (such as the market or bureaucratic or political interests) which determine the vari-ous objects. The object itself determines the intermediate goals needed for its achievement in conjunction with the division of labour which is determined internally to the activity. However, in general it is the societal means of distri-bution which ultimately provides the motivation for all the actors.

For the workers engaged in the activity, the object is the "merely known motive" of the activity, but their *really effective* motive will more likely be to earn a wage, while the really effective motive for the business owner is the expansion of their capital. Obviously, in some cases in some activities, or pro-jects – such as political movements or charities – the object is indeed the effec-tive motive, but Leontyev did not have these kinds of activities in mind.

I use the word "project" *synonymously* with "an activity" or "a project," but "project" tends to connote an activity which is not yet institutionalised and therefore presupposes voluntary participation. In a project, generally, there is no difference between the merely known motive and the really effective motive. This is an archetypal activity in my approach. Under certain circum-stances, a project becomes *institutionalised*, and rewards are needed to engage the collaboration of employees or volunteers. On the other hand, the orthodox concept of "an activity" tends to take the institutionalised project as the arche-type. But I use both terms to cover all kinds of projects, practices or activities and the same theoretical ideas are used in each case.

All human actions are mediated by the use of artefacts – material objects which are both products of human labour and in turn used in human actions. Often, one and the same artefact may mediate the *entire activity*. The artefact mediating the activity, its object, cannot in principle be separated from the entire social situation, but is a feature of it. The artefact which mediates the entire activity is sometimes referred to as the "raw material," or in German, the *Arbeitsgegenstand*, the thing being worked on. But this terminology may obscure the fact that the *Gegenstand* in question may not be a pile of steel, but a human being, such as a patient in a hospital, or itself an activity, such as the government of the country. In the latter cases in which the object includes a human being, the subject-object relation must be conceived as a collaborative activity or project.

The mediating artefact in a given *action*, however, differs in principle from the object which mediates or controls the whole activity. It is a *means*. For example, the body of a patient may mediate the activity directed at resolving the patient's illness, but the actions making up that activity may be mediated by scalpels, medicines, spoken words, scripts, etc., as well as the hands and voices of medical practitioners.

The mediating artefact in an action or activity may be *part of* the object, but there is a difference in principle between that element of objectivity which is taken up as a means and possibly *consumed* in the process of being used, and the *Arbeitsgegenstand* which *persists* but is *changed* and bears the marks of the subject's intentions.

6.2   *Activities Which Fall Short of Leontyev's Ideal-Typical Activity*

In reality, there are many activities to be seen in the world which on the face of it fall short of this representation of an activity; actions may lack coordination and achieve a collective outcome either not at all or unintentionally; there may be no "merely known" motive for the activity distinct from the joy or otherwise-compelling attraction of taking part or the object may be the on-going subject of dispute.

Using our dialectical approach, we do not say that such phenomena are *not activities*, but rather that they are activities which (as yet) fall short of the concept of "an activity" – they may be activities in an early stage of development or in a late stage of degeneration or simply a malformed activity. Activity Theory needs to be able to encompass activities which are not the archetypal collaborations aimed at a well-known, explicit motive. A theory of *the development of activities*, not just a definition, is necessary.

Even when the concept of "activity" has been generalised in this way, Activity Theory appears to be a theory adapted to a *specialised kind of social phenomenon* and something quite distinct from psychology. People tend to think of psychology as being just about thoughts and feelings rather than activities, but emotions are the springs of action and concepts are *forms of activity* and exist whenever people are *active*. Even when you just sit and think you are active, even if that activity is only manifested later when you put your thoughts into action, so to speak. When properly conceived, Activity Theory can be a general theory of all human life and an immensely powerful lens for a wide spectrum of research projects and the solution of a wide variety of problems, from clarifying the foundations of mathematics to improving the training of doctors to motivating children to learn to read or overthrowing capitalism.

7   Motivation

This is how a researcher or in fact any human being approaches the world and tries to understand it. At first what you see is a lot of actions. You can see what people are doing, that is, the outcome of each of the actions and the extent to which the outcome corresponds to the evident goal of the action, fulfilling the actor's purpose. This will be evident from the emotional expression of the actor and the coherence of the operations which are normally unconsciously controlled towards the achievement of the goal. But what is still unclear is this: why are people doing these actions? what are their reasons? what is it all for?

The world is not full of people just doing things. People do things for a reason and it is these reasons which bind them and their actions together into coherent activities and communities.

In Activity Theory, motivation is what gives us reasons for doing something: the object, which produces the internal emotional conditions of the psyche which are in turn the springs of action in the mind. But we do not see the object which is providing the reason for an action as a material or natural thing, an objective condition lying *outside* of human activity, motivating activity from outside, so to speak. In this I part ways with A.N. Leontyev's dualism. Although Leontyev agreed that human needs are produced by society, that is, by activities, he saw the motivation for any given activity as something objective, lying outside the given activity, drawing the activity towards itself, so to speak. This was seen at the time to follow from Marx's philosophical materialism. But it is mistaken; a theory of social life which sees human activity simply as a response to objectively existing *needs* is a vulgar materialism, not Marxism. I align with Leontyev's student Fedor Vasilyuk (1984) – the units of an actor's mind are the same as the units of their life-world, or more precisely a *selection* of those units. That is, it is not a hamburger as such which stimulates me to go into the restaurant but my concept of the hamburger which I expect to find in the restaurant which elicits an emotional response and action. It might turn out that I am deluded and when I go into the restaurant I find that it is a Chinese restaurant which does not serve hamburgers, and my search must continue elsewhere, watching the signage outside the restaurants this time.

The source of the motivation, the reason for doing something, is the *object-concept*. The object-concept is *implicit* in the material activity of the participants in an activity. That is, people carry out some action to contribute to a whole collection of actions, by themselves and by other people, which tend to bring some *Arbeitsgegenstand* – some material product, activity, person or relationship – into correspondence with a concept of how it ought to be: the *object-concept*. From a psychological point of view, the motivation of an individual action is a concept of the object, at the heart of which is a moment of volition, emotion, a commitment. The object-concept is an ideal form of activity, a norm of activity, which is acquired by individuals in and through their participation in activity. Their actions are realised as material actions by means of the mediation of artefacts incorporated in the action, and as such are objective.

The motivation, the actions, the object-concept and the artefacts are all elements of the activity; they are internal to the activity. But the actions are *material* actions, and as such they are part of the material world, interconnected with everything else in the world.

7.1   The "Unconscious"?

The concept of the Unconscious long ago entered into popular consciousness mainly thanks to the work of Sigmund Freud.

For decades, psychologists had wrestled with the problem that conscious awareness did not seem to be explicable from itself; awareness flipped from one thought to another and then brought back thoughts which had been left behind and at times seemed to be driven by motives which the subject themself was unable to explain. Freud took the bold step of hypothesising that one could speak of ideas of which one was not conscious, despite the fact that for the psychology of the time this was a contradiction in terms. That is to say, he broadened the subject matter of psychology to include consciousness beyond conscious awareness.

At first, Freud raised the hypothesis that these ideas of which one was not conscious at the moment resided in some *physiological* structure from which ideas could move into and out of conscious awareness. This was a misconception because consciousness is in any case inseparable from the physiological processes which realise it. Attention moves from one thought to another, but it is all part of consciousness – an integral psychic process. Both consciousness (including subconscious thoughts, thoughts of which we are not aware, as well as the thought of which we are aware), physiology and behaviour are all inseparable parts of the broader, more complex process of *activity*, and make sense only as aspects of activity.

For us, the Unconscious is not a psychic process which *pre-existed* conscious experience and determines motivation "behind the back" of the conscious actor, so to speak. Freud's idea that dreams, hypnosis and "Freudian slips" reveal this otherwise inaccessible realm is largely a myth and does not stand up against the evidence, despite the popularity of the idea. Vygotsky and his associates were able to demonstrate that the origin of the *sub*conscious lies in prior conscious awareness. The origins and *development* of the subconscious are key to understanding its place in the overall pattern of activity.

As said I above, "consciousness" in Activity Theory means the *totality* of the psychic processes mediating between physiology and behaviour, and our physiology and behaviour are in turn part of the totality of *activity* in which we are participants. "Totality" is important. Our starting point is the totality, not some part which has to be added to other parts to make the whole. There is indeed psychic activity which lies "below" conscious awareness but it is not something deposited without ever having passed through experience. That "subconscious" psychic activity had its origins in experience and can be recalled even if sometimes the aid of a therapist is required.

A variety of situations intervene to mean that an experience of which the subject was consciously aware is no longer accessible and yet continues to underlie the subject's motivation. Chief amongst these situations are:

i.   Mastery: it is no longer *possible* or *necessary* to consciously control an emotion or action. I distinctly remember the moment I first learnt to tie my own shoelaces (or rather, I remember boasting about it to my father). It took intense concentration and attention to every movement. But not too long afterwards I could do it without interrupting a conversation and being hardly aware of the shoes within my field of vision. The characteristic of this process is that mastery is *effortful*, but once achieved, no special effort is required so long as you do not pay attention to it. Throughout life we confront little challenges; we stop and think and pay close attention, but soon pass through like situations without a second thought.

ii. Second, we all acquire ways of acting which could hardly be called effortful; young men learn to talk over women and women learn to be nice when they would be better advised to be disagreeable. Once acquired (effortlessly) these social mores generate or suppress inhibitions and thereby shape motivations which are as elusive as any. Activity theorists grasp these prejudices and subconscious conformity to norms in terms of *concept* development, which occurs through participation in activities, and at the heart of every concept is a moment of volition. Generally, we are broken from prejudicial conceptions and the behaviours which flow from them when our actions are subject to criticism and we are made aware of conflicting norms.

iii.   The third source of the subconscious and the one to which Freud looked is trauma or at least humiliation or embarrassment falling short of trauma. In this circumstance, it is no longer *possible* to deal with a painful experience consciously. Remembering an incident or an inappropriate desire causes such painful feelings of humiliation, anxiety or whatever, that we suppress memory of it, while at the same time avoidance of the unpleasant emotion continues to provide motivation which seems inexplicable to the subject themself. This activity with inexplicable motivation continues until some disturbance brings its source back into conscious awareness where it can again be brought under conscious control and the disturbance overcome. Recall the section above on operations. The task of the psychotherapist is to disturb the activity in which the experience is suppressed and help bring it back into conscious awareness and control.

But frequently the extreme of a motivation originating in a past trauma is not suppressed to the extent that it is inaccessible. I am someone who is a little too obsessive about being on time for appointments. But I *know* that I acquired this motivation in my earliest experiences in politics when more experienced cadres routinely turned up half an hour late to appointments, which I found insulting. The motivation is subconscious but it is not necessarily inaccessible.

The point is that it is a mistake to hypothesise the Unconscious as a distinct psychological organ. All our motivations are more or less conscious, more or less acknowledged, more or less accessible; motivations slip in and out of awareness minute by minute. Anything that is in the subconscious is potentially something of which we can be aware because its origin was in conscious activity even if at the time we were not aware of it and/or unable to verbalise it.

• • •

To understand the broad scope of Activity Theory and how it achieves its status as a monist theory of human life, it will be necessary to briefly reflect on its genealogy and the connections between the ideas of its historical precursors and proponents.

8   The Genealogy of Activity Theory

The origins of Activity Theory lie in the philosophy of Hegel. Hegel was writing at a time when Darwin's theory and the discovery of the cell still lay in the future. All that was known of non-European cultures were reports of missionaries and slave traders and nothing at all was known of the origins of human life. Anthropology and comparative linguistics were only in the embryonic stages of their development. Hegel's philosophy rested solely on the history of European society and philosophy and what was available to anyone able to observe the activity of people living in a modern secular state in the 1790s-1820s.

All activity theorists are aware of the origins of their theory in Hegel, but few have actually read Hegel. His work is difficult and arcane. Nonetheless, all the fundamental concepts which I am outlining in this introduction come from Hegel.

Hegel's most enduring contribution was his Logic. The distinctive feature of Hegel's Logic is that it is a logic of *concepts* rather than Formal Logic which is effectively the logic of sets – collections of objects grouped together according to some shared attribute. It is like the difference between *knowing* (*wissen*) someone, in the sense of understanding what that person is about, their personality and so on, and *knowing* (*erkennen*) someone in the sense of being able to pick them out in a police line-up. Hegel's Logic is the logic of how people actually think and act, whereas Formal Logic is the logic of bureaucrats with their check boxes and rule books, who replace the concept of a human being with a list of their characteristics. Dialectics is like Darwin's categorisation of creatures according to a theory of evolution which lies *behind* appearances, as opposed to Linnaeus's taxonomy in which creatures are categorised simply according to their attributes. The employer who interviews prospective employees, asks them about their past, tries to get to know them and what brought them to apply for the job is thinking like a human being, dialectically. The HR manager who simply gives all the applicants a form to fill in and then processes the forms with a software app. is thinking with formal logic, like a bureaucrat not a human being.

It is frankly impossible to explain dialectical logic in a phrase. If that were so, there would be no need for Hegel. I try to exhibit dialectical logic in the way I argue for and explain the ideas in this book, and there is no shortcut. There are lots of maxims: always begin from the whole; see everything in movement, rather than fixed; contradiction is the root of life, etc. Engels offered his "Three Laws of Dialectics":

The law of the transformation of quantity into quality and *vice versa*;
The law of the interpenetration of opposites;
The law of the negation of the negation.

ENGELS, 1883

But these "laws" have caused more harm than good over the 140 years since they were written, not because they are wrong, but because they are over-simplified. However, every time you see through that rigid, mechanical, bureaucratic box-ticking way of thinking, you are learning some dialectical logic.

Hegel called himself an Idealist because his work was primarily concerned with the categories and forms of thought before the *content* of ideas. Philosophers were led to an examination of the forms of thought in the late 18th century because science had reached an impasse, torn between scepticism and dogmatism, riven by dualisms and contradictions, and a new Logic was required to find a way through that crisis.

The subject matter of Hegel's philosophy was *spirit* (*Geist*, also translated as *mind*). The idea of *Zeitgeist* – the spirit of the times – gives an idea of what is meant by *Geist*. We could say that spirit is the system of norms – the practical, semantic and theoretical norms – of a community, simple common sense in the view of the majority of people. These norms Hegel calls "thought objects," and indeed it is hard to say exactly what kind of thing a norm is; it is not just a material thing (like a law written in a book) but nor is it just a thought in people's heads. Norms are implicit in human activities, especially when we look at the activity of people *en masse*. Norms can be said to represent the *expectations* which guide and constrain activities in much the same way that material objects and processes do. The trick of reading Hegel is to understand that the subject matter he is writing about is *forms of human activity*, how they change and develop and how they relate to individual actions and activities. Hegel's contemporaries understood this, and his philosophy has inspired almost all radical political currents ever since, even though Hegel himself was quite conservative.

Hegel's successor in philosophy, though not in politics, was Karl Marx. Marx gave Hegel's philosophy an explicitly "materialist" form in that the subject matter was now no longer categories of thought but explicitly human activity en masse, and rather than being an advocate for the constitutional monarchy, Marx was an inveterate revolutionary. Marx's ideas were the inspiration behind the Russian Revolution and in the decade after the Revolution there was a kind of cultural revolution in which Marx's ideas spread among the masses and new ideas flourished in all the arts and sciences.

Among those inspired by Marx was Lev Vygotsky, a young Jewish-Ukrainian psychologist, who had probably never read Hegel, but had studied Marx, Engels and Plekhanov and was unique in his generation for being able to extract from his reading of Marx the essential ideas which Marx had appropriated from Hegel and applied in the writing of *Capital*. Vygotsky famously declared that "Psychology needs its own *Capital*," and set out to found a completely new general psychology. Vygotsky revolutionised at least five branches of psychology.

Vygotsky's (1930) key innovation was the *artefact-mediated action*, universally recognised as the founding principle of Activity Theory. An artefact-mediated action is mediated by a product of the wider culture, originating usually from beyond the horizons of the individual actor. By observing how a person's action is mediated by symbols and tools selected by the researcher from the wider culture, Vygotsky opened the way to the study of the mind under laboratory conditions. Rather than trying to isolate the subject from their normal, cultural environment, he observed exactly how culture plays the central role in their shaping activity, and consequently in the very formation of the human personality.

Vygotsky's *Thinking and Speech* was published after his death from tuberculosis in 1934. The first chapter of this book was a short discourse on the concept of a "unit of analysis." Under a new name, this was in fact Hegel's most important legacy: the One, central to Marx's *Capital*, but never previously examined in its own right. The unit of analysis for the study of the relation between thinking and speech was *word meaning*, that is to say, doing something with a (spoken) word. Here Vygotsky, for the first time, put *spoken words* at the centre of his psychology, rather than tools and signs. A spoken word is, said Vygotsky, "a unity of thinking and speech ... a unity of generalisation and social interaction, a unity of thinking and communication," highlighting not one but three contradictions at the heart of the meaningful word. Although the unit of analysis or the germ cell of *Thinking and Speech* was the meaningful word, the subject matter of the book was the intellect, i.e., concepts, which are the units of the intellect.

One of Vygotsky's students was A.N. Leontyev, and while Vygotsky's work was suppressed by Stalin's regime after his death, Leontyev survived and went on to build a following and hold eminent university positions. A.N. Leontyev is widely recognised as the founder of Activity Theory as distinct from Vygotsky's Socio-Cultural Theory. Vygotsky had approached the cultural formation of the mind in terms of how artefacts, including language, originating in the wider culture, are used by individuals to resolve situations, also the product of the wider culture. Vygotsky did not, however, investigate how these situations, including a person's motivation which is a key element in constituting a situation, originate in the social environment itself. This issue was taken up by Leontyev.

Leontyev continued Vygotsky's work beginning from the idea of the tool-and symbol-mediated action. However, whereas Vygotsky had gone on to focus on the mediating artefact as a *sign* (a spoken word in particular), Leontyev took the archetypal artefact-mediated action to be a tool-mediated action, i.e., a *labour action*. This turn towards labour rather than the intellect was well adapted to the new regime in the Soviet Union and was key to the survival of Leontyev and his ideas. As I explained in my article *Tool and sign in Vygotsky's development* (Blunden, 2021c), this tension between words and tools expresses a deep-seated contradiction in the development of Marxism which persists to this very day, reflecting changes in the labour process and with that, changes in the composition of the working class.

With the tool-mediated artefact as the basic unit of analysis, the subject matter of Leontyev's work was no longer the intellect, i.e., concepts, but *activities*, thus coining the term "Activity Theory." Among the conquests of the Soviet Activity Theorists were a re-opening of Hegel's work to a reading in terms of human activity, the idea of the "germ cell" to conceptualise developing practices, and a theory well suited to spread from psychology into the broader social sciences.

Despite his limitations, the introduction of three units of analysis (operation, action and activity) in an hierarchical structure was a brilliant move. Although both micro-and macro-unit are implicit in the work of both Marx (commodity and capitalist firm) and Vygotsky (word meaning and concept) neither of these writers made this explicit.

Nevertheless, much of the philosophical insights of Vygotsky were lost in Leontyev's work. According to Leontyev's son: "an ambiguous understanding of the units and levels of activity organisation can be seen" (A. A. Leontyev, 2006), and Leontyev's work is riven with dualism and dogmatism.

In the 1980s, the Finnish Activity Theorist, Yrjö Engeström, relaunched Activity Theory with the idea of an expanded unit of analysis in which each of the mediating links of the artefact-mediated action is in turn mediated – by norms, tools and division of labour respectively – with this new unit conceived of as a "system of activity." At the present day, three broad currents of Activity Theory co-exist, that of Vygotsky, Leontyev and Engeström.

It will be necessary now to look a little closer at the relation between Vygotsky's Socio-Cultural Theory and Activity Theory in the narrow sense.

9   Activity Theory and Vygotsky's Socio-cultural Theory

It is impossible to assess Leontyev's contribution to Activity Theory and particularly his relationship with Vygotsky without first understanding the toxic
conditions in Stalin's USSR which made scientific discussion, even between
friends, impossible. Every moment one risked denunciation over a misplaced
word, followed possibly by exclusion or a bullet in the back of the head.
Vygotsky's psychology was a sensitive issue in the USSR. Vygotsky's other most
influential student, Luria, survived only by changing discipline and becoming
a neuropsychologist. Luria's survival into the 1970s made possible the publication of Vygotsky's work in the West.

The priority Leontyev gave to tool-mediated action as opposed to communicative action is the first difference between Vygotsky and Leontyev. Vygotsky
was well aware of the danger of demoting communicative action to a genre of
tool-mediated action. He summed up the relation as he saw it on the last page
of *Thinking and Speech*, expressed in terms of word and deed:

> "In the beginning was the word." Goethe answered this Biblical phrase
> through Faust: "In the beginning was the deed." Through this statement,
> Goethe wished to counteract the word's over-valuation. ... [W]e can agree
> with Goethe that the word as such should not be overvalued and can con-
> cur in his transformation of the Biblical line to, "In the beginning was the
> *deed*." Nonetheless, if we consider the history of development, we can
> still read this line with a different emphasis: "In the *beginning* was the
> deed."
>
> VYGOTSKY, 1934, p. 281

Developments in technology shape the terrain on which human beings work
and communicate with one another, and develop a practical intelligence, but
it is through communication that intellect develops along with the capacity to
think, not just in potential concepts, but in true concepts.

As I remarked above, Vygotsky revolutionised five different domains of psychology, and in each case he used a different unit of analysis.

In his analysis of personality he used *perezhivaniya* – experiences; in his
analysis of child development he used "social situation of development"; in
his analysis of disability he used defect/compensation; in his analysis of the
acquisition of culture he used the artefact-mediated action; in his analysis of
the intellect he used word meaning.

In Leontyev's Activity Theory, however, we have only the hierarchical structure of three units explained above – operation, action and activity – a kind

of monoculture when compared with Vygotsky and Hegel's rich and diverse deployment of units. Further, Leontyev did not really understand units. In his theory, "an activity" referred to a *type* of activity – "work" for example – rather than a specific activity. As a loyal Soviet citizen he did not distinguish between what was *objectively* true and what was *universal*, i.e., the policy of the Politburo. His concept of an "object" lying outside the activity which was motivated by it was confused in such a way that his version of Activity Theory became a variety of Functionalism, and his conception of an activity was limited to the reproduction of existing relations, transformative projects lying beyond his horizons.

Nonetheless, all these defects and shortcomings are solvable if we understand his theory in the context of its time and as a phase of development of Activity Theory beginning with its origins in Hegel. Further, Leontyev made it possible to take Activity Theory from the domain of psychology into social theory as such, even though he himself remained a psychologist and his own incursions into social theory were miserable.

An important aspect of Leontyev's move to Activity Theory, however, was that it made explicit the reading of Hegel in terms of *human activity* en masse. In Chapter 5 of *Thinking and Speech*, Vygotsky explicitly presents concepts as *forms of action*. The internal mental activity commonly associated with concepts arises through the in-growing of these forms of action and growing facility in their use. So already for Vygotsky *concepts are forms of activity*, including speech activity. This simple realisation gave us a *monist theory of psychology*. Behaviour and consciousness are both *abstractions from* activity. However, few readers of *Thinking and Speech*, I think, notice this.

It is easy to read Chapter 5 of *Thinking and Speech* as if Vygotsky was talking about mental shapes whose traces are exhibited in behaviour, rather than themselves being forms of activity. The chief subject matter of this chapter is the artificial concepts which children form in a laboratory setting. Children are observed sorting blocks into groups based on their shape, size, colour, etc., or signs marked on the underside of the blocks. The forms of action which the children manifest are categorised according to the phases of development they exhibit. What is observed can be characterised as "concepts in the child's mind manifested in their actions," or "forms of action in which a form of consciousness is implicit." There is no objective way of saying one of these formulations is wrong and the other correct. Both descriptions are valid, depending on how you grasp the concepts of "actions," "activities" and "concepts."

But it is only in the final chapter, 7, that Vygotsky begins to talk about forms of consciousness, and explains that thinking is pure meaning (not words), tied up with emotion and volition, non-sequential, like a "hovering cloud that gushes a shower of words" when we speak. Nonetheless, it is through its origin in speech – an activity by an individual using sequential actions mediated by spoken words to do something in the world – that we can understand the intellect.

But concepts – by which we mean entities with a social existence that are *acquired* by people as we participate in activity and *learn* – are special *forms of activity*. Leontyev's Activity Theory is *also* a theory of concepts, but one which begins with the societal existence of concepts, rather than their acquisition by individuals as internal forms of thought.

Thus there is essentially no contradiction between Vygotsky's Socio-Cultural Theory and Leontyev's Activity Theory, provided that both are implemented as a consistent and comprehensive, monist theory of human activity.

The rectification of some of the defects of Leontyev's Activity Theory and its use as a *social theory* was accomplished by Engeström, by the conception of an activity as a "system," marginalising the significance of other activities outside of an organisation ("system of activity") which is the subject matter of intervention. The whole idea of activities as *units* of analysis is negated, however, if there is only one activity. More on this presently.

10   Germ Cell and Unit of Analysis

I have already referred to "units of analysis" and "germ cells," concepts which are so central to Activity Theory it is impossible to talk about Activity Theory without reference to them. I will now endeavour to explain where these terms come from and clarify exactly what is meant by them.

The two terms – "unit of analysis" and "germ cell" – both refer to the same entity, but in a different sense, and both terms have their origin in 19th century German science – *das Eins* and *der Keim*. "Unit of analysis" is widely understood as the smallest entity which figures in analysis as an instance of a phenomenon for a given theory; typically it would be an individual person, a group, a class or a nation. Although originating in 19th century German science, the term "unit of analysis" was rarely used at the time Vygotsky first used it in 1934, and only came into widespread use in the social sciences after World War Two.

The idea of the "germ cell" has its origin in the work of Johann Gottfried Herder (often regarded as an early founder of anthropology) and the great naturalist and poet, Johann Wolfgang von Goethe, before Hegel gave the idea a systematic philosophical formulation. Hegel referred to it as the One or the First in his Logic. The idea was subsequently taken up by Marx, Vygotsky and the Soviet Activity Theorists. (Blunden, 2010; 2012; 2021).

The term "cell" in this context was used by Marx for the basic entity of Economics, by analogy with the cell of Biology:

> In the analysis of economic forms, moreover, neither microscopes nor chemical reagents are of use. The force of abstraction must replace both. But in bourgeois society, the commodity-form of the product of labour – or value-form of the commodity – is the economic cell-form.
>
> MARX, Preface, 1867

But neither Hegel nor Marx ever presented an explicit definition of either "unit" (*die Einheit*) or "germ-cell" (*der Keim*). In *Thinking and Speech*, Vygotsky gave a definition of "unit of analysis" which united the sense of Hegel's "the One" (*das Eins*) and "the First" (*das Erste*). In his Logic, Hegel shows that the crucial point in analysing some phenomenon is the determination of the One: the single instance of the phenomenon. That One then becomes the First: the starting point for a conceptual reconstruction of the entire phenomenon. That is, the unit represents a *concept of the whole* "in embryo," and the selection of the unit determines how the whole process is conceptualised. As the starting point for analysis, the unit is the simplest instance of the phenomenon which can be perceived without reference to a concrete theory of the phenomenon.

Vygotsky cleverly redeployed the already known term "unit of analysis," the smallest entities recognised by the analytical microscope, so that it also represented an abstract (embryonic) concept of the whole phenomenon. Not just the smallest unit of the phenomenon, but a potential concept of the whole phenomenon. I say "abstract" because the "unit of analysis" is as yet undeveloped. It is just an embryo, a "germ cell" of the whole, developed phenomenon, *der Keim* in Hegel's expression. But it is "concrete," in the sense that it is immediate, even visceral, and available as an everyday conception in the context in which the activity arises, that is, at a level of theory *below* that of which the cell is the germ. It is at hand; you don't need to know the theory as a precondition to understanding the unit or germ cell. You don't have to be an economist to grasp what a commodity is and how it is a really-existing value. So that's why I say that the germ cell is a "potential concept." It is available to practical or everyday intelligence, not just as a pseudoconcept, but a potential concept which can grow into a true concept by means of theoretical reconstruction.

It can be said that unless the concept of a phenomenon can be shown to be rooted in such a One, a single instance which is comprehensible without reference to the theory or concept for which it functions as the unit or germ cell, then the concept is just an abstract concept. By "abstract" I mean a concept detached from experience and lacking in definite content, a superficial concept based on appearances alone, a bad concept, an incoherent concept. Any valid *concrete* concept, any concept with genuine explanatory power, must have its One. This does not exclude concepts which are subordinate or specialised concepts *within* a well-grounded theory which in themselves are abstract since they rely for their meaning on their place within a broader theory.

The evident ambiguity in the word "abstract" I will deal with presently.

So the importance of the "germ cell" in Activity Theory is two-fold. First, it allows us to form an everyday or visceral understanding of a social practice by stripping it back to its simplest form. This simplest form or "germ cell" of an activity is rooted in a form of human action, and as such, the germ cell will necessarily embody a contradiction, typically the difference between the goal and motive of the archetypal action. So the germ cell does not rely on the theory itself to be understood, but arises from the lower level of activity, the context from which the activity in question arises. Such a germ cell can shed light on the whole form of activity which unfolds from it and allows it to be grasped concretely – a simple concept of the process as a whole. A *concrete concept* like this is distinguished from a pseudoconcept which simply indicates a field of objects according to a shared attribute.

This understanding opens the door to practical *intervention* in human development. A germ cell can be utilised for intervention in a social formation or institution by introducing a simple "germ cell" practice which takes root in the environment and grows spontaneously without further intervention to *transform* the environment. Or a tool which enables some simple action which has the potential to transform an activity. Or complex fields of study mastered by school students who are introduced to the basic concept in the form of a germ cell, and assisted through problem-solving methods of pedagogy to reconstruct step-by-step, germ cell by germ cell, the conceptual framework of the entire theory.

At the same time, the idea of the unit of analysis is that some complex social practice is nothing more than an aggregate of "units." It orients our approach to understanding a phenomenon. Identifying and understanding a simple unit and how different units can relate to one another allows us to form a unifying concept of the phenomenon and build up an understanding of how a whole complex process works.

Because we see the unit as a germ cell, we expect to see that the broader phenomenon develops as the unit itself develops.

Marx's analysis of political economy in terms of the commodity relation provided the model for Vygotsky and the Activity Theorists. Marx opens *Capital* with the words: "The wealth of those societies in which the capitalist mode of production prevails, presents itself as 'an immense accumulation of commodities', its unit being a single commodity." But the appearance of wealth in capitalist societies (money, credit, services, contracts, intellectual property, shares, etc.) differs widely in appearance from the simple commodities from which that wealth has developed. By making the commodity the unit *and* germ cell of value he made his starting point such a simple relation that anyone who has had even the most rudimentary experience of economic life will immediately understand without recourse to any prior theory about money and value. The single commodity is "the simplest social form of value" (Marx, 1881). And yet understanding how value arises from being a commodity, i.e., a product of labour to be used for exchange, is the foundation for understanding the entire dynamics of capitalism.

The germ cell offers an approach to understanding any social phenomenon. The first task Marx set himself was to show how a commodity is both an exchange-value (i.e., it contains a definite quantity of necessary labour) and a use-value (i.e., has a certain utility for a buyer). The goal of the act of production (in Leontyev's terms) is the use-value, but the motive for the act of production is its exchange-value. Marx was the first to see that these two determinations of value were not identical and were in conflict with one another, and the contradiction between the two determinations of value drives the development of capitalist society. This is an example of using the unit/cell as a method of analysis and conceptual reconstruction.

Hegel showed that, in outline, any science has this same structure. Further, at nodal points (*Knoten*) in the unfolding structure of a science, *new* units/cells appear, marking the development of the various branches and subfields in the science.

Consequently, the unit/cell can also be used as a method of teaching and learning. For example, typical mathematical expressions and problems differ vastly from counting, but it is from counting which most of mathematics grew. Awareness of this structure of mathematical knowledge allows a school to design the curriculum so as to lead pupils through the whole of mathematics by gradually building on the practice of counting, determining new units at each step.

Further, understanding that the germ cell is the active essence of a real process, an elementary social practice can be introduced into a community or institution, and, if the soil is propitious, it will grow and may ultimately transform the entire social formation. It depends of course on whether the context really is propitious. For example, the introduction of trade into a hitherto isolated tribal community can be relied upon to pretty quickly undermine traditional relations and draw a community into the world market. As the terrain changes under the impact of the proliferating germ cell, so the germ cell itself must change. Word meaning changes as the intellect develops. The labour process changes as the products being exchanged develop and as the production process changes the people doing the work change and their needs change. Germ cell and environment develop in interaction with one another.

Leontyev's students Petr Galperin (1902–1988) and Vasily Davydov (1930–1998), pioneered the use of "germ cell" in Activity Theory, and this idea has proved to be very productive over the decades since.

When Engeström developed his own version of Activity Theory, he overcame a number of problems in Leontyev's version, but the understanding of "unit" was now lost altogether. The unit of analysis was transformed into a "root model" for a "system of activity" (more on "system" below). Nonetheless, Engeström and European and American followers of Leontyev's theory have made fruitful use of the concepts of "artefact-mediated actions" and "activities" as well as the concept of "germ cell" both as a method of analysis and as a method of intervention and extended Activity Theory into a variety of fields of research and intervention.

Whereas the concept of "systems of activity" is commonly used for diagnosis of problems in institutions followed up by well-targeted changes in the system, intervention using "germ cells" is central to many applications of Activity Theory in projects for educational and social change. Meanwhile, European and American Activity Theorists use Leontyev's ideas about motivation and the development of personality to do important work.

11   Activities and Concepts

I need to emphasise a point made above: an activity is a concept, and a concept is an activity. The only difference between an activity and a concept is the *connotation* on the one hand of behaviour, and on the other of consciousness. But actually, each subsumes the other: an activity is an aggregate of actions which include the reason for doing something, the shared concept binding all the actions together. The concepts a person has acquired are a subset of all the activities to be found in their life-world.

What it means when we say we have a concept of something is that we understand a particular combination of actions, or more precisely, the *norms* determining a certain aggregate of actions with an established place in the given social formation, i.e., culture, institution, science or other social practice. To fully understand the activity means to grasp the concept, inclusive of the reasons for the various actions making up the activity. This fact is somewhat obscured by our habit of *reifying* concepts. For example, we take it that a chair is a certain useful object and we can recognise it by the usual shape of a chair. But people know how to make them, know the price they sell for, know where to place them around the house and how to sit in them. In reality, this whole ensemble of practices is what constitutes the concept of "chair." Taken out of the social context in which people make and use chairs, an object of chair-shape is not a chair at all. Likewise, a "university" is constituted not by build-ings and grounds and academic staff and students, but by the set of practices constituting a university.

Any *culture* (or science, or institution) is an aggregate of *activities* (practices or projects), or more precisely by certain *norms* of activity. Theories and nar-ratives are abstracted from those activities. A *mind* is an individual instance of the culture, an aggregate of concepts making up the intellect of a person and what Vygotsky called the "potential concepts" making up a person's practical intelligence based on the use of the artefacts on which the culture is built.

But these concepts which make up the minds of people participating in a community did not generally *originate* in the minds of its present day citizens. People are born into a community in which these concepts/activities already exist, and as they grow up and participate in the general life of the community the individuals *acquire* the concepts as they learn to do things according to, or in mindful violation of, the norms of the community embodied in its activities.

Further, concepts are not merely mental entities; they exist only insofar as they (eventually) manifest themselves in action. And actions are not merely physical entities; an action essentially includes the reason for doing it. The idea of a body of knowledge that exists like some kind of static neural filing system is not tenable. Knowledge as something self-sufficient alongside the parts of the nervous system which actuate the body in action or perception is dubious. Insofar as there is any distinction at all between a concept and an activity, they are intimately tied together through the processes of their development.

When we compare the work of Vygotsky and Leontyev we see Vygotsky's most important work was the study of the development of *concepts*, while Leontyev's most important work was on the development of *activities*. So both writers in fact studied the *same object*, though taking it in a different sense: one as forms of subjective consciousness, the other as forms of objective practice. But the frame in which they studied their respective topics is such that they were in reality both studying the same thing: both studied activity. Activity Theory is a *monist* theory of psychology, and it makes no difference whether you call that one substance *Geist*, mind, or activity. There is no *essential* differ-ence between the two bodies of work.

The idea of a "germ cell" ties "activities" and "concepts" together. The germ cell is an action (or an artefact which is the goal or means or symbol or name of some action), something done for a reason, namely, the object-concept of an activity. An action always contains at least one internal contradiction, that between goal and motive. It is this contradiction which is at the root of any concrete concept. The germ cell being an action shows why a concrete concept can have different *senses* according to the social context in which the action is done. This also shows why an entire activity is represented in germ cell as an *action* – because the reason for doing the action is the concept of the activity. This also shows why there is always moment of volition at the heart of any concept.

> Thought has its origins in the motivating sphere of consciousness, a sphere that includes our inclinations and needs, our interests and impulses, and our affect and emotion. The affective and volitional tendency stands behind thought. Only here do we find the answer to the final "why" in the analysis of thinking.
>
> VYGOTSKY, 1934

For example, the motive for producing a commodity is to realise its *exchange* value, but this is only possible by producing it as a *use*-value. This is the concept of commodity production. The reason to exercise is to be able to move around safely and easily, but it is precisely those movements which you *can't* do safely and easily which you have to exercise. A germ cell action can only function as a germ cell of a given activity, for example science or economics, if it is situated within a relevant activity, for example science-like practices of observation and measurement or making and exchanging for needs.

To continue Leontyev's Activity Theory today means that we must critically appropriate Leontyev's work in the light of its place in the genealogy of ideas lying behind it, from Herder, Goethe, Hegel, Marx and Vygotsky (Blunden, 2010).

12   Abstract and Concrete

I indicated above that the word "abstract" is used in Activity Theory in two contradictory senses which have their origin in Hegel. A very common expression amongst Activity Theorists is "rising from abstract to the concrete." This expression is often used to describe the scientific process which begins with an "abstract" concept (i.e., a simple, undeveloped concept, e.g., commodity or word-meaning) and on this basis reconstructs in theory the entire "concrete" process (e.g., bourgeois society or intellect). The expression describes the relation between a simple unit or germ cell and the concrete process that grows out of that germ cell, by analogy with a seed and the tree which grows from that seed if conditions are propitious. It expresses both a theoretical and a practical relation. That is, it refers both to the reconstruction of a phenomenon *in theory*, and the way an actual germ cell practice can transform an *actual* form of practice or produce a new form of concrete practice. "Abstract" means cut off from or lacking a variety of facets or connections with the world; "concrete" means having a rich variety of facets and connections.

The same expression also represents how a branch of science can be *taught* by giving the students a germ cell to begin with and guiding them through the discovery of successive transformations leading them to acquire and understand of the whole body of knowledge. Or alternatively, a simple form of practice meeting an immediate need can be introduced and allowed to grow until it effects a *real* transformation of the whole social environment. Or alternatively, the expression describes the *historical* movement of science beginning from that moment when its epoch-making discovery (germ cell) is made, such as the development of biology after the discovery of the cell.

The expression "rising from abstract to the concrete" was coined by Evald Ilyenkov (1960) but originates in Marx's *Grundrisse* (1858) and reflects the structure of all the books in Hegel's *Encyclopaedia*. To fully understand this expression, it is important to know that in dialectics "abstract" and "concrete" have very specific double meanings.

"Abstract" means both far-removed from everyday, immediate experience, lacking in connections and relations to other concepts: abstracted from reality, *and* simple in the sense of representing a single, undeveloped idea or relation, stripped of contingent attributes and variety.

"Concrete" on the other hand means both given to immediate sensuous experience, *and* with multiple connections to other things, with aspects and tendencies within itself, as Marx says: "the concentration of many abstractions."

The movement of science is therefore a double movement. It begins with *concrete* experience (e.g. observations) which are nonetheless *abstract* in the sense that on their own, each datum has little significance. Science then goes through a process of combining data in multiple different ways, averaging, categorising, and filtering and contrasting data, and so on. The final outcome is a simple idea, such as "collaborative learning," "Neoliberalism" or "value." This outcome is both *abstract* in the sense of being a general principle only more or less instantiated in any given instance, but *concrete* in the sense of being the concentration of all that data, history and investigation. The implementation of an abstract idea, e.g. implementing a program of collaborative learning in a certain school, means taking the original idea, which is a mere abstraction, and "concretising it" in definite circumstances demanding numerous modifications to deal with difficulties and special conditions. A study of this project would again be beginning with abstract data (such as a list of test results) with the aim of producing a more refined (concrete) concept of collaborative learning. So the movement is always a double movement from abstract to concrete and concrete to abstract and continues in successive cycles of experience.

13   Analysis by Units and Analysis by Elements

Engeström's seminal work, his PhD Thesis *Learning by Expanding* (1987), marked the beginning of a new current of Activity Theory, the current which is probably the most widely known today. In this work, Engeström had conducted an immanent critique of American Pragmatism and Soviet Activity Theory. Beginning from Vygotsky's (Figure 3) triangular conception of artefact-mediated action as a unit of analysis, Engeström (Figure 2) "expanded" this triangle by adding mediating links to each of the links in the original triangle. The result was his famous triangle-of-triangles which presented a network of relations between subject, community, tools and signs, rules, division of labour and object, all connected each to the other, and to the object, outcome. Each of the links in the triangle potentially harbours a contradiction.

Engeström (1987; 2015, p. 65) characterised this as the "root model" of a "system of activity," arguing that "the model is actually the smallest and simplest unit that still preserves the essential unity and integral quality behind any human activity." So the triangle was formulated as a "root model" but then incidentally referred to as a "unit" without any reflection on the difference between a system model and a unit of analysis.

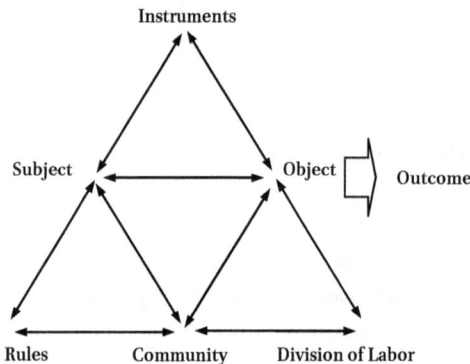

FIGURE 2   Engeström's root model

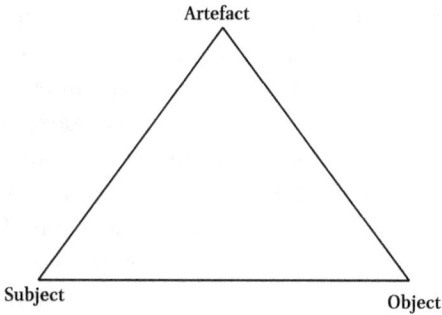

FIGURE 3   Vygotsky's unit of analysis

What is the difference between a model and a unit? In the model, for example, all of the elements are categorically different, but none of these elements are actions, and yet an activity is nothing but units, i.e., it is an aggregate of actions. H_2O is a "model" of water in which H and O are the elements, but "water molecule" is a unit, because water is nothing but water molecules in one or another type of aggregate whether or not you know of or have any interest in H or O.

Yet nowhere does Engeström contradict the definition of an activity as an aggregate of actions.

–   The model *includes* the context in the form of "community" but the context is *other activities*, not just an abstract generalisation like "community." Activity Theory requires that a community is taken to be an aggregate of activities, and making bonds with a community entails making bonds with definite local projects.

–   The model includes the rules, instruments and division of labour *in addition to* the object, but in Activity Theory these elements are integral to the object-concept of the activity; they cannot simply be added together as separate elements. An activity is like a "field" in Bourdieu's theory, in which all the normative expectations and rewards operative within an activity or practice are determined by the object-concept of the field.

–   The "subject" is the person whose point of view is taken in the research; that is, the graphic is a *subjective* view of the "activity system," not an objective model of an activity at all. Does this mean that what is represented is the activity of one person, one of a multiplicity of such systems each with their own object, etc., or is a representation taken to be an average of all the subjective representations, or do we take it that the "subject" is that subject position which has the "objective" or "official" point of view presumed in A.N. Leontyev's theory?

A model is a completely different way of grasping an entity rather than the concept of it in terms of units. There is no true concept of the whole in a model, only its analysis into different elements. At a certain point in analysis, however, an object cannot be conceived of as so many like units. In the classic example of water, a water molecule is found on analysis to be a heterogeneous system combining the elements hydrogen and oxygen atoms in a specific structure. The *concept* of the water molecule, however, is that it is the smallest unit of water. In the analysis of an action we face the same situation: an action is a complex system of internal psychic activity, physiology, behaviour, and material artefacts in a social situation. But in Activity Theory we take an action as elementary for our science and it is defined as a process whose goal differs from its motive.

Since 1987, Engeström and his followers have come to routinely refer to Figure 2 as "the unit of analysis." Not "the unit of analysis of ...," just "the unit of analysis." Each of the *elements* of the system is qualitatively different from the others and all are necessary for a working system of actions. Problems in the system arise from contradictions within one of the elements or contradictions in relations between elements.

The "root model" is a classic representation of an activity as a *system of elements*, in contrast to Vygotsky and Leontyev's insistence on the representation of activity by *units*. One could say that there are two types of scientific analysis: analysis by units and analysis by elements – that is, dialectical analysis or systems theory. Engeström's system represents the entirety of the field of investigation. The system is analytically isolated, connected to the rest of the world by boundary conditions, although these are generally not included in Engeström's representation, except for "community." There is only one system. When other systems are added to the field of observation, then each system has "boundary objects" connecting it with each other system.

In Vygotsky's analysis by units, however, the field of enquiry is made up of *many* units; the units develop as do the relations between the units. Analysis by units "simplifies" the field of enquiry by means of the common characterisation of all the units making up the larger, unbounded field of enquiry as units. Likewise, in Leontyev's Activity Theory, the relevant activities exist alongside and in active relationships with *other* activities.

Engeström's innovation was therefore a fundamental break from the tradition of Hegel, Marx and Vygotsky. However, he clothed the move in the language of Activity Theory. Since what was represented was an activity, it represented a *unit of analysis*. However, what was being analysed was not a social formation made up of *many* such units, but the unit itself. It was a unit *for* analysis, but not a unit *of* analysis. He analysed the unit by means of *systems theory*.

An activity became a system constructed from subject, community, division of labour, etc., no longer an aggregate of actions or subordinate collaborating activities. In any real institution, however, there will be *multiple activities* working side by side, multiple projects in conflict with one another, each with their own motivation. In Engeström's system theory approach there is only one activity, and any conflicts arise from contradictions within or between the *elements*, and which need to be eliminated.

In order to analyse the *social formation* of which the activity is a unit it becomes necessary to present numerous *coupled systems*, usually theorised through the idea of a *boundary object* shared by two or more systems. To analyse a typical social formation with a multitude of such systems entails the impossibly complex system of multiply coupled systems, now a system with millions of elements, the very problem which analysis by units was intended to overcome. More recently, Engeström has proposed a unit of analysis which is "multiple-interconnected activity systems" (Engeström & Sannino, 2021) – a so-called "Fourth Generation of Activity Theory" whose unit is explicitly plural in itself.

The "root model" constitutes a kind of template to be imposed on any given research subject. In this form, the triangle has been used as an artefact in Engeström's interventions in his Developmental Work Research (DWR) in which his institute acts as a change consultant for organisations (usually public service bodies) experiencing difficulties. Engeström has done some fine work with his DWR approach and it is widely emulated across the world. All those who have successfully emulated DWR have improvised on the original protocols in some way, however, and this work has proved to be a rich source of knowledge in the broader realm of socio-cultural analysis. In reality, what remains of the so-called "unit of analysis" is a mnemonic which reminds the researcher to pay attention to all the different elements which may generate problems within the system. DWR work belongs to Activity Theory (i) because it historically arose from Activity Theory, and (ii) because its ontology – artefacts, artefact-mediated actions and activities – is that of Activity Theory. However, Engeström made a fundamental break from the dialectical tradition by adopting systems analysis. On the other hand, Engeström has conducted some exemplary studies based on the expansion of a "germ cell," again justifying his identity as an Activity Theorist.

The reader should not however draw the conclusion: "analysis by units good, analysis by elements bad." In Vygotsky and Luria's analysis of the brain, that is, the material neurological processes which underlie psychic processes, they pointed out that the newborn's brain is a *system* of organs, each with a very distinct function. The diversity and specialisation of these organs is surprising;

different organs perceive colour, movement, trajectory and shape of moving visual images, and other organs correlate these with sounds, etc., for example. All these organs combine to allow animal-level functionality in a newborn or infant.

As any of the higher animals grow up, their involvement in activity – playing baby games or going along with the adults – builds "alliances" between these basic modules to equip them for the experiences they are going to need in their life. Among humans, we have developed childcare and educational practices using cultural artefacts and the forms of action they enable to "program" these neurological alliances and young humans spend many years undergoing this "programming." Human infants are hard-wired to play close attention to what the adults around them are doing. Over time, basic hard-wired functions like memory, thinking, attention, perception, etc., are *superseded* by *higher psychological functions* which facilitate the replacement of "native" involuntary memory, attention, and so forth with *voluntary, culturally mediated* memory, attention and so on, which are based on "alliances" of the basic neurological organs. By the time we become adults, all our mental functions are executed by whole alliances entailing the participation of areas all over entire nervous system, even "gut feelings." *Localisation* of brain functionality is quite limited.

Now this brain structure, called a *Gestalt* by Gestalt Psychologists, forms a *system* of quite distinct elements, no longer separate hard-wired elements, but elements which are already in themselves systems. They cannot be treated as units. But they *do* exist in a world full of other brains in active bodies in the process of "programming" these brain-and-bodies to work together in a social and cultural formation. And the nature of these social formations, made up of millions of broadly similar people, are eminently appropriate phenomena for analysis by *units*. That is, the first way we understand minds is as units of a cultural community, something we can do without the aid of MRI machines and scalpels.

Likewise, there is a place for analysis of institutions and organisations as systems. Especially from the point of view of the leadership or regulators of an institution who hold the levers of power over a *system* but not the life-projects of all their employees, their unions and professional associations and so on. So system analysis of institutions and psychological functions does have a place. But in the wide world of social and cultural conflict and cooperation, "system" is more a hope than a reality.

13.1 *Monism Again*

This might be a moment to reflect on whether Activity Theory has really overcome Descartes' paradox, whether we are still contemplating objects as passive observers. The short answer is that we are *part of* human activity, we have an inside view of it. To understand particular institutions, ethnic communities and political projects, etc, we have to get involved and help. But still, it is a fact that we can walk into a hitherto isolated valley in New Guinea and meet local people who have never seen outsiders, and we can still make each other understood, because we are humans. What the world looks like to a snake, we can only speculate, but we do have privileged access to those activities in which we can participate. To put this in philosophical terms, the subject and object are part of the same activity and can only be grasped on that basis.

This insider viewpoint has its downsides. What is most familiar to us we don't even notice. We look straight through it. So the study of activities in other communities and how people explain the reasons for what they do is especially useful for making what is familiar stand out in relief against its absence.

But when we look at a material object, we see it terms of its being an artefact, a material entity which is or can be included in practical human activity, including experimental activity, and it is by this means that we can understand it. Perception is essentially active.

14   Subject, Object and Participant Research

True to its Hegelian origins, Activity Theory understands both the research subject (a.k.a. the object) and the researcher (a.k.a. the subject) as first of all and essentially moments of the culture of which they are a part. Any effort by the researcher to *isolate* the research subject from the culture and society of which they are a part is doomed to fail and in doing so will despite themselves obscure the essential nature of the situation being studied. Further, any attempt to abstract the researcher's activity from the situation they are studying is generally vain and false.

This standpoint of Activity Theory is in contrast to the traditional, mainstream research paradigm in which the researcher aims to insulate their research subjects so far as possible from "outside influences" and to make their own intervention as inconsequential as possible. The conception of the research subjects is that their nature is independent of their environment and subsequent observations in other situations can be interpreted on the basis of a fixed nature determined in isolation in the laboratory, interacting with an external environment. This is false. Human beings are what they are in the context of the activities they engaged in, and a human being isolated from the activities which animate and sustain them (and have done so in the past) are not fully human beings at all. In any case, observation is an essentially *active* process. All the traditional positivist research paradigm achieves is to remove people from the context of their own life-projects and insert them into the context of the experimental laboratory where they will try to behave as good research objects.

Activity Theory "puts culture in the middle," seeing that all human interactions are mediated by artefacts which originate from the wider culture, either deliberately introduced by the researcher, or part of the research activity simply because both the research subjects and the objects of research are creatures of their times. Activity theorists both study *how* cultural objects and processes determine the activity of research subjects, and *use* cultural objects in order to bring about desired changes in the research situation, that is, they *intervene*. They learn not only what the research subjects do, with assistance, but they learn what they – as both researchers and activists – *can* do.

Ideally, activity theorists are *participant observers*. This stance differs from the stance of the anthropologist (for example) who aims to share insofar as possible the lives of their research subjects but to do so as invisibly as possible so as to have minimal impact on the activity they are studying, observe it as if in disguise and then uncritically report it. Activity theorists prefer to address themselves to the same problems and aims which the research subjects are addressing. While they do so, their aim is not to solve a problem themselves, but to offer their assistance to the research subjects, working with the research subjects, to solve the research subjects' problems and help them achieve their goals. But activity theorists are completely open in their commitment to their research aims in addition to the indigenous goals of the research subjects. Ideally, though not necessarily, the research subjects will themselves come to value the research aims and themselves become *participant-researchers*. The participant researcher is simply someone who takes note of all their experiences, shares them, and learns from them as they pursue their life-goals.

To participate in a project for the purpose of accruing publications is suspect. To do so when the participants find your observations and your questions inconvenient and distracting is unethical. To carry on research in secret is utterly unethical unless the objects of the research project are white supremacists or corrupt police or something where no pretence of solidarity with the participants is possible.

15   Activities Have a Life Cycle

We have learnt from A.N. Leontyev that an activity is an aggregate of collaborative actions all immanently tending towards the realisation of a common object using a division of labour. Engeström has further observed that such activities entail specific immanent means and norms. Such activities represent an *ideal* – the concept of "an activity." But no activity comes into the world fully formed and already conforming to this ideal, and might in fact *never* fully conform to this ideal. This raises the all-important issue of the *development* of projects (or practices or activities).

At first, the activity does exist not at all; people are just carrying on their lives unaware of the object in question. Up to a certain point the conditions for the existence of the activity may not be present. When the conditions are found to be present, that is, some problem arises for which the conditions of its solution seem to be present, then people will begin to act in an effort to overcome the problem, at least insofar as it affects them personally. Initially, their actions will not be coordinated; there will simply be so many independent actions tending towards some common object, each initiated under unique conditions. The actions produce something more like a crime wave than a social movement. The development from here is merely quantitative and qualitative: more and more people act with greater and greater vigour. This is the first phase in the *life cycle* of an activity or project. Researchers are just as interested in *emerging* activities like this as they are in fully formed activities, already conforming to a model such as Engeström's "system of activity." Maybe even more so.

At a certain point, the actors begin to be aware of each other's actions and begin to collaborate. But this is still far from being a project with a well-formed, shared object together with appropriate shared ethical norms and common means. Most likely the activity does not even have a name or a shared symbol or leader far less a coherent concept of where it is going and according to what principles. Actions become coordinated, but sporadically, and sometimes at cross purposes. It still remains to adopt some definite means of organisation and agreed means and norms, some principles and possibly some kind of stable leadership.

At a certain point, the activity really "finds itself." It enters upon the scene of social life behind its own banner, with its own concept of its demands, alongside all the other institutions and movements in the wider society which must take a position for or against the new activity, and adapt to it, cooperate with it or strive to extinguish it. The activity then enters into a process of development in which it *penetrates* every other institution and milieu with its own ideas. Meanwhile the activity itself becomes *domesticated* and eventually it is simply a feature of the existing social formation alongside other practices with no separate existence. It is simply *one concept*, one practice, within the culture of a whole community.

At any point in this development, if and until it becomes completely objectified in the entire life of the community, an activity can "die." Not until the activity is so integrated into the life of the community that it shares the fate of that community can the *effort* to further the activity – and conscious awareness of its trajectory – be relaxed.

That is the life cycle of an activity (or practice or project). Activity theorists are interested in the entire life cycle of activities, not just the "normal" and "ideal" activities that have settled into being a fixed institution reproducing the given social formation, and nor just during that tumultuous phase where ideas are objects of contention on the streets along with the excitement of activism and social change in motion. Figure 4 illustrates this life-cycle.

So when considering an action, activity theorists need to determine its motive. In ideal conditions – the conditions presumed in the work of Leontyev and Engeström – we will find that the action draws its motivation from the activity of which it is a part and that activity will be a well known feature of the existing social formation.

But frequently this will not be the case. If the action in question arises during the first phase in the life cycle of an activity it will be motivated as an immediate response to an existing situation but without any consciousness of

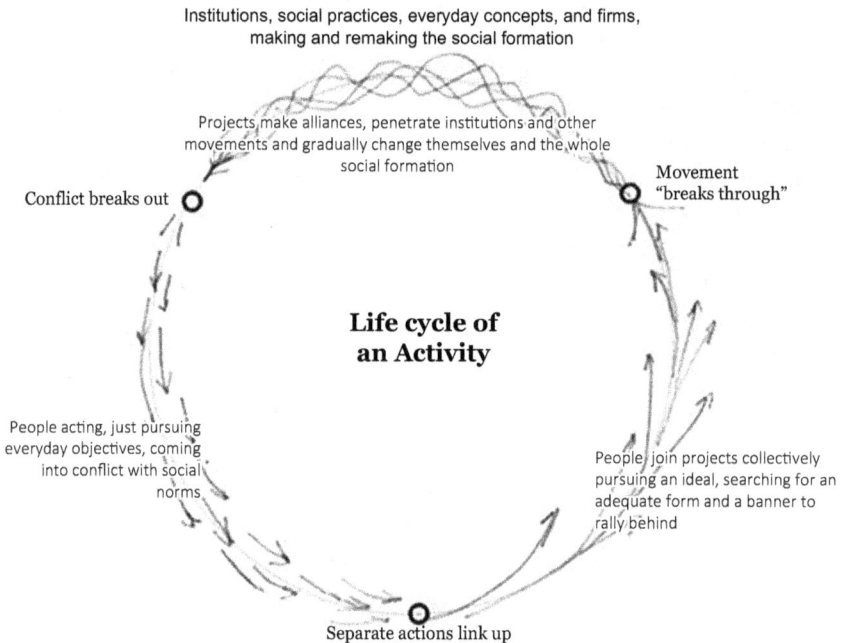

Institutions, social practices, everyday concepts, and firms, making and remaking the social formation

Projects make alliances, penetrate institutions and other movements and gradually change themselves and the whole social formation

Conflict breaks out

Movement "breaks through"

Life cycle of an Activity

People acting, just pursuing everyday objectives, coming into conflict with social norms

People join projects collectively pursuing an ideal, searching for an adequate form and a banner to rally behind

Separate actions link up

FIGURE 4   Life cycle of an activity

how that situation could be resolved, without the aid of a developed object-concept. If the action arises during the second phase of the life cycle of an activity, then the action may well be motivated by a consciousness of how the situation can be resolved, but at that moment this resolution is not available within the existing social arrangements.

Thus we should always be able to identify the motivation of an action, but the nature of the motivation will vary according to the development of collaborative relationships in the given social context.

16   The Context of Activities

It is fundamental to Activity Theory that every activity is part of its context; an activity is responding to the conditions which surround it and its object, norms and mediating artefacts are inevitably drawn from those same social conditions. But if we are serious about this claim, we find ourselves in a quandary: how can we know about the infinite, unbounded context surrounding an activity when our aim is just to study one finite activity? What is the point of analysis by units if we are obliged to analytically *isolate* the activity from its context?

It is the approach of *Systems Theory* to isolate the system of interest and represent the context in terms of boundary conditions, in the hope that the boundary conditions are knowable, fixed and there is no "feedback" from the environment and the activity in question is not "coupled" with other systems.

For Activity Theory, the whole is represented as an aggregate of activities. The context is simply *other activities*. This does not eliminate the problem of an unbounded context, but it frames the problem of conceiving of the relation of the activity to its context in the same terms in which we conceive of the research subject itself, *as activities*. It is an immanent property of activities the way activities relate to each other, the way the object-concepts of activities are modified by other activities, the way the norms of activities are modified by the activities around them.

All activities exist in an unpredictable and unbounded world, and *there is no shortcut* which can insulate the observer from this uncertainty.

What we have to understand is the extent to which an activity is capable of generating the conditions for its own reproduction. It is this which makes an activity a "living organism" capable of surviving the exigencies of its environment: institutions like states, families and religious faiths which somehow survive revolutions, along with economic and gender hierarchies which also prove to be exceptionally resilient, even while economic and family systems change. An activity which fails to reproduce the conditions for its own existence, is either short-lived, or is a dependent product of other activities.

Any activity which is a dependent product of its conditions, reproduced by the conditions but otherwise incapable of reproducing itself, is like the government departments which are created and destroyed overnight on a change of government or those small businesses which come and go every day according to economic conditions. In such cases, the conditions of existence remain of primary importance in analysing the activity.

16.1   *The Immediate and Societal Contexts of Activities*

A culture or nation does not produce individuals like some kind of cookie-cutter. The relation between a universal activity and the individual actions which make it up is mediated by a multiplicity of particular activities and institutions. It is this multiplicity of activities which constitutes the context or activity.

Mariane Hedegaard (2009) has drawn attention to the fact that the context of an action is always at least two-fold.

In the first place there is the collaborative activity which constitutes the immediate context of activity and provides the "merely known" motive for all the constituent actions. Hedegaard refers to this as the "activity setting." It could be a hospital, a kindergarten, a business or a family home, for example. Such settings are typically "institutions," understood as collaborative projects each with a certain concept of itself such that all the actions are collaborating towards the realisation of the normative conception of its goal. So for example, all the specialist departments and social classes working in a hospital contribute to making patients healthy; everyone in the family contributing to raising the children and sharing the burdens of everyday life, and so on. This is

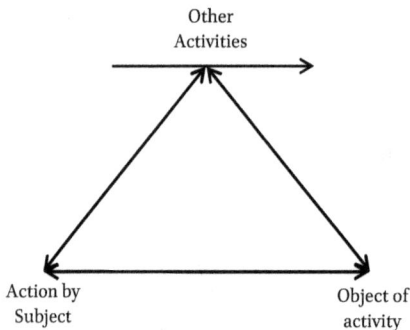

FIGURE 5   Activity setting

the immediate context which provides the merely known motives for all the actions taking place in the setting. The norms operative within such an "activity setting," determined by the object-concept of the activity, are a "field" which Bourdieu uses to theorise the rules and rewards active within an institution.

But in the second place there is the wider society, culture or community – that universal activity which subsumes all the particular activities going on within its sphere of influence – all the hospitals, kindergartens, businesses and families which participants in the "activity setting" participate in at *other* times. Typically this "wider society" is conceived of as the nation state – a collaborative activity which is more or less self-governing, mediated by a shared artefact such as a geographical territory – and an official language, bound together by a shared history, and constituted by governmental activities which to a greater or lesser degree determine the character of all the institutions within it. This universal activity in which everyone is also participating mediates all the actions determined by the object of the particular institution.

But this conception of the wider context can be problematic.

I do not see this as concentric circles of context: micro-, meso-and macro-contexts. All there is is Nature and other activities. Each activity has a concrete concept of its self. An investigation of an institution's self-concept will reveal the impact on this *particular* institution of *numerous* other activities. Most important in the generalised surrounding culture is what is *universal* across all the relevant particular activities. There is no master activity determining the whole thing and there is always the possibility that a war will break out, or a pandemic or economic crisis will cut through normal life and disrupt an institution. To understand the institutions in a given country you have to study all the various activities, how they see themselves, and how they support each other. There is no short cut. The context is an open-ended totality and there is no possibility of definitively capturing it in some finite theory. Events on the global stage can derail your project to improve the work of your kindergarten; the government can change the funding arrangements for your school. This ultimately unpredictable condition of the wider cultural context is ineliminable, but the focus is always on the capacity of the activity to reproduce itself out of the conditions of its existence.

But in addition, Hedegaard makes the following observation: *individual people* in this situation *move* from one "setting" to another; the child who is participating in the kindergarten teacher's lesson this morning spends the rest of her day in the family home; the hospital's patient may happen to be also head of a household or an essential worker somewhere else in the economy. The actions of an individual are comprehensible only in the light of their participation in the *range* of activities in which they are participants, and their actions, and therefore their personality will vary from one setting to the other.

We can express this another way. A universal activity (e.g. Denmark, or Social Media) is grasped as an aggregate of activities. The individual action (by a Dane or by a social media actor, for example) is *mediated* by the *particular* activity (working in a hospital or making a webpage, for example) in constituting the universal activity. But likewise, the individual action within the "activity setting" is mediated by a range of life experiences outside the given activity. That is, we see the concrete universal activity as a unity of many particular activities which together stitch all the individual actions into a universal whole. There is no master activity. Not yet anyway.

16.2   *The Historical Context of Activities*

Activities appear at a certain historical juncture but the world in which they appear was not created just in time for them. All the institutions and cultural elements around them are the product of a long history. Every activity also has its historical antecedents and precedents. And all the participating actors also have a history. Activities arrive in a world which already "knows about them," so to speak. This historical context is just as essential as the synchronic (structural) context. Meaning is "path-dependent."

The activity of interest may be one which itself has a long history, and that history is an important key to understanding the activity and in particular the contradictions which it harbours within it. It is the identification and understanding of these contradictions in an activity as it is before us now which is of interest to activity theorists. It is these contradictions which transform a seemingly solid structure into something which is in motion, unstable and vulnerable to collapse or transformation. The study of the history of an activity gives us insight into these contemporary structural contradictions.

Contradictions have their origins in history, so analysis of an activity will impel us to look back into its history. Looking back into history for a germ cell of the activity opens analysis to the danger of being subjective and arbitrary. Somewhere in the past you can find some phenomenon which you think typifies the present state of the activity. For example, bourgeois historians of economics believe capital originated in antiquity with the birth of commerce. On the contrary, Marx has shown that over the centuries various forms of society had succeeded one another and the place of capital was subordinated to the dominant relations of the time; capital had only become the dominant relation subordinating all other relations to itself in recent centuries. The Enclosures had created the mass of labourers without access to means of production whose exploitation would be the basis for the rule of capital, but Marx did not take the forced seizure of means of production from the labourers, as in the Enclosures, to be the central contradiction of capital because such theft is not a *self-sustaining* mode of production. It was only when capitalists began gathering impoverished artisans together in workshops and appropriating their labour that marked the origins of capitalism. Marx conceived of capital as an activity which reproduced the conditions of its own reproduction through the exploitation of the labour power of proletarians who were only ever paid just enough to live on, and therefore ready for exploitation next week. This provided a sound basis for determining its historical origins. Another example. Foucault regarded modern society as an elaborate system of social control so he took it that modernity had its origin in the invention of the prison and military conscription. The question this raises is this: does one germ cell exclude another? It seems to me that one and the same phenomenon (e.g., modern society) can be validly analysed by different germ cells. However, the implication of this is that the theoretical reconstruction of the phenomenon from the abstract germ cell to the conceptual representation of the concrete phenomenon will produce different results, each of which may be judged to capture the existing concrete phenomenon more or less truly. The theoretical concrete representation is never identical with the original immediately given sensual-concrete phenomenon which was the object of analysis. The aim of theoretical reconstruction from a germ cell is to provide an insight into the essential dynamics and basis of the given concrete subject matter as an integral whole. In reality the concrete existing phenomenon will exhibit aspects which are *inessential* and are not captured by the integral, conceptual reconstruction and these may be more or less significant.

To take another example. An historical study of the 1920s and 1930s leading to World War Two would function as an explanation for a post-ww2 world divided up between the USA and the USSR. However, such an explanation contributes little to understanding the post-ww2 situation, which was created in 1944–1948 by the range of institutions put in place at Bretton Woods and Yalta. Only an analysis of *these* arrangements and the conditions in which they were implemented can shed light on the dynamics of the post-ww2 world and its basis.

Likewise, the essential contradictions in the Islamic Republic of Iran did not originate in the 1979 Revolution which was led by a group of students and progressive intellectuals but in 1981. When the Iranian workers formed shuras and occupied their factories, the Mullahs mobilised the poor into a religious militia to terrorise the shuras and put the industrialists back in charge of their factories, but under the terroristic domination of a parasitic layer of clergy. This created a system of exploitation which was self-reproducing, concentrating wealth in the hands of the Islamic clergy. The 1979 Revolution created the *conditions* for this regime, but it did not create this regime as such.

Vygotsky showed that the intellect originated not with the child's first words, and not with the child's pre-linguistic practical intelligence, but with the intersection of speech and thinking manifested in the child's first *meaningful word*.

So, identification of historical origins of an activity or concept must look to its origins as *a self-reproducing system* of actions, not simply the historically-first instance.

Secondly, activities arise in conditions which make the emergence of the activity necessary and viable. Activity theorists must look to the conditions – that is to say, the array of other activities – which constituted the soil on which the new activity flourished. If industrial technology was all that was required to stimulate an industrial revolution and the growth of industrial capital, then capitalism would have originated not in Britain, but long before, in China. But Chinese labourers maintained access to their land; only in Britain where the nobility had brutally robbed their own people of their land were the conditions for exploitation of wage labour in existence. Thus, in examining contradictions in an existing activity one must have an eye to the conditions which fostered their appearance in the first place and whether these conditions continue to exist or have in fact disappeared.

Finally, contradictions could be classified as follows: (1) Contradictions like those just discussed which lie at the very foundation of an activity (e.g. exploitation of proletarian labour power, or word meanings which are *both* means of thinking *and* communication). (2) The object-concept of an activity is not (any longer) in accord with dominant norms, that is, the conditions which sedimented themselves in the founding of the institution have changed and the institution is now out of step with its socio-cultural environment. An example of this would be a hospital found to be discharging victims of domestic violence back into the conditions in which they sustained injuries. Such a restricted conception of the hospital's object would be out of step in a society which is now acutely aware of the problem of domestic violence. (3) A contradiction which is secondary to a more fundamental contradiction. For example, the low pay of workers in the care industries which is secondary to the pre-existing feminisation of care work as a by-product of the traditional gender division of labour. The care industries we see today originated in the socialisation of care work which had hitherto been carried out by women under conditions of domestic servitude. The socialisation of care work was a necessary concomitant of women escaping domestic servitude. Ironically, the low status of care work followed them from the domestic sphere into the economy. Care work needs to be defeminised.

Most of the contradictions researchers will need to deal with are of types (2) and (3). However, the contradictions of type (1) are fundamental to how Activity Theory understands history.

In short, it is not valid to just search back in history for an "explanation" of the contradiction, its apparent germ cell. A *backward and forwards* movement is necessary: looking back speculatively for possible origins, and then tracing the relevant relations forward to establish if there is an intelligible narrative connecting the conditions in which a relation first appeared with its present-day form, and having an eye all along to the surrounding conditions which have fostered changes or exposed latent contradictions.

• • •

All the actors who will participate in the activity have a pre-history in which they have grown up, had experiences, and formed their personality and their commitments. Participation in the given activity is generally merely one episode in their life. This biographical context is also essential material for Activity Theory. Indeed, the biography of every participant, and episodes within their life, are activities, and are subject to the same methods as any other activity.

17   *Perezhivanie*

Russians have a word for "an experience" – *perezhivanie. Perezhivaniya* (plural) differ from *opit* which means "experience" in the sense of "work experience," something generally conceived of as *continuous* rather than discrete, as something which is accumulated. *Perezhivaniya*, on the other hand, are best conceived of as *discrete episodes* which transform or at least affect the person to some degree; *perezhivaniya* are emotion-laden and meaningful. A *perezhivanie* is an activity, *work* done in going through and surviving some situation, mentally processing it, and absorbing it into one's personal development. In Activity Theory, *perezhivaniya* are the building blocks, the *units*, of personality, in just the same way as the chapters of a novel are the units of a narrative (See Blunden, 2016b).

In Russian psychology, *perezhivanie* is a very basic concept, representing the active relation between a person and their situation; it entails the whole of the personality, not just one or another mental function. It differs from "lived experience" which emphasises only the subjective aspect of experiences while a *perezhivanie* is a person's active *relation to the world*, rather than something purely internal. This feature of the word – its bidirectional character – is quite common in the Russian language, like обучение, which means both instruction and learning.

Vasilyuk (1984) gave definite shape to the concept of *perezhivaniya* in his theory of psychotherapy (See Blunden, 2021b). For Vasilyuk, *perezhivaniya* are not just everyday experiences, but rather episodes in which a person is facing an *impossible situation* which they can only live through by a radical reshaping of their personality.

These are not two different concepts of an experience. A *perezhivanie*, as Vasilyuk describes it, is a fully developed experience together with its catharsis. On the other hand, we all go through "little crises" every time something happens in our lives. Perception, in Activity Theory, is an *active* process. Unless we actively respond to some stimuli it will simply pass us by; every stimulus that we remember, we remember because we reached out to it actively and incorporated the event into our person. These active experiences are *perezhivaniya*.

Recently I visited a restaurant with a psychologist friend and when we sat down I asked her how many hairdressers she had noticed as we walked past all the shops (there are 3 or 4 of them) and had she noticed the graffiti (which was abundant) – no. And then I asked did she remember the whole foods shop? Yes! All the other sensations she had seen on that walk had just come and gone, but this one sight, a young Asian woman taking barrels of exotic grain back into the brightly light and well-stocked shop, had stuck in her memory. She will remember that. It was a little *perezhivanie*.

In Activity Theory, when we refer to a *perezhivanie*, we generally mean a more or less traumatic, transformative episode of activity, inclusive of the build up and subsequent "adjustment" after the crisis is overcome. These are the ideal-typical *perezhivaniya* which constitute the fully developed concept for which the passably memorable little experience is the germ cell.

18 The Development of the Personality

The development of the personality is characterised in Activity Theory by an evolving structure and hierarchy of commitments, commitments to objectively-existing life-projects/activities. In Leontyev's view, over the course of a lifetime these commitments tend to become less personal and egocentric with more and more commitments to projects serving the social good and fostering social virtues. Over the course of an active life, these less egocentric commitments normally work their way to the peak of the hierarchy of motives.

Vygotsky's theory of the personality sits very comfortably with this idea of the personality (*lichnost*) as a life-project. Vygotsky (1934a) theorised that these commitments which make up a person's persona undergo crises at different points in their life. During such periods of crisis the subject engages in a specific kind of work called *perezhivaniya*, in which their commitments to relevant projects – *otnoshiniya* – are restructured.

Although the individual person is at the centre of their own life-project, all these *perezhivaniya* are collaborations, implicitly if not explicitly, and arise from real conflicts in the objective world around them.

When we are studying the development of a personality across a person's life, we have a macro unit and a micro unit. The macro unit is the personality or *lichnost*. The micro unit of analysis are the *perezhivaniya* in which individuals, usually in concert with others, reorient their *lichnost* and restructure their *otnoshiniya*. That is, we see the life course as a series of *perezhivaniya*, each of which is itself a specific activity. *Perezhivaniya* mark out the episodes or chapters in a person's life, or in the life of a project.

Lichnost (личность, etymologically linked to лицо, or *litso*, which means face) is a polysemous word, just as is "personality" in English. In Activity Theory, *lichnost* means a kind of persona (a theatrical mask in Latin), rather than psychic processes like temperament, intelligence, extroversion, etc.

Otnoshiniye (отношение) is also a very polysemous word; dictionaries list English translations as: affiliation, attitude, concern, relation, reference ... and more. In the context of Leontyev's theory of personality development however the word is best translated as a *commitment*. Alex Kozulin (1991) interpreted it as one's "life-relation," the "life-project" to which a person is committed. For example, for much of my recent life my *otnoshiniya* have included my late partner Vonney, Socialism, Activity Theory, Marxist Hegelianism, etc., a group of friends in their 70s all suffering from isolation, Vonney's niece, as well as a number of principles such as intellectual honesty, solidarity, sustainable living. These *otnoshiniya* form the structure of my personality, in certain situations one *otnoshiniye* predominates over the others in generating my motivation, while other *otnoshiniya* will modulate my emotions and responses. In other situations, other *otnoshiniya* will determine my emotional responses and actions. As Vygotsky emphasised, at the heart of every *concept* is a moment of volition, and the emotional content of this volition is the *otnoshiniye* embodied in that concept. Every concept evokes some kind of emotional response which is connected to the structure of a person's *otnoshiniya*, their *lichnost*. Consequently, a situation which generates a *perezhivanie* for a person makes sense only in the light of the person's *otnoshiniya*.

19   Narrative Analysis

The modern theory of the narrative begins with the Russian Formalist Vladimir Propp, who published his *Morphology of the Folktale* in 1928. Mikhail Bakhtin continued the study of narrative, introducing the notion of genre. French literary theory continued work on narrative and in the late 1970s and early 1980s the "narrative turn" exploded into social theory and psychology.

The drift of the narrative turn was not that narrative was a means of grasping concepts or part of the developmental process of concepts, but rather, "narrative rationality" was an *alternative* form of knowledge to what was variously called the "paradigmatic mode of knowing" (Walter Fisher), "scientific knowledge" (Lyotard) or the "logico-scientific" mode of knowing (Jerome Bruner). Some writers proposed that both narrative and conceptual rationality were necessary components of the whole knowledge of a topic. Bruner observed, for example, that a psychiatrist needs to bring the skills of the literary critic together with knowledge of theories of psychology in order to understand a patient, both skills being equally necessary, and that relying on just one kind of knowledge could lead to absurdities. Nonetheless, the main finding of the narrative turn seemed to be that narrative rationality and conceptual rationality were two qualitatively different, competing kinds of knowledge, counterposed to one another. The central role of narrative was highlighted in politics (Walter Fisher), psychology (Jerome Bruner and Donald Polkinghorne), sociology (Laurel Richardson), economics (Deirdre McCloskey), and the philosophy of science. Narrative developed as a distinct domain and style of enquiry and a lens through which every aspect of human life could be viewed. The focus on narrative came to be seen as an *alternative* to focus on concepts.

In the view of Activity Theory, narrative analysis and conceptual analysis presuppose one another; every concept relies on a narrative for its validity and no narrative can be coherent without grasping the concepts it generates and deploys.

The idea of *plot* is of central importance for Activity Theory, for the plot of a narrative brings events into a meaningful whole (Polkinghorne, 1988), by selecting events and placing them in chronological order and thereby *suggesting* a connection between them. In general, narrative has an ambiguous relation to truth, an ambiguity which is essential to its function of suggesting and negotiating meanings, leaving itself open for interpretation, without pre-empting what is taken up into conceptual rationality. "We interpret stories by their verisimilitude" (Bruner 1990, p. 61), rather than their veracity. In this way narrative is particularly suitable as a vehicle for the imagination which presages developmental processes under way in both the subject matter and the teller.

Paul Ricœur (1984) told us that it is a *predicament* and its resolution which constitutes the plot thereby bringing a whole complex of experience into a whole. This coincides with the view of Activity Theory that concepts rely for their explanatory power on internal contradictions. Thus, narrative may be understood as the explication or "unfolding" of predicaments, with the characters and their actions functioning as "emblems" (Bruner 1990, p. 60) for the predicament and the series of situations which emanate from it.

The leading alternative to positivist "laws of history" is what Ricœur (1984) calls "emplotment," which entails arranging heterogeneous narrative components together into a plot, in such a way that one situation follows from another in an intelligible and convincing way.

As to the characters acting out a narrative, we have already indicated that we take projects (or activities) to be a basic units of social life, and projects fit the description for what Ricœur (1984, p. 194) calls "entities of participatory belonging," which are the quasi-characters of an historical narrative. It is these quasi-characters which mediate between the actions of individuals and their cultural-historical determination by their life-situation. So activities, taken as the actors in an historical novel, form the frame in which activity theorists grasp the historical context of activity.

Narrative rationality presents concepts to us as *predicaments* or *situations* and the unfolding of their resolution in human activity. Every plot therefore presents us a concept and an understanding of the predicament which drives the plot. The predicament produces the drama and represents the concept in a narrative frame. The whole project through which the predicament plays itself out and is overcome conveys the meaning the concept has for us.

The scripts and schemas introduced into psychology by Jean Mandler have considerable appeal in this light as elementary psychic structures, and seem to be crucial in understanding how people grasp concepts practically, as elementary units of practical action appropriate to a situation.

Over and above the perception of narratives as activities whose micro-units are episodes, the discipline of narrative analysis has identified *structural* elements of narratives which give insight to the researcher beyond a simple series of events and demonstrate what a rich source of data narrative data can be.

Subject, researcher and context narratives are well established as data for Activity Theory, but the practice of generating data by means of survey forms and coding of narrative data continues. While there may be special circumstances warranting such methods, on the whole, coding destroys data, eliminating from the research natural language material which does not survive coding. Survey forms likewise prejudice data in favour of researchers' preconceptions and ensure that the richness of narrative data and material which may be surprising never make it into the research. If surveys and word-counts were the most effective way of conveying meaning, then natural language would have no place in our lives and would never have evolved.

Daiute and Lightfoot (2004) present an overview of the rich data which a familiarity with narrative analysis can draw from the study of subject narratives. Narratives alone are able to convey succinctly the complexity of human life, and can do so in the natural language without specialised training.

For example, the ambiguous relation to truth characteristic of narrative allows subjects to talk in an "as if" mode of narrative in which imagination and emergent development can manifest itself. Subjects will choose a genre to present their story, be that the genre of journalistic reporting or *Bildungsroman*, which tells us more than the words themselves can convey. Subjects may use metaphor, which are both creative and communicative; subjects report on their experiences from a definite subject position, as victim, hero or dispassionate observer; they also tell stories within their own stories, conveying knowledge of events reported in its rawest possible form; they not only report what happened but evaluate their experiences; they express themselves in the terms of a particular cultural milieu and class standpoint, invaluable data when interpreting experience; even the level of narrative skill they display in telling their story provides information of interest to the researcher.

Generally speaking, subjects relating their own experience will spontaneously focus on the events which were most challenging for them and which obliged them to actively respond, creating the episodes of interest to the researcher. In doing so they will identify the dilemmas they faced. Dilemmas are not constituted objectively, that is, without reference to the commitments of the subjects involved, and the identification of dilemmas and their resolution or not not only structures the narrative but places the subject in an ethical space which no other form of reporting can do. All the skills we acquire in our lives, listening to other people's stories and reading novels and other literary genre, can be brought to bear in gathering an understanding of the research material, all of which can be lost in coding and survey forms.

Leontyev and his student Vasilyuk have given us a theoretical structure for the analysis of *perezhivaniya* which is unique as an approach to biographical writing. The techniques of critical analysis applied to novels or historical narratives or the reports an individual gives of their experiences provide means of understanding the personal or societal life-project which is the subject of the narrative.

Narrative analysis is a well-established critical genre and so offers rich resources for Activity Theory. Conversely, the approach of Activity Theory to narratives, which are seen as projects undergoing a series of *perezhivaniya*, is a unique contribution to narrative theory and historiography.

20   Summary: Motivation

One of the most important aspects of Activity Theory is the insights it provides into the sources of motivation underlying activities. Below is a summary (Table 1) of the different concepts that we find in Activity Theory to represent motivation.

TABLE 1   Conceptions of motivation

Really effective motive	The motive for which a person participates in an activity, in contrast to the "merely known" motive of the activity itself.
Merely known motive	The normative situation which the activity is directed at realising, which determines the component actions and norms and constrains the motivation of an individual actor.
Object-concept	The normative concept of the object being worked on, which the activity is directed at realising. (This is what Leontyev called the "objective motive.")
Effective demand	The difference between an external object and the normative object-concept of it which provides the motivation for an activity,
Goal	The intermediate situation towards realisation of the object-concept of an activity which orients an action. The goal of an action always differs from its motive – the object-concept.
Norms	The widely-held concepts, generally unspoken, of what is the right and expected thing to do, the meaning of words and signs, and how the world works. Norms provide motivation often without conscious awareness.
Concepts	At the heart of every concept is a volitional moment, exhibited in the object-concept of an activity, guiding all the actions within an activity, and the norms which determine what people are expected to do in the context of this or that activity. Concepts may provide motivation subconsciously.
Commitment	The disposition of a person to support an activity and which, together with other commitments, makes up their personality.
Motif	A recurring theme which characterises an activity which may not have a clearly delineated object-concept. The motif drives the development of the activity.

TABLE 1   Conceptions of motivation (*cont.*)

Stimuli	At the most basic level of interaction with the material world, sensual interactions which come to trigger particular learned responses. A person acquires and fixes these responses in consciousness so that they are able to control their own activity "from the outside" so to speak.
Internal rewards	Sometimes people just enjoy some activity, or are even unaware of doing it, and there is no motive other than the pleasure of its internal rewards.

The above considerations have shown, I think, the need for a general concept of "an activity." The classical conception of an aggregate of actions by different individuals all consciously oriented to the same object is a *limiting case*. Other aggregates of actions which do not (yet) conform to this norm can nonetheless be theorised by Activity Theory, suitably generalised. Such a generalised concept of activity is the aim of this work.

PART 2

Diverse Research in Activity Theory

∵

Introduction to Part 2

Whereas Vygotsky's ideas have widely taken root amongst people living and working in child development and school education, the emphasis in the content to follow is more on adult life, which is, after all, the chief determinant of the outcome of child development.

Activity theorists are united in believing that if someone has a problem, then usually the best thing that can be done for them is to help them change their situation rather than medicating them or subjecting them to a "talking cure." Identifying the predicaments in which people are caught and finding ways of resolving them requires us to identify the activities motivating people. This we do by first observing people's actions. My point is that the concepts of an activity used both by Leontyev and Engeström are too narrow to be useful in most cases where Activity Theory does in fact have something to say.

Accordingly, I will examine 18 exemplary research projects and activities in which the relation between the component actions and the concept orienting the activity is in some way problematised:

1. a child learning to read and a young professional putting book knowledge to work;
2. a patient facing an impossible situation seeking psychotherapy;
3. a wage worker and the capitalist enterprise in which they work;
4. the life course of an individual person;
5. narratives of patients and trainee doctors;
6. the history of a practice, such as a science or profession;
7. people reframing their lives and taking an active responsibility for their situation;
8. using a germ cell to understand or teach a practice or theory;
9. using a germ cell to transform a practice;
10. a trade union organising in a workplace;
11. rival political parties competing for public opinion or government;
12. the women's liberation movement;
13. an activity sharing a *motif*;
14. the construction of utopian forms of activity;
15. postcolonial projects;
16. the ethics of collaboration;
17. a social class;
18. the struggle for Socialism.

CHAPTER 2

Building Institutions

The first group of research topics I will consider are activities which are at the opposite ends of what we call "institutions" – the nuclear family, taken together with other child carers who take responsibility for raising the new members of the community, and the capitalist firms which later employ them for the purposes of making a profit while incidentally producing something for which an effective demand exists in the community.

What these institutions have in common is that the child or worker who comes into the institution does not generally arrive with a really effective motive to fulfil the goals of the institution. The object-concept of the institution is set by societal processes with a very long history to which the neophyte has as yet no commitment.

The parents and child educators have a legal and moral authority to raise the child so that they will become a productive and responsible member of the society. In particular, the child must learn to read. But the child has no interest in learning to read as such. Even if they could be convinced that in order to become an engine driver they must learn to read, they don't yet have the developed psychological structures for such a belief to motivate struggling with a text.

Likewise, the typical employee applying for a job as a car salesperson doesn't really care whether customers get good prices for good cars so long as their own remuneration is worthwhile. They most likely don't even aspire to a career or reputation as an honest sales rep.

This is the classic conception where A.N. Leontyev's idea of the "really effective" motive and the "merely known" motive comes into play. Whoever is in charge of the activity or project must see to it that the neophyte is motivated to do what they are needed to do and their expectations for reward are indeed met. We could say that the source of the merely known motive – the object-concept of the institution – is societal in its character, while the really effective motive is psychological in its character. But ideally, over time, the subject begins to embrace the merely known motive in its own right. The demand for the product of the firm and the demand for literate responsible young adults come from societal processes on the broad stage of cultural-historical life. The really effective motive is able to generate that volitional, emotional affect at the core of a conceptual structure in the child or worker's psyche. However, it

© ANDY BLUNDEN, 2023 | DOI:10.1163/9789004541245_004

too has its origins on the broad terrain of social life and is transmitted to the neophyte by the responsible teacher, parent or manager.

Alasdair MacIntyre (1981) has said that all institutions require some system of reward to maintain themselves once the circumstances which first brought them into existence have passed, and in his view, such systems of reward inevitably corrupt the institution at the same time as maintaining it. It seems that this applies as much to the nuclear family as to professional sport. It is this disjuncture between effective and "objective" motives which characterises what we call "institutions." The situation is never straightforward, but this is the essential question: how do activities exist and develop productively without the participants being spontaneously motivated to fulfil the mission of the institution?

1 A Child Learning to Read

Any parent or teacher knows that a young child cannot be motivated to work at reading if the only motive they have is to equip themselves to be good citizens when they grow up, or even to pass an exam which will give them the admiration of their parents and eventually admission to a paying job. The young child has not yet matured sufficiently such that by means of psychic reflection these more remote objects can generate the motive to keep their nose to the grindstone. Doubtless, the child will have been told many times that they need to learn to read in order to be fire fighter or whatever when they grow up. But this motive cannot be effective for the child. The educator will devise a situation – some kind of game perhaps or merely sit the child on mummy's lap while she reads – where the child is motivated to collaborate with the educator in the reading activity because it is enjoyable in itself (i.e., initially, for the child it is a collaborative action enjoyed *for its own sake*, for the internal rewards offered by reading with mummy, but not yet an action). Leontyev says that the teacher provides a really effective motive distinct from the "objective motive" which at this point in the child's development is known only by the educator. The really effective motive is conceived of as individual and subjective; the "objective motive" is that which is societally produced and "approved," and the teacher or parent acts here as the agent of the nation, blessed with understanding of and the psychological capacity to be motivated by this object: the production of literate adults. As the child matures they become capable of acquiring more remote motives. Hopefully, in the initial phase the child becomes able to enjoy reading in itself and over time, as their personality develops, they acquire commitments to social goals such as passing their exams, graduating and earning their own living and promoting the welfare of the nation at large, and their reading becomes a subordinate action in furthering these commitments. Leontyev says that the aim of the teacher is to see that the really effective motive more and more merges with the "objective motive" which is eventually enjoyed for its internal rewards as well as instrumentally for the contribution reading makes to leading a good life.

This is fine so far as it goes, but two things. (a) The situation of the child is conceived in an unmediated individual/universal dichotomy which Leontyev wrongly casts as subjective/objective. In reality, the child is not just an individual but already a member of a definite social class and ethnic heritage, and the child's relation to the activity of reading is mediated by the conditions and social expectations imposed on a member of their class. (b) The teacher is not an agent of "objectivity," but (even leaving aside the teacher's motives as a wage-earner) is the agent of the Education Department and other relevant institutions which are riddled with their own social interests.

That is, Leontyev's Activity Theory is, despite itself, dualistic and asocial. Leontyev sees society as an aggregate not of activities but of individuals. Individuals shaped by the use of culturally sourced artefacts in societally constructed activities. However, there are no classes – economic or otherwise – in this utopian society, which is modelled on the self-image of the Soviet Union. In real present-day societies, teachers must be sensitive to the social situations of students and critical of their own bosses. (This line of criticism is to some extent answered in Leontyev's theory of the personality, in which a person is seen as committed to various activities, but the above remarks remain true with respect to the usual reception of Leontyev's theory).

Leontyev's version of Activity Theory is particularly strong on *motivation*, in part because of its distinction between the immediate goal of an action and the concept which provides its motivation. Vygotsky was well aware that volition, emotion and motivation lie at the heart of even seemingly intellectual activity, but Leontyev's notions of effective and merely known motives make the question of volition much clearer and more specific.

> Thought has its origins in the motivating sphere of consciousness, a sphere that includes our inclinations and needs, our interests and impulses, and our affect and emotion. The affective and volitional tendency stands behind thought.
>
> VYGOTSKY, 1934

Left unanswered in the above quote is where the "inclinations and needs, our interests and impulses" come from. They come from the activities to which the subject has some degree or kind of commitment. Also, we see in the way a teacher organises the child's reading activity that even the motive for reading *develops*: at first simply being an immediate, individual response to an interaction and only later becoming participation in a shared cultural project.

I will now look at a deep study of how to diagnose and remediate learning difficulties developed by American Activity Theorists in San Diego.

1.1   *Question Asking Reading (King, Griffin, et al.)*

Question Asking Reading (King et al., 1989) was an epoch making study which developed an approach to simultaneously diagnosing and remediating reading difficulties in primary school children of normal intelligence. The study aimed to differentially diagnose the underlying cause of reading difficulty among children who could "de-code" written text, and had sufficient oral skills to understand the world around them in adult terms, but could not read texts for *meaning*. That is, they could not mediate their understanding of the world with text, they could not bring what could be learnt from a text to bear on a real world situation.

King et al. point out that although all human beings have the ability to learn to read and use what they read for real-life purposes, none did so prior to a few centuries ago, and many otherwise normally developing people *never* do: it requires deliberate instruction. Learning to read is therefore not regarded as a phase in child development, even though it rests on developmental processes and in many respects must be seen itself as a developmental process.

The "zone of proximal development" is the developmental gap between what a child can do with assistance and what the child can do unaided, indicating the potential for a child to make a "developmental leap." The authors use this concept to describe their activity with the children, despite reading not being a stage in child development (the context for which Vygotsky designed the concept), and they take care to differentiate their work from the idea of "providing scaffolding." The aim of the teacher's work "is not for the child to 'learn' a particular interpretation from the teacher" but is rather "an opportunity for the children to develop relevant and coherent interpretations ... as they struggle to de-code individual words." The means devised for this "opportunity" is to divide the process of reading for meaning into five different tasks and having a group of teachers and children, each taking on one of the component tasks, interpret the text collaboratively. Disturbances in the collaborative process give clues as to the underlying source of the learning difficulty in each of the subject children.

The five tasks are: asking about words that are hard to say; asking about words whose meanings are hard to figure out; picking the person to answer the questions asked by others; asking about the main idea; asking about what is going to happen next. The tasks are redistributed after each chunk of text has been dealt with. In this way children get to differentiate, focus on and make explicit the different components of using a text meaningfully to understand something in the world. By dividing up the tasks of reading for meaning the specific difficulty can be isolated. It also allows the learner to grasp each phase of reading for meaning in its own right.

The authors believed that learning to read meaningfully "reorganises" existing innate psychological functions to create a new "higher" psychological system not present to begin with. The creation of this new psychological system justifies the use of the concept of zone of proximal development, because it implies the *development* of a new psychological structure, or "neoformation."

1.2   *Putting Academic Knowledge to Work*

Young people struggling to turn their ability to "de-code" texts to using the text to navigate the world is just like the situation of a medical student who has mastered the medical curriculum and has normal abilities in general interaction with the world around them but can't yet use their book knowledge as a means of navigating real-life clinical situations. As in King et al.'s paper, this is distinct from students who have difficulty dealing with people in any case, or students who have not mastered their book knowledge: these are different problems. Nonetheless, medical educators would be interested in a differential diagnosis, if a junior doctor is failing to develop adequately.

People in modern societies need to read to have a fully functioning adult life, and most people become functionally literate. But for a professional, such as a doctor, the knowledge they gain from books is central to their lives. However, it is not until the medical student arrives at the hospital that they must confront the need to rely on their academic knowledge in interacting with other people. Although the ability to "read" human beings for signs of their mood, intentions, health, strength, etc., develops normally in human beings, to use a large body of academic knowledge to read a human being and act accordingly is not inherent in a human being; it is an ability which has to be fostered with the support of more experienced others. The same issue arises for a student who has studied Activity Theory at university and then wants to realise these ideas in their activity as a teacher or as an activist in a social movement or whatever.

The medical student is required to "see" the patient as a case, indirectly, refracted through their medical book learning, and *simultaneously* engage the patient and their context in the normal practical-sensuous linguistically-mediated way, relatively directly. Generally speaking these two perceptions will be discoordinated, generating the need for further enquiry and development.

King et al. quote Luria (1932), and it is relevant here as well:

> the consideration that a voluntary act can be accomplished by "will power" is a myth ... the human cannot by direct force control his behaviour any more than "a shadow can carry stones" ... Voluntary behaviour is the ability to create stimuli and to subordinate them; or in other words to bring into being stimuli of a special order, directed to the organisation of behaviour.
>
> 1932, p. 401

The task of learning to use academic knowledge to direct your action requires the creation of stimuli generated in the clinical situation which "trigger" access to the appropriate academic text. Initially the student will require assistance to develop these stimuli but later will be able to generate them internally. These new stimuli become "indexes" to their academic knowledge. All neurotypical people have the ability to "read" facial expressions and other signs embodied in another person's habitus so as to understand things about them. That deeply embedded psychological structure has to be *restructured* for the use of the student's academic book knowledge, so as to be able to read the world *as a doctor*.

Likewise, a student who learns Activity Theory at university or by reading books or web pages, even if they have well understood what they have read, will not as a result be able to effectively intervene or participate in a social movement or run a kindergarten class, or whatever, using their knowledge of Activity Theory. Some kind of apprenticeship will be required such that their book knowledge can be "restructured" by clinical experience.

These case studies point to how the people in charge of an institution must arrange for the neophyte to participate in activities for which they do have the effective motives and stimuli to systematically build the psychological structures required for the neophyte to develop motives aligned with institutional goals. An indirect route must be taken. The neophyte cannot be directed to the necessary goal; they need to be supported and presented with tasks that they can, with support, achieve at the present stage of development, until they can accomplish them autonomously.

Providing support for a learner, providing an effective motivation, and dividing up a task into separate elements provides the opportunity both to learn one step at a time, in safety, and to isolate the elements which may be the source of difficulty.

2   Vasilyuk's Work on Resolving "Impossible Situations"

Vasilyuk was a postgraduate student at the Faculty of Psychology of Moscow State University when he wrote his PhD thesis later published as *The Psychology of* Perezhivanie (1984). As he saw it, patients came to a psychotherapist because they faced *impossible situations*. Basing himself on Leontyev's theory of the personality, Vasilyuk saw such impossible situations as resulting from one of four types of dilemma arising from the fate of the life-projects to which the patient was committed. The set of life-projects to which a person is committed constitutes their "life-world." These life-projects are selected from those activities existing in the society and arranged in the structure of the person's *lichnost*.

He defines a *difficult* life-world in which a person's life-project is blocked in some way, and a *complex* life-world in which a person finds life-projects in conflict with one another. The easy/difficult and simple/complex dichotomies provide him with a four-part taxonomy of archetypal crises. In each case, the relevant commitments have to be identified and the subject must engage in a *perezhivanie* – understood as the cognitive and emotional labour required to re-orient their commitments so as to resolve the impossible situation. In each case a particular kind of work has to be done and a particular virtue developed according to the type of life-world the patient must restructure.

2.1   *Types of "Life-World"*
i.   *Stress* is the crisis of the *easy-simple life world*. Here the subject has no goals and pursues no project because they demand and receive immediate gratification. Having no direction in which to strive they express diffuse anxiety which is manifested as stress. A person may have many commitments, but so long as the subject pursues each commitment only one at a time and encounters no resistance, the subject's world is simple and easy. Vasilyuk call this a hedonistic crisis; it is rampant in the leafy suburbs of the wealthy capitalist countries.
ii.   *Frustration* is the crisis of the *difficult-simple life world*. The subject is focused on their life-defining project, but achievement of their goal is blocked and nothing can be done about it. The typical example of this crisis is a disaster in a treasured career which has hitherto defined a subject's life, or the subject's partner may have died, and the subject may find themself unable to go on in a life which has become pointless.
iii.   *Conflict* is the crisis of the *easy-complex life world*. The subject is committed to more than one project, both of which are immediately attainable, but the two options have nothing in common by means of which

to compare them, except that the subject has a commitment to both and must choose which to pursue: should I have a child or should I continue my career?

iv. The crisis of the *difficult-complex life world* is a *life-crisis*, combining features of the two preceding sectors. The subject's chosen life-project is blocked and there is a temptation to abandon former strong commitments to overcome blockages in others, and only a creative response offers the possibility of recovering a meaningful life.

On the basis of these four types of crisis, Vasilyuk defines a typology of four kinds of *perezhivanie*, respectively hedonistic *perezhivanie*, realistic *perezhivanie*, value *perezhivanie* and creative *perezhivanie*.

2.2 Types of *Perezhivanie*

i. The prototype of the *easy-simple* life world is that of an *infantile* person. *Perezhivanie* is impossible in the purely easy-simple life world, because everything is provided and the pleasure principle faces no resistance. With immediate satisfaction there can be no contradiction or any situation creating psychological challenges to be worked over. However, as soon as some small difficulty arises in this infantile life-world, the only psychological resources available are those already freely available in the easy-simple world of hedonistic, here-and-now satisfaction. Whatever the nature of the difficulty or complication which has arisen, the infantile response will be manifested in diffuse, senseless *activity*. This can only be resolved when those conditions are no longer present or the subject takes on some commitment.

ii. The prototype of the *difficult-simple* life world is the *fanatic*. The *perezhivanie* in this world begins with *patience* but culminates in *realism*. Patience differs from denial in that although it believes in a good which is not present and does not deny the problem, it believes it can be solved. But when patience runs out, and frustration sets in and the subject is faced with the impossible situation, the reality principle offers two alternative ways out. The first is to postpone satisfaction, or lower one's sights and make do with a substitute for what is impossible according to the reality principle. In the second way, the subject abandons the former pursuit (the meaning of their former life) and takes up a coping behaviour to substitute for the loss of the first or continues it by other means.

iii. The *easy-complex life world* is an aesthetic and moral world. The *perezhivanie* of the easy-complex world is *value*-perezhivanie. The critical situation may arise when an activity which is attractive to the subject comes into conflict with the subject's life-project. Either the offending activity is morally discredited and abandoned, or the subject finds a way of reconciling it as not really in contradiction to the life-project. Alternatively, value-*perezhivanie* is required in the wake of a wrecked life-project, searching amongst other projects for that which is most valued and could restore meaning to their life, such as a project in memory of the lost life-project. Alternatively, the crisis may be resolved by a radical restructuring of the subject's entire value system, maintaining continuity through forgiveness and redemption. The principle of value-experiencing is *phronesis* or wisdom.

iv.   The *perezhivanie* of the difficult-complex life world is creative *perezhivanie* and entails an entire reconstruction of the *lichnost*.

- The first alternative is to continue the pursuit of the *values* which had hitherto defined one's life but were identified with a particular person or project which is no longer available; however, the identification of the life-intent with this particular form of realisation can be overcome by reframing these values in more general, abstract terms, so that they can be realised in some other form (or person), realising that the fixation on that former particular embodiment was unnecessary.
- The second path is to discover that life has hitherto been based on false values and to formulate a new value system, but in such a way that preserves the meaning of the past life, showing how the subject has conquered error and at last won through to life's true intent, like the defrocked priest who sets up a charity.
- The third type of creative *perezhivanie* is connected with the highest stages of personality development as the life-intent moves away from egoistic projects and places the self in the service of higher motives, proof against any misfortune and for which, ultimately the person is prepared for any sacrifice including life itself.

The leading psychological function in difficult-complex life world is the *will*. The integrity of the person as presented in self-consciousness is not something present and achieved, but has to be *actualised* in life-activity and the will is the only organ which can achieve that actualisation. The will is therefore the central psychological function in the formation of the personality, and constitutes a higher psychological function encompassing numerous psychological organs. The will not only develops a mature capacity to achieve its ends despite difficulties, but most importantly it is able to freely determine the ends it pursues.

The will is first developed in childhood, according to Vygotsky, in the passage through the series of childhood crises which separate the successive phases of childhood, when the social situation of development which defines the social position of the child must be transformed for the child to grow up and break through to the next station in life. In these childhood crises the will is formed as a concrete, higher mental function, and the various forms of psychic reflection which characterise a person are formed.

This highly schematic synopsis of Vasilyuk's approach is meant only to demonstrate how Vasilyuk identifies the source of psychosis in the predicaments people find themselves in as a result of the development of the commitments which constitute their personality. I also appreciate Vasilyuk's idea of an individual *lichnost* as a life-world being one instance of the life of the community of which the person is a part, conceived as a psychological structure built from a *selection* of the projects constituting that community. This nicely solves the problem of how a community is simultaneously conceived as an aggregate of projects *and* a collection of individual people.

3   A Wage Worker Employed in a Capitalist Firm

A wage worker employed in a capitalist firm turns up to work each day and is diligent at their given role, archetypically, because they expect to be paid, and will as a result be able to pursue their own aims outside of work. At the same time, the worker collaborates with fellow employees so as to successfully and efficiently produce the relevant product. Leontyev expresses this by saying that the worker is motivated by the really effective motive as well as the merely known or "objective motive." With good management, the employees will develop so as to fully embrace the "objective motive": providing some product or service to the community.

The capitalist owner is in the same situation. The capitalist participates (if at all) in order to ensure capital accumulation. However, capitalists, like other human beings, may come to value their contribution to the nation, but obviously this is not always the case. All collaborate in the enterprise – be that peddling party drugs or healing patients – and social arrangements beyond the enterprise are entered into which see that all the participants receive a monetary reward for their effort.

Putting this another way, the object of the firm mediates both the workers' activity of earning a living and the capitalists' activity of amassing capital. All going well, societal processes will ensure that the object also mediates between demand for their product and its consumption.

The object, which Leontyev calls the "objective motive," is the reproduction of the means of some social need. These needs are not restricted to any kind of "basic need," but arise from the social process itself. In the planned economy of the USSR, these "objective motives" were set in five-year plans determined by the Politburo. The needs of the worker – their career, their living and their family's needs – are met by whatever system of distribution the Politburo determined, either a labour market or a centrally determined scale of wages or the distribution of products according to need. Thus needs and their satisfaction are mediated by the *societal arrangements* made for distribution and management of the economy. In present day capitalist reality, the process by means of which the social product is distributed appears to be more of an objective process, as described by political economy, moderated to one extent or another by government policy and trade union bargaining, namely, an *effective demand*. Thus, casinos, criminal enterprises and the provision of fattening food, tobacco and liquor, pornography and so on, for which there is an effective demand, take on the status of "objective motives."

Everything that happens in building and maintaining these institutions happens because people in the appropriate social positions *make it happen*. Everything that is done passes through human minds. These are not *natural* processes. As Anthony Giddens said:

> there is no such entity as a distinctive type of "structural explanation" in the social sciences; all explanations will involve at least implicit references both to the purposive, reasoning behaviour of agents and to its intersection with constraining and enabling features of the social and material contexts.
>
> 1984, p. 179

The necessity in these processes arises from the historical distribution of resources and rights among social actors. It is said that if the capitalist decides not to pay wages, they go out of business, so their decision is made for them, so to speak, but they *could* decide otherwise. If social arrangements are made which place people in unequal situations, as rational human beings they act appropriately to their situation. This is not to say, however, that an agent can give a coherent and logical verbal explanation of their actions. But their situation does not *force* them to act in a certain way.

The fact remains that everything has to pass through human minds in which people weigh things up and deploy the resources their social position affords them so as to make things happen. It all depends on the motivation of the strategic actors, the resources they have at their disposal and their commitments.

So *Activity* Theory, not Behaviourism or Economic Science, is needed to understand the workings of capitalist firms and the economy.

In general, most people in an enterprise do strive to actualise the object of the enterprise: not only because it mediates their own project, but because as human beings they have accepted a contract with the employer and accept an obligation to the person whose demand is being met, and as Leontyev says, over time they will generally come to embrace the "objective motive." But this is not guaranteed. Some won't. And if the workers' needs are not met or for other reasons they will generally take strike action and if the capitalist does not make a profit they will generally withdraw their capital.

Public services are generally structured so as to set up proxies for meeting their social functions – promotions, bonuses and salaries linked to Key Performance Indicators, for example – in the hope that if civil servants achieve their KPIs and are duly rewarded, then the relevant social need will be met. The point is that the object has arisen from an outside social process and arrangements must be made to generate effective motives. That is the task of managers and legislators, who in turn have their own motives.

And the idea of *extending* the psychological concept of "motive" to include ends (such as obesity-inducing and addictive foods) which are merely mediating the activity of capital accumulation elides the process by means of which the object of the enterprise is formed. The so-called "objective motive" is a *societal* category, more or less identical with "effective demand," masquerading as a psychological concept. Leaving out this link in the circle of social determination of motives leaves Leontyev's theory as a variety of Functionalism: "people are fulfilling this function because otherwise the present state of things would be inexplicable." This is the logical fallacy of reverse causality.

Public service institutions and capitalist firms are *collaborative projects*, or activities, in which a number of distinct activities are collaborating towards the shared, relatively remote aim. The aim or concept of the project (or activity) has a different sense for different collaborating projects. The alternative view is either a "flat" conception of collaborative activity in which everyone is motivated in exactly the same sense, or every individual participates with their own unique individual effective motive. What is omitted is the variety of collaborative projects which may be at work *within* the enterprise, not just the private aims of individuals.

The objective tendency of the project can be determined with scientific precision by closely observing the collaborative tendencies in all the constituent actions. Collaboration may produce a kind of "compromise" aim, a "second best" aim, or it might produce an unstable and varying aim, or one view of the aim may override all others or the project may be headed for self-destruction. This may be determined by observation.

The difference between the motives of the capitalist owner or senior civil servant and the motive of an employee are the *archetypes* here. Each has their effective motive met by means of societal arrangements depending on the actually incidental product of the firm: meeting an effective societal demand.

The capitalist wants to accumulate capital and use the product as a mediating artefact in that action (M-C-M')*; the worker is furthering his or her project of raising a family and building a career (C-M-C'); some workers – especially more senior professionals – may be motivated to produce some social good and enjoy the internal rewards of that activity, while building a career; all are trying to minimise the burden of work on their own lives. The senior public servant is trying to meet some arbitrary performance criteria and the rewards that go with success. The actual work activity which results from this collaboration is the outcome not only of cooperation (despite differing motivations) but also of class struggle and struggle between various interest groups, whether or not explicitly organised, reflected in ideology.

The main idea which Leontyev offers to deal with complexities like these is to say that the *personal sense* of the object is different for each participant in the activity. This preserves the object as something *objective* while allowing that for each participant the object has a personal sense. This personal sense is formed by means of ideology, which expresses meanings appropriate to one or another social position, in interaction with the life experiences of each individual in the course of their activity. As Leontyev saw it, all the meanings expressed by ideologies are *objective*, but are *more or less adequate* to the lives of the individual, to the extent that the ideology expresses a broad *social interest*. This is how social classes enter into motive formation for Leontyev.

These ideas go part of the way towards a genuinely social conception of human activity, but only on the side of the individual, of psychology. As a social theory, Leontyev's version of Activity Theory cannot comprehend anything beyond a planned economy run by a disinterested bureaucracy. It cannot explain *why* some collaborative activity has come into existence and when it might disappear. Leontyev just assumes that an activity springs into action because there is a social need which must be met.

We have "objective motives" (effective demand masquerading as a human need) of which one person (e.g., the teacher or senior administrator, ...) is the

---

* In this symbolism, which Marx uses in *Capital*, M means Money and C means a Commodity. So C-M-C' means selling labour power to buy the means of subsistence, and M-C-M' means buying commodities in order to sell at a profit.

agent and another person not. Furthermore, the theory is essentially one of stasis: the continual consumption and reproduction of a given array of socially and culturally produced products answering to a given and static array of social needs. There is no place for an activity whose explicit aim is to *transform* activity, abolishing some needs and creating others, and expanding the horizon of activity; and yet many activities nowadays are of this kind, be they simple capital accumulation or radical projects for social change. And even if we allow for the social formation of every participant's personal sense of the object of activity, there is *no* "universal person" here whose "personal sense" can be deemed to be the "object" or "objective motive."

I sometimes use the words "a project," which is synonymous with "an activity" and "a practice" except that (i) "project" does not carry the connotation of stasis, but of transformation, (ii) "project" is not generally taken to be institutionalised, and (iii) a "project" is generally taken to be collaboration towards a *shared* end, and there are a several distinct paradigms of collaboration which are excluded by Leontyev's dualistic conception. But I use all these words (activities, practices, projects) as synonyms, while each term suggests one or another ideal or archetype.

What is needed is a specific analysis of *collaboration*. I see projects, such as public services or capitalist firms, but also the whole range of activities underway in a modern society – charities, political parties, NGOs, pressure group and so on – as *collaborations* between a number of projects, each with their own motives.

It remains the case that a collaborative project, i.e., a project in which the constituent actions are motivated by a *variety* of motives, nevertheless has a "merely understood" object, such as curing an ill patient, teaching children to read or governing the country according to liberal principles. In order to achieve their own object (e.g., pay, profit, or career) participants collaborate to achieve the object through which their own object is realised, if all goes well, thanks to societal arrangements.

"Personal sense" as a way of expressing the different meanings of the object of an activity for different participants is OK so far as it goes. But in connection with analysing collaborative projects I prefer to not use this idea alongside "objective meaning." I allow that *all* participants (shaped as Leontyev says, through the interaction of ideological meanings more or less adequate to their life experience in having a certain social position) have a different concept of the object being worked upon, that is, a different normative concept of the object. But this *object-concept* is not to be conceived of as a mental entity, but rather is itself *a form of activity* because *a concept and an activity are two expressions of the same social reality*. Only by this means can Leontyev's dualism be overcome. This object-concept is *implicit* in the activity and can only be determined by observing the tendency of the collaborative actions. Conflicts arise within an enterprise from time to time as a result of the participants having different normative concepts of the object. This is over and above the fact that different participants may have different motives for simply participating in the collaborative project. One does not follow from the other. A radiologist, an oncologist and a social worker may all share the motive to earn a living and contribute to the health system, but for professional reasons they will conflict over the actions best suited to achieve the shared end.

I have talked about motives, and in particular I have referenced *archetypical* motives which are taken to be monetary gain. But I have qualified this. The aphorism "follow the money," so beloved of conspiracy theorists, is a relative truth. In general, for example, scientists seek the truth as they see it, and not monetary rewards; people on the whole take their jobs seriously. Economic factors influence affairs in general *indirectly*. The capitalist economy determines the entire context in which research and production takes place, but this is far from being the same as direct monetary reward in exchange for corrupt or dishonest research. Developed capitalist nations have multiple layers of checking on what people do, from shopfloor workers who might take products home with them to bureaucrats who might take a bribe to pharmaceutical companies who are happy to market dangerous goods, and this limits the impact of direct corruption by money. All this hardly needs to be said as a careful attention to motives will always be able to demonstrate the truth.

To summarise, the distinction between the *really effective motive* – a psychological category, relevant to the motivation of an individual person, and the *object-concept* of an activity – a societal category implicit in the objective tendency of the actions constituting the activity – is basic to all kinds of activity. As Vygotsky said, (and he is here talking in psychological terms):

> The affective and volitional tendency stands behind thought. Only here do we find the answer to the final "why" in the analysis of thinking. ... A true and complex understanding of another's thought becomes possible only when we discover its real, affective-volitional basis.
>
> VYGOTSKY, 1934

Anyone engaged in recruiting people to an activity – a teacher, manager or branch secretary – has to understand the distinct considerations entailed in each category. Recall Luria's words cited above "the human cannot by direct force control his behaviour any more than 'a shadow can carry stones'."

As an individual personality develops and as they take on more senior roles in an activity, then the distinction between the motive to fulfil effective demand and the motive to meet personal goals may disappear. In their role as a leader or self-conscious social actor, the person may become directly motivated by the social outcome of the activity to which they are committed.

The key to understanding institutions with Activity Theory is to understand the source of *motivation* of all the actors and the location of motivation at the heart of all concepts, concepts understood as both forms of activity and forms of consciousness. But we need a *consistent* Activity Theory in which needs and motivations arise from activities not the other way around. But Leontyev's distinction between the official motive (so to speak) and the really effective motive is crucial. A person's social position does not *compel* them to act in a certain way, even though it defines the resources they have at their disposal and the predicament they must resolve.

CHAPTER 3

Activities Characterised by a Narrative

Activities are *collaborative* projects. But as Hegel (1821) said: "A person is the series of their actions." A person's life is itself an activity, a project, *and* a narrative. A person lives their life in continuous relations of collaboration with others, but while each of the projects to which a person commits themself is an activity which generally first exists independently of the subject, one project to which every person is committed is that in which they themselves are the object, their own life.

There is nothing in the concept of an activity which excludes the case in which one person is at the centre of every action making up the activity, and that activity is in fact their life-project. As it happens, the life-activity of an organism was the archetype of an activity from which Leontyev derived the concept of an activity by introducing division of labour. And how better can a life-project be represented than as a narrative?

Equally, the heroes of a narrative can be projects – social movements, political parties, firms, nations, aggregates of actions which form so-called "collective subjects" – which, like individuals, have a life cycle, beginning with a twinkle in the eye of a founder, gaining support and finding their way in the world and an identity, learning, growing, eventually changing the world in their own way, and finally fading away with old age and leaving the world to their descendants, their life nothing more than a memory. These projects, as well as the lives of individual people, can be grasped through the concept of narrative by means of Activity Theory as well as concepts already elaborated in the discipline of narrative analysis.

Activities fit the description of what Ricœur (1984, p. 194) calls "entities of participatory belonging," which are to be the quasi-characters of an historical narrative. But "participatory belonging" notwithstanding, a "collective subject" is not to be understood in terms of people belonging. Commonly, but by no means universally, people who are participating in an activity *may* be identified in some way, as members, employees, supporters, or whatever. In this way, a "group" could be conceived of as a "collective subject." But this is never really the case. People's membership of whatever kind (unless the person is a slave) covers only their actions during working hours, or in relevant interactions. A person is only ever partially engaged in an activity. In reality, it is more true to say that the subject here is *an activity*, which is an aggregate of *actions*, not persons. Likewise, the individual subject is also an aggregate of actions, the temporal succession of actions for which they are morally responsible, their biography, so to speak.

Together with concepts, narratives are how we conceive of the human world. Concepts and narratives, inseparably connected by volition, constitute the stuff of human life, manifested in activity and reflected by describing, narrating and explaining human life. They are activity taken synchronically and diachronically. But as indicated earlier, narrative data communicate far more than a series of experiences. Essential to a coherent narrative are the plot which ties all the events together into an intelligible whole, and the characters, whether individuals or activities. Narrative analysis tells us the subject's response to and evaluation of situations and points to emergent developments. It also reveals the subject's own social position.

None of the projects reviewed here have entailed passing the narrative data provided by subjects through the filter of survey forms and coding. They have valued the irreducible richness of narrative.

We have already noted that concepts are units of analysis for understanding either an individual psyche or a socio-cultural formation (understood as an aggregate of activities). It is equally true that *narratives* can be units of analysis for understanding people's experiences, their personalities and their social formations. It is by means of narratives that we grasp concepts and forms of activity in time, as *historical* entities. Understanding social situations historically is fundamental to Activity Theory, so narratives are crucial units of analysis for Activity Theory. A narrative *is* an activity. In fact, in most research projects conducted in the socio-cultural paradigm, the raw data are acquired in the first place as subject narratives in the form of qualitative interviews. This *is* the material to be analysed and the first step in analysis is to determine the unit of analysis. "Unit" applies in the first instance to the data of perception; subjected to processing, these data can suggest new units of analysis in the outcome of the research project. But the organisation of the input data into units is also a precondition to analysis.

We have said that a concept and an activity merely express different senses of the same thing. In the same way, a narrative and the series of events which the narrative relates are the same thing, expressed on one hand as mental product and on the other hand as a series of intelligibly interconnected events. Narratives are of course selective and some narratives will stand up to critique better than others, some are more partial than others. But there is not some "objective" series of events out there, "objectively" selected independently of the motives of the participants. Every intelligible historical narrative is an abstraction from millions of events each of which may or may not be given its due. Even the most comprehensive narrative is not "objective," but it is what we have.

Once we allow that narratives can be units of analysis, quite different approaches to analysis are opened to Activity Theory. In particular, narratives can be seen as composed of *episodes* (larger than the micro-unit of single actions but smaller than the macro-unit of an entire life). This is a new and distinctive unit of analysis and the first task of Activity Theory is to work out how to segment a narrative into episodes. More on this shortly.

In designating narratives and episodes as units of analysis it should be noted that I do not list genre, positioning, plot, etc., as *units*. These are the *elements* of narrative analysis and elements belong to *systems theory*; each of the elements characterises one essential aspect of a whole episode or narrative. Every narrative unit can be analysed in terms of these elements, but it is the narrative units which allow us to segment data into a series of self-standing wholes, one after the other, each of which can be analysed in terms of a multiplicity of elements.

There are four kinds of narrative which activity theorists have used as units of analysis: entire lives of historically significant individuals, the life-course of individuals suffering from some significant social or medical condition, episodes which shed light on an institution either from the inside or from the outside, and the narratives of movements, institutions, sciences, ideas, etc., the narratives of activities themselves.

1   The Life Course of an Individual Person

The life course of an individual person can be grasped in many ways, but one important way a life can be conceptualised is through the development of their personality (*lichnost*). The development of the personality is characterised in Activity Theory by an evolving hierarchy of commitments, commitments to objectively-existing projects. These commitments are created at particular, crucial junctions in a person's life. It could be said that each chapter in a person's biography is the story of how a person encountered a situation, how they dealt with that situation and how in the medium term it changed their personality as they "processed" that event. At the end of the story we can understand the subject's personality because we have traced all the formative experiences in their life, how they overcame impossible situations and/or seized momentary opportunities and *made* their own life out of the circumstances that were given to them. An understanding of such a personal narrative is how we come to know a person and what we can expect from them.

According to Vygotsky (1934a), in these critical episodes the subject engages in a specific kind of work called *perezhivaniya* (Blunden, 2016b). Vygotsky is at pains to point out that what may be a catastrophe for one person may mean nothing to another person, depending on the relation of the person to the relevant circumstances: their social situation. The critical nature of the situation depends on the stage of development of the subject's personality and (in the case of an adult) their *lichnost* – their personality, with their commitments – *otnoshiniya*.

This conception of *perezhivaniya* was given finished form by Vasilyuk (1984) but for Vygotsky *perezhivaniya* included all the little episodes in one's life which were to one degree or another memorable, having had some impact on the formation of the personality. According to Vasilyuk, A.N. Leontyev did not have a place for *perezhivanie* in his system, but the reader will see from my description of Leontyev's theory of personality, above, that the notion fits very well with his theory. Nor does *perezhivanie* play a significant role in the Activity Theory of Engeström.

Although an individual is at the centre of their own life-project, all these *perezhivaniya* are collaborations, implicitly if not explicitly, and arise from real conflicts in the objective world around them. Being late to work every day one week may mean nothing to me, but if I am starting a new job, or I'm the manager of my work unit then the loss of prestige in the eyes of my colleagues may pose a serious crisis for me. If I decide to criticise my boss in public, it will make all the difference in the world whether my work colleagues support me or not. Every action is a collaborative action; its implications for me depend crucially on my relations with others around me. If I get promoted, it may be because of the support I had from colleagues when I took some initiative. And so on.

A *perezhivanie* is not just an episode which *happened* to you, it is what you *did* in the face of some challenge. To a greater or lesser extent every *perezhivanie* entails a change on one's commitments and one's priorities. Generally speaking this change in *lichnost* is not an instantaneous change, but happens over a period of time as the subject reflects on the experience and "works over" it, so to speak. It is these critical episodes which divide a person's life into "chapters."

So, if the subject matter is the biography of a person, the units of analysis are the *perezhivaniya* which mark out the episodes in the subject's life. If the subject matter is some historical event, then one of several possible approaches to analysing this event or more protracted experience is to take as macro units of analysis the narratives of each of the relevant participants, and in this case the micro units would be all the *perezhivaniya*, which are more than likely shared experiences.

There is no contradiction in using narrative analysis as part of Activity Theory. Narratives can represent the life of an individual, the course of a developing social movement or a personal experience or any other activity. As activity theorists, we look to cognising a subject's life as a series of phases of *gradual adjustment to their social situation,* separated by critical periods of re-formation (*perezhivaniya*) in which a person *changes their relation to the world* by changing their commitments (*otnoshiniya*), deepening or weakening them, rearranging their relative value or transforming commitments altogether. Although each commitment is personal, the life-projects to which a person commits themself are universal and objective. The units of the personality make up a substructure of the units of the entire social formation. Thus, in this approach the development of a subject is comprehended in intimate connection with and a part of the development of the whole social formation.

To study the history of the Russian Revolution, for example, your project might begin by studying the life-course of each of the individuals who played a significant role in the Revolution and follow up by tracing the trajectory of all the projects active at the time, not just the actions they took in October, but the conditions out of which they grew, their ideals and their rising or falling trajectory. This would not in itself provide a definitive history or analysis of the Revolution, but such a history would be one important *moment* of a concrete history of the Revolution. If instead one were to write the history, say, of the Russian Revolution event by event, then it gives the appearance that individual participants exist only for that moment in which they play a decisive role and their motivation is mystified. Abstracted from a knowledge of the life-course of participants, the analysis of the event in question will lack depth.

In what sense is the life-course of a person an *object-oriented* activity though? How do we understand the "object" of a person's life? In the first place, it is like the typical activity envisaged by Leontyev in that throughout the life course a person renews themself every day just as a baker renews the supply of bread every day as bread is consumed. But that is surely the lowest level of human existence. We understand a *life-project* as a project whose meaning only gradually evolves and finally tends to become clear in the rear vision mirror, "when the shades of night are gathering." To define the project of an individual human life in terms of an object or goal which makes sense of the life *in advance* (as we usually characterise activities), is rarely tenable. The meaning of a life is surely an outcome, usually not a precondition.

So should we take this wisdom gained from the way we understand the lives of persons – that the reason for an activity only becomes clear in retrospect – and apply it to how we understand the unfolding object of activities? Every clinic, every public service, every educational institution or productive

enterprise strives to achieve excellence in the delivery of some service, inno-
vate and develop long term plans, often proudly reflecting on their history and
the achievements of their founders. We reflect on our lives, the achievements
of our forebears and try to leave the world a better place for our descendants. It
is true, that at any given moment we don't generally have a clear image of our
future; very often we find ourselves in some job to which we had never given a
moment's thought in our youth. Nonetheless, we strive to lead a good life and
in doing so become more conscious of the reasons for our own existence. An
activity *is* a life-project, and as a life-project its real meaning is discovered only
in the course of life itself.

An activity (or project or social practice) has, as an integral part of its existence, a concept of its object. This concept is *reified* as part of an objectively
existing world, and it *changes* in the light of the experience of the project.
Any activity (or project or social practice) is like a personal narrative in how it
learns from experience and its conception of the reason for its own existence
evolves accordingly. The reified object – what a life was aiming at – is more
truly grasped as the moral character of a life, which is present throughout but
only becomes clear over time.

1.1 *Luria's Romantic Science*

In *The Mind of a Mnemonist* (Luria, 1968) and *The Man with a Shattered World*
(Luria, 1972), Vygotsky's close associate, A.R. Luria, presented paradigmatic
examples of "Romantic Science" in the form of two books each tracing the life
of an individual living with an extremely disabling neurological condition. This
is *idiographic* science is called "Romantic Science" in reference to the natural-
ism of Goethe. Goethe advocated the exhaustive and "gentle" empirical examination of a single case, as opposed to "nomothetic" science – the subsumption
of an entire class of phenomena under a covering law. This commitment to
Romantic Science lies at the very foundation of Activity Theory, reflected in
our commitment to qualitative methods.

Luria referred to these studies as "concrete psychology" because he did not
study just one neurological function or disorder in isolation, but studied the
development of the subject's entire personality and life-world over a period
of 30 years. This approach is in contrast to Leontyev's concept of *lichnost*
which focuses merely on the subject's persona. Luria's study sheds light on the
extreme interdependence of all the distinct psychological functions. When the
structure of psychological functions is disturbed, the startling changes in experience and personality which result teach us much about the structure and
development of the mind.

Luria founded modern neuropsychology, who formulated the theory of how the fundamental building blocks of the nervous system are reconfigured into functional units each composing the system underpinning the various higher psychological functions. So Luria is remembered for a theory, a set of broad principles for understanding neurological development tied up with participation in social practices. But what was the experience on which this epoch-making theory was built? It did include an array of novel psychological tests and a mass of empirical data accumulated in the lab. But the real meaning and content of the neurological processes was revealed concretely by following the entire life of some exceptional individuals, individuals whose lives were shaped by their counter-normative neurological condition. How different the world looks to someone who cannot forget *anything*! How do they cope? How do they cope having lost the capacity to even locate different parts of their own body? They *did* cope, with enormous difficulty; they found ways to go on living, efforts which shed great light on how the nervous system works and the ways in which human beings can collaboratively repair damage to their nervous systems. These individuals throw the achievement of an ordinary human life into sharp relief.

In *The Mind of a Mnemonist* Luria studied S, a man whose mind had developed from infancy in a very unusual way. S had unlimited memory: he could reproduce 1000 digits read to him 30 years before effortlessly and faultlessly, and his memory stretched back to infancy, even before he had acquired speech, for his memory was not verbal memory, but immediate sensory memory. He had thoroughgoing synaesthesia: every sensation correlated taste, sound, colour, and complex emotional colouring and association. By the power of imagination, he could alter the temperature of his skin or change his pulse rate. His ability, indeed compulsion, to imagine a scenario was so powerful that his body responded to imagined stimuli and he could not tell where his imagination ended and reality began. He observed his own behaviour as if from the side. S did not *think* in the way we do. He *saw* before his eyes what he imagined and observed what he saw. Words carried a multisensory load, so in order to correlate a word with its meaning, he had to associate various shades of feeling the word gave him with the meaning, and he "chained" meaning like a small child – using the same word to indicate a series of linked impressions which otherwise have no common feature.

Luria studied S's whole personality and learnt to understand his world. This gave Luria a deep insight into the way in which the various mental functions interacted and depended on one another.

This kind of concrete psychology might be worth considering in connection with recent pathological developments in public discourse. For example, rather than anecdotes or surveys about conspiracy theories, post-truth, hyper-partisanship, antivaxism and so on, what about some longitudinal observation of the whole life of someone caught up in these pathologies?

Traditionally, Activity Theory looks to deep qualitative data, as opposed to superficial gathering of data across large numbers of respondents. It was Luria who pioneered this approach. These deep data necessarily come in the form of narratives. Oliver Sacks is another well-known researcher who has continued Luria's approach.

2 The Narrative of a Patient Visiting a Hospital and Receiving Treatment

The narrative of a patient visiting a hospital and receiving treatment for their complaint provides an important insight into the functioning of even a large teaching hospital. Indeed, this is how most of us get to know how hospitals work. Researchers can gather narrative knowledge from patients visiting the hospital which, while incomplete, in combination with insider knowledge of the hospital can give important insights otherwise invisible to insiders alone. Furthermore, since a successful patient experience is the *aim* of the hospital's work, these narratives are of particular importance. *"Successful" patient narratives* are in fact units of the *object-concept of a hospital*. So it makes complete sense to collect data in the form of patient narratives. This conforms to Vygotsky's idea that the unit of analysis is a spontaneous concept of the whole, a concept grounded in immediate everyday perception.

Public teaching hospitals are vast and complex, even chaotic institutions. To theorise a modern teaching hospital as a "system of activity" is wishful thinking; a single clinic perhaps, but a modern hospital is a "system" only in the broadest definition of the term, though very likely the senior administration of the hospital sees it this way. Each of the hospital's specialist medical, paramedical, auxiliary and administrative departments has its own motives, hierarchies and norms; each is itself *an activity*. Every department interacts with every other department and as a patient passes through the hospital – from referral and admission to discharge and rehabilitation – they engage in collaboration with a succession of hospital officials acting as agents for their department or profession. The hospital must be theorised as a complex collaboration of many distinct projects, but the most important project of them all is that expressed in the *therapeutic narrative*: the story of one patient's experiences as they pass through the hospital, committing themself to collaborations with a succession of hospital departments and their agents as well as interdisciplinary teams, going through a series of more or less critical experiences which constitute their diagnosis and treatment. "Successful" therapeutic narratives are the object of the hospital's work, that is, the hospital's aim is to admit people in need of medical care and discharge them, as soon as possible, either well or with a positive program of rehabilitation before them, and with the patient understanding and satisfied with the hospital's work. The hospital's idea of a dischargeable patient, generally taken in relation to the more or less grave condition in which they were admitted, represents the hospital's concept of a patient who is well for the purposes of a public hospital (not necessarily from the point of view of a social worker, psychologist or policeman). How does the hospital's concept align with that of their patients? How does the hospital's perception of the extent to which they are meeting their goals align with their patients'?

Manidis and Scheeres (2012) followed *a single patient* from admission to discharge and her story shed invaluable light on what was going on in the hospital and lent itself immediately to proposals for a productive intervention. The same approach can be used in connection with a "collective subject," a single unit within the hospital. Lingard, McDougall, Levstik, Chandok, Spafford & Shryer (2012) followed *a single specialist team* through a series of difficult interactions with other specialist teams in the course of dealing with one complex case, producing one of several possible therapeutic narratives relating to the various hospital departments. This study brought out in sharp relief the fact that different units within a hospital have different concerns and have conceptions of their role within the hospital, and different norms of interaction with others: different object-concepts.

It is possible to define a motive for each of these narratives: the patient is suffering and wishes to get well, the team wants another team to adapt their actions to ameliorate the difficulties the patient presents for their own discipline, etc. But this could be an extraneous post facto exercise. Understanding narratives is as basic a mode of human cognition as is understanding concepts such as objects of activity. It is through narratives of difficult interactions like those presented in the above two papers that the divergent self-conceptions of the various groups of health professionals is manifested. This knowledge has to be *abstracted* from the narrative and combined with other information to produce a generalised conclusion to the research.

In fact, the two modes of knowing mutually constitute one another: you can't make sense of a concept without knowing the story behind it and you can't follow a story so long as you are unfamiliar with the concepts and personae being deployed. The patient narratives, medical narratives and administrative narratives, all the narratives which make up the life of a hospital, allow us to abstract the rules and objects and identities of all the projects making up the hospital and make sense of how they interact and how contradictions emerge and can be resolved. These narratives are the substance, the units of analysis, the real subject matter for analysis.

Having a unit of analysis gives the researcher purchase on a forbiddingly complex process. Manidis and Scheeres' patient narrative did not in itself elucidate why things are done the way they are, but it did highlight in very sharp outline what the contradictions were. The problem brought out in the patient's narrative was a critical lack of communication between health professionals, not listening to the patient, and in particular, the responsible doctor not seeking insights from nursing staff who had spent far more time listening to the patient. Once identified, fixing the problem would require either (1) an analysis of the hospital "system of activity" identifying the source of failures in communication in the division of labour, perhaps, or the norms governing the self-conception of agents, or perhaps the technical means of record-keeping and communicating, or (2) introduction of a germ cell tool or word into interaction with patients and nurses that would stimulate listening. But generally speaking, once the contradictions are brought into relief, corrective action tends to immediately suggest itself. The same comments apply to the study of the medical narrative.

But the fact remains that narrative analysis can be a means of identifying the relevant activities, understanding how the constituent actions cohere meaningfully, and understanding the shared experience as a whole. A clinical team has a "personality" analogous to that of an individual person, a personality which develops historically through *perezhivaniya*; an accident happens one day, an anaesthetist is sanctioned and the modus operandi of the unit is changed forever. How do different projects interact and support one another? As independent subjects, their interaction is either governed by some system of rules, possibly negotiated between them, or one or the other project subordinates itself to the other. Or some combination of all of these. There is no basis for assuming that the norms of collaboration-as-such apply to all such collaborations. (See the section below on relations between projects.)

Of course, all the professions engaged in these interactions within a hospital have a long history in medical systems across the world; each specialist unit brings their own culture, points of pride and vulnerabilities with them when they set up in the hospital. The hospital administrators are working in a larger world where multiple projects intersect their own work.

2.1   *The Story of a Female Trainee Surgeon Who Chooses to Leave Training*

Rhea Liang and her colleagues (2019) enquired into why so many well-qualified female trainee surgeons abandon the discipline before completing training, a longstanding phenomenon which has led to only 11% of surgeons being female, despite high levels of female participation in other medical disciplines.

The researchers used professional networks to recruit research subjects who had already chosen to leave surgery and these subjects helped recruit others and also participated in analysing the data; they were *participant observers*. The inclusion of research subjects in the research team itself was possible because the researchers approached the topic with a *feminist perspective* consistent with aims of the Women's Liberation Movement (WLM) to identify and break down barriers to female participation in the professions. They adhered to the maxim: if it's not suitable for women it's not suitable for anyone!

The research team collected trainee narratives which began from the time when the women first formed the idea of becoming a surgeon and carried through to the moment at which the trainee abandoned this ideal. The narratives identified 11 types of experience (six of them newly reported with this study) which were shared by a number of the women and which contributed to the ultimate decision to leave the discipline. They found that the impact of these experiences was *cumulative*. Three or four such experiences produced a threshold condition where just one more experience, possibly relatively minor – an incident of bullying, a denial of leave or a gender-based slur – had a critical effect, triggering an irreversible decision to leave. Here the concept of *perezhivanie* is crucial; although none of the subjects had sought psychological treatment, several were suicidal at the time of their decision to leave. The study highlights cumulative as well as the critical effect of *perezhivaniya*.

Liang and her colleagues found that surgeons' *habitus* (Bourdieu, 1979) – "the deeply ingrained habits, skills, and dispositions that develop through life experiences" in professional settings – a habitus imbued with upper class, male norms of behaviour, was the primary source of difficulties faced by surgeons, male as well as female. This observation highlights the fact that surgery training programs are characterised by the conflict-laden collaboration involving two social movements – the patriarchy and the WLM – a reality obscured if training is viewed as a "system of activity."

Liang et al.'s research did not solve the problem but it went much further than generalisations. They identified a number of the behaviours and administrative arrangements which were driving women to quit the profession.

Sohrab Rezvani (2022) sought to understand how environmental activists *became* activists and the well-known phenomenon of "burn-out." He recruited to his research project a group of students who had formed an environmental activist group. These problems were of pressing concern for the activists themselves and they readily acted as "participant researchers," conducting interviews and helping to interpret the results. Rezvani also found *perezhivaniya* had a cumulative effect. Again, solutions remain outstanding but the problem has been clearly posed.

This is frequently the case; there is a gap between analysing the nature of the problem: the causes of dysfunction, the location of contradictions, the origin of barriers, on the one hand, and on the other hand, the intervention required to fix the problem. Having identified the key contradiction facing female surgeons, it remains to identify the germ cell which encapsulates and transcends that situation. This is the point at which real creative thinking is required.

Given a rich, immediate, visceral representation of reality which identifies the crucial contradictions, it is generally possible to develop principles which capture the problem as a whole, and from there you can design an intervention. In cases like those just mentioned, social movements such as the WLM or anti-racist movement, trade unions, professional or other representative bodies can provide concepts and strategies to aid research and interventions.

2.2   *A Medical Student in Their First Months as a Hospital Doctor*

The story of a medical student experiencing their first months as a hospital doctor also provides an invaluable insight into problems of the professional development of newcomers in a profession.

Traditionally, doctors served an apprenticeship just as in other trades, even while training in medical schools became more widespread. Nowadays, doctors invariably complete an academic course at a medical school which generally takes five or six years, mostly made up of long hours of lectures and "book learning," before completing a year or more of training in teaching hospitals. Medical schools often use problem-solving groups and simulation exercises in an effort to introduce students to clinical practice before they enter the profession as junior doctors in a teaching hospital. Other professions also use various kinds of practical exercise, such as mock courts, environmental surveys, cadetships and so on, to prepare students for entering the profession.

Tim Dornan et al. (in progress) have collected the narratives of a number of either newly-qualified or final-year student-doctors who entered the British NHS hospital system at the height of the COVID19 pandemic in 2020. At the beginning of their stories they were university students who had been taught protocols for clinical practice, but had little clinical experience. They were, nonetheless, young adults already with a strong commitment to medicine; they were not children in any sense of the word. They found themselves filling the role of junior doctors with responsibility to diagnose and treat patients. The advice of more senior doctors was normally available, but doing on-call shifts they found themselves in charge of wards with limited access to support and advice. Further, they were in the midst of enormously complex institutions alongside medical specialists, consultants and technicians, nurses, administrators and auxiliary staff, in unfamiliar spaces where necessary equipment and information was secreted in unknown places, and subject to complex norms, rules and procedures for which they were completely unprepared. Their relationships with nurses – generally far more experienced than they, but supposedly receiving direction from them – was problematic. Meanwhile, senior doctors and specialists may or may not have been disposed to help. They had had to manage complex presentations, patients providing unreliable information, or screaming in pain, or dying in their hands, and having to inform grieving relatives.

Initially, their medical knowledge was purely *formal*. They could answer questions on anatomy, physiology or pharmacology, but could not *use* that knowledge to guide their clinical practice in the hospital context. They seemed to be starting from scratch.

We know that the concept of "knowledge" abstracted from the practice it is meant to inform, is unreal, an abstraction; it is purely formal knowledge. And yet, professional training is almost universally based on the opposite assumption, that theory can be learnt in one context and then unproblematically applied later in a context different from the context in which the theory was learnt.

When we engage in a practice, each action is made thanks to mediation by psychic reflection, in response to stimuli generated by the situation. Recall Luria's words cited above: "Voluntary behaviour is the ability to create stimuli and to subordinate them ... to the organisation of behaviour." The situation is constituted psychically by a complex of stimuli which access neural pathways and interact with previously acquired "scripts" (to use Silvan Tomkins' term), a form of operational knowledge which connects situations with stereotyped responses. For a student whose knowledge is still formal, the scripts are purely formal. They relate formal situations to formal responses, for example, answers are connected to questions, names are connected to physiological images, and so on. Prominent among these scripts are *checklists* which give a practitioner a series of actions, usually captured by a mnemonic (for example, First Aiders learn DRSAB for applying CPR: Danger, Response, Send for help, Airway check, Breathing). Checklists are intended to provide stimuli which move a novice practitioner through a series of actions which ought to be appropriate to a category of situation. But even these scripts can *distract* the junior doctor from stimuli emanating *from the situation itself.* In order to perform as a clinician, the junior doctor requires a completely new set of scripts connected to the stimuli which arise in real clinical situations, stimuli which connect relevant action-scripts to the real situation. That is, their formal knowledge must be *restructured.*

This is the process Vygotsky described in terms of a "scientific concept" acquired through instruction developing into an "actual concept" in the course of professional experience – "rising from the abstract to the concrete." The scientific concept is acquired "top down," beginning from a formal name or principle, while everyday knowledge is acquired "bottom up," beginning from immediate experiences and organised in the course of reflection. The process of professional apprenticeship is a process of *merging* book learning with immediate everyday experience.

Like mountaineers who see the peak continuously retreat as they mount each slope, doctors never reach a plateau on which they shall never face another entirely novel situation. However, the junior doctor is all at sea to begin with. Faced with an emergency they resort to checklists and miss vital cues in the situation itself. They try to carry off the impression of being in charge of the situation but their activity takes on an infantile appearance in front of nurses who are supposed to be their subordinates. Learning never ends, but if completed successfully, the "steep learning curve" entailed in the initial months of a junior doctor's experience constitutes a *development* in the sense Vygotsky gave to this term in his theory of child development.

At the same time, they are undergoing an *identity crisis.* They are already dedicated to their profession, but they soon become aware that that commitment (*otnoshiniye*) is purely formal. There are commitments and commitments. They now must really *become* doctors. It appears that despite the fact that junior doctors are already adults, the development that they must make in order to become real doctors entails a zone of proximal development. During this period, the guidance of more experienced professionals is essential, and failure to provide that guidance and support can result in trauma with life-long impact. From being all at sea they must "find their feet." Confronted with novel situations, a doctor must always be willing to ask advice but such moments will be occasional and will stand out from the background of the normal course of practice in which the doctor is working on familiar territory. But the newly qualified doctor is not on familiar territory. A critical clinical situation ought normally to stimulate an action, an operational script, not book knowledge. Only unusual or surprising turns in therapeutic episodes should cause the doctor to think about research papers, text books, images from anatomical diagrams, lists of diagnostic options or pharmacological indications. This restructure of medical knowledge entails a development, a complete restructure of their medical knowledge.

Dornan et al.'s study of junior doctor narratives in terms of the *perezhivaniya* which marked the experience of their first six months in a hospital brought out in sharp relief the problems in longstanding current practices of medical training in the NHS.

The interviewees did not have to be prompted to relate the *perezhivaniya* endured during their experience in the NHS. These traumatic moments – crises, humiliations, revelations, moments of panic or confusion – all stood out in sharp relief. Their memory of the time was structured around these experiences, and how they worked over them and struggled to learn from the experience and do better next time. But every one of these *perezhivaniya* was a pointer to a potential time bomb in the training regime of junior doctors. How could they have been better supported? Was it possible to avoid situations like this?

Frequently, young doctors struggled with mnemonics designed to manage critical procedures and found them more helpful in retrospect than in real time, but had no viable alternative to using them. Teams used mnemonics more effectively because calling out the triggers can facilitate a division of labour. The research is ongoing. The point is that the data are narratives of participants, the units of which are *perezhivaniya* each of which points to a contradiction latent in the procedures and principles of the hospitals. These contradictions are revealed through *activities*.

• • •

Hitherto I have considered only personal development and psychology on the assumption of a more or less static social and cultural environment. However, as is well known, activities, a.k.a. practices or collaborative projects, are themselves subjects which develop through all the phases of a life cycle and in so doing are transformed by the changes affecting the social formation at large and themselves participate in changing the social formation.

I will now move to look at the historical development of activities and their place in the historical development of social formations. In the first instance I will consider the history of a project simply from the point of view of being an object of study.

3   The History of a Practice, Such as a Science or Profession

The history of a practice, be it a science, a profession, a sport or an institution such as a family or a government, provides an invaluable insight into the present state of that practice and its latent contradictions. Such contradictions may be taken for granted or simply implicit in the practice without any obvious expression. Frequently, it is by looking into the history of the practice that such contradictions are revealed. Indeed, it is impossible to understand any social practice without tracing its genealogy through preceding generations, and through the resolution of various conflicts and crises which have successively transformed the practice, set new priorities, defined new concepts and made new discoveries. Hegel's philosophy, for example, makes sense only in the context of its prehistory in European philosophy, oscillating between theories of the immediate relation between mind and the world (thanks to Reason or Faith) or theories of the mediation of the relation between mind and the world (Kant and the Empiricists). Past crises are sedimented in existing practices in the form of concepts and norms which originated as germ cells in the form of solutions to problems now lost in the past.

To illustrate the importance of understanding the practice of a science or profession as an activity by tracing its life story I will refer to the history of medicine and the related training of doctors in the 25 years prior to the present moment. In a video interview, Dornan (2021) analyses the problems confronting medicine in 2021 by beginning from the 1990s.

In the 1990s, the neo-liberal ideology which had become rampant over the previous decade flowed over into tertiary education, but there were surprising side-effects of this shift. Consultants who had battered down management hierarchies within the capitalist economy in favour of outsourcing, deregulation, one-line budgets, quality control and so on, now turned their attention to the universities. The traditional relationship between teacher and student was subjected to critique and replaced with the conception of the student-as-customer, casting the teacher as a service provider: the student was buying a qualification and the teacher was selling it. Unlike earlier critiques of university education, this movement was enthusiastically embraced by university corporate leaderships. The surprising side-effect of this reactionary attack on traditional hierarchical conceptions of higher education was that it provided an opening for other more egalitarian conceptions of the student-teacher relationship which had hitherto been unable to penetrate the university, despite collaborative learning, for example, having conquered school education 20 years before (see Blunden & Arnold, 2014).

One such novel approach which took advantage of the moment was Problem Based Learning (PBL). This movement had its origins in John Dewey's Laboratory School in the 1920s which had survived, however, only for a short time. Bruner in the 1960s and later followers of Vygotsky had introduced the idea in the related form of "project learning" in school education. Universities were slow to adopt these new approaches to teaching and learning. As early as 1969, however, McMaster University, Canada, had created PBL rooms in its Medical School with the aim of promoting self-directed, self-motivated, self-assessed groups of students working collaboratively on clinical problems. As described in 8.4 below, this idea only reached the University of Melbourne where this author was working in the 1990s.

This conception was remote from the idea of student-as-customer, but it did respond to the now-established tendency for medical professionals to be university educated before qualifying to work in hospitals, by introducing elements of clinical practice into the book learning paradigm of traditional university education.

PBL, collaborative learning and project learning entered the university as a result of contradictory factors. They resonated with the desire to "democratise" learning and make it more open to "market forces." Collaborative learning was a conception of teaching and learning with its origins in Activity Theory which responded to the same spirit, and was well known to most people who had undergone teacher training. Collaborative learning had become widely adopted in Medical Schools by the 1990s. Neo-Liberal managements welcomed collaborative learning into universities because they thought it would undermine the traditional authority of university teachers, who had hitherto been able to dominate curriculum and teaching practices. Collaborative learning was seen to prepare students for collaborative relations at work and university leaders believed that teamwork was a marketable skill in itself and employers were demanding universities equip their graduates with skills in "teamwork."

This move was undoubtedly a positive one. It was well known to Activity Theorists that collaboration was essential to *learning*. PBL also offered a practical means of teaching clinical practice outside of the context of real health care, including the practice of simulation which boomed and continues to boom with improvements in technology. However, PBL was based on the false assumption that problem solving was a *transferable skill* that could not only flow from one discipline to another but also from one context to another, from the PBL room to real clinical practice. This misconception had a perverse effect in the context of the next wave of Neoliberal attack on education, medical education included.

In the 2000s, Neoliberalism launched a wholesale attack on education, partly in order to "take the teacher out of teaching" (opening classroom activity to bureaucratic control) and partly to marketise the education industry by means of external testing, commercial professional training services and "upskilling." Central to this appropriation of education was the conception of *transferable skills*.

Further, the ethos of "quality control" which had penetrated most other industries focused attention on adverse outcomes in medicine and appealed to public opinion and common sense for the need to reduce adverse outcomes. The Hippocratic Oath was rewritten to suit the spirit of Neoliberalism. The command to "To hold my teacher in this art equal to my own parents; to make him partner in my livelihood" was quietly forgotten and the promise that "I will use those [treatments] which will benefit my patients according to my greatest ability and judgment, and I will do no harm or injustice to them," was reduced to "Do no harm." Minimising harm in the practice of managing a fleet of aircraft is one thing, but quite another in the Accident and Emergency Department.

The conception of the college or university as a seller of qualifications had taken root. Because their future depended on performance in standardised tests, medical students were disinclined to take advantage of opportunities for practical experience before applying for their first placement. Meanwhile, educators relied on the false premise that clinical practice could be broken down into elements – transferable skills – which could be taught with simulations and check lists. As a result, medical students were arriving at hospital utterly unprepared for what they were to face in their profession. Doctors do learn and become doctors nonetheless, but not without considerable pain, trauma and confusion along the way.

Unwinding this accumulation of misconceptions is impossible without understanding the social basis and *interests* – especially economic interests – entailed in the various conceptions and practices embedded in present-day medical education. These can be made visible only by tracing the origins of these conceptions in earlier phases of its life history. Even simply *understanding* where these bizarre practices come from helps the young doctor survive the system with their integrity intact, even while they lack any capacity to change medical practice. Perhaps at some future time the damage done to medicine by Neoliberal economics can be undone on a systemic basis?

Similarly, in *Origins of Collective Decision Making* (Blunden, 2016a), I sought to analyse problems arising in the social justice milieu around the conflict between majoritarian and consensus approaches by tracing the genealogy of collective decision making from its origins in traditional society. What

I witnessed was movements otherwise united around a social justice issue split into mutually hostile camps over the question of *how* collective decisions should be made. Protagonists usually justified their claim for a majoritarian or a consensus approach by appeal to pragmatic concerns: how to get the best decisions, how to maintain unity, how to respect the variety of concerns. But the intractable character of the disagreement pointed to something more deep-seated.

Investigations revealed that Majority had its origins in the earliest formation of voluntary associations among artisans and merchants in the interstices of feudal society dominated by hierarchies of blood and land. It was only after hundreds of years of organising mutual aid via Majority that Majority penetrated government via the establishment of parliaments. Although Consensus had had a precursor in the Quakers of 17th England, Consensus had originated in Myles Horton's work with African American activists, the Peace and then Women's Movement in the US in the 1950s. It was simply not true, as had been claimed, that traditional communities had used Consensus. In fact, traditional decision making by Counsel had relied on hierarchy. The displacement of Majority by Consensus within social justice movements in mid-century had its origin in the historic compromise between the workers' movement and the Comintern on one hand and imperialism on the other. The workers' movement had lost its authority before the most oppressed and excluded of the world. A new ethos had come to dominate social justice struggles: the ethos of inclusion and respect rather than the ethos of solidarity and tolerance. I took the view that *understanding* the origins of this ethical conflict would allow participants in movements to be able to adopt one or another mode of decision making pragmatically in accordance with the demands of the moment, rather than making a matter of principle out of it at the cost of splitting the movement. See the section below on decision making within projects.

In both the above instances, the study of the history of a practice leads to understanding, but does not necessarily, in itself, lead to solutions to the contradictions. Self-evidently, however, understanding the historical origins of a contradiction, and therefore the conditions under which a contradiction embedded itself in a practice, is a precondition to transforming that practice.

In order to understand how a reactionary political regime remains in power and the conditions which make that im/possible, it is likewise necessary to study the history of the regime in question. In an unpublished study of the Islamic Republic of Iran and with an Iranian collaborator, I found that the origins of the regime did not lie in the 1979 Revolution which created the Islamic Republic, which had been led by left-leaning urban people, but two years later. The workers' movement had seized factories and placed them under the control of shuras (communes). The clerics now used their religious following among the rural poor to terrorise the workers and return the factories to the employers. The employer was now captive of an Islamic terror wielded by a parasitic layer of clergy, which more and more bled them dry. As the rural people became disappointed in the regime, the regime more and more relied on their clients *outside* the borders of Iran to maintain the ranks of the religious militia. It then became possible to see how changes in neighbouring countries, whose fate was less and less tied up with that of the Islamic Republic, and the impact of sanctions were beginning to destabilise the regime. It was not the Islamic Republic *as such* which was the problem. The *germ cell* of the oppressive regime was in the conflict between the shuras and the religious militia now sourced from countries presently finding their own road to modernity. Whatever follows the Islamic Republic, be it the return of the Shah, a European-style parliamentary republic, a US occupation, a failed state, or whatever, it seems that the fate of the ordinary people of Iran would again depend on the shuras, whose defeat had opened the way to the regime of terror which has ruled Iran since about 1981.

In my (2010) study of Activity Theory, I made an immanent critique of the development of the theory. I observed that the germ cell of the approach was in Vygotsky's concept of a germ cell or "unit of analysis" – not any one version of the unit, but simply the practice grounding of a theory in a unit. Tracing the origins of this concept in Goethe, Hegel and Marx, and following its use by Vygotsky, Leontyev, et al., made it clear that the "unit" was not just an incidental or idiosyncratic feature of Vygotsky's work which could be adopted or not, but was the very essence of the theory. The unit of analysis of the theory was the unit of analysis of the theory. Consequently, my critique of Activity Theory through the lens of the unit of analysis was an "immanent critique."

Bringing an understanding of "germ cell" grounded in a study of the entire history of the concept through a number of diverse writers to bear on contemporary work in Activity Theory revealed that none of the contemporary writers understood the term. People were using Vygotsky's insights but could not generalise from them because they did not understand the germ cell or unit. As a result, I was able to bring out how the understanding and successive misunderstandings of the concept of "unit of analysis" in the context of the changing social situation in which Activity Theory operated, had produced the current situation where a number of different currents exist side-by-side with quite different concepts of the legacy of Lev Vygotsky.

These studies demonstrate how the historical critique of practices can yield insights which facilitate transformation.

CHAPTER 4

Transformative Projects

Hitherto, the research projects which I have considered have been aimed either at helping an individual adjust to a social practice or at *understanding* a social practice, but as Marx famously said, "the point is to change it." Studying the development of a practice is simultaneously a study of the practice itself and a study of how that practice changes and therefore how it *can be changed*. The teaching of the history of a practice can be a transformative practice in itself. Understanding the history behind the practice into which a young person is being inducted undoubtedly stimulates a critical attitude to that practice inasmuch as the practice ceases to be fixed and normative, but inherently subject to challenge and contradiction. Vianna (see below) and Dornan (above) have both used this approach to generate critical consciousness in groups of their students.

But the practices still have to be changed, and teaching and researching leaves all the work still to be done. I will now move to those projects where Activity Theory is being used to change the world.

Activity Theory has been used for the purpose of bringing about social change in the following ways. (1) By identifying the conditions out of which new committed activists are formed and actively intervening to foster the development of such activists. (2) Introducing from outside some change in practices which research has shown can function as a germ cell, growing and proliferating so as to improve a practice or even transform it altogether. (3) By actively participating in a practice, especially a social justice or emancipatory struggle, alongside and in solidarity with others, but doing so as a reflective and theoretically informed participant who is able to transform practices using Activity Theory. (4) By offering education and training services directly into social movements and struggles. (5) By simply participating as equals alongside others engaged in social movement activism. (6) Initiating and leading projects aimed at a specific social changes. (7) By contributing to the development of social theory by participating in political and philosophical debates in public and interdisciplinary forums.

As I move from research and teaching to effecting social change, the idea of "agency" comes into focus. Activity Theory is one of those currents of practice which believes that through collaborative activity individuals can and do bring about changes in the conditions of their own existence and even in domains beyond the horizons of the individual's own activity. The world is currently in a critical state. New initiatives, novel ideas and refusals have ramifications far beyond what could be expected in a stable world.

1   The Activist Stance

The "activist stance" was introduced by Anna Stetsenko working at the City University of New York as a response to urban youths facing exclusion and disadvantage. The essential idea of the activist stance to tackling social problems is threefold. First is the idea that a person can only be free thanks to their own efforts, whereas freedom on the gift of another party is essentially only a new form of subordination (the principle of self-determination). The commitment to challenge oppressive social conditions invariably changes the lives of the youth even while those conditions remain in place. Second is the principle that meaningful social bonds – essential to human flourishing – are fashioned and secured only by participation in collaborative projects, not merely by the proximity or identification with others on the basis of commonality. Third, the oppressive social conditions under which the youth suffer can be abolished only thanks to the efforts of such activists steeped in the lived experience of these very conditions.

These were the ideas behind my book, *Collaborative Projects. An interdisciplinary study* (2014) in which both Stetsenko and her colleague Eduardo Vianna were contributors. As I argued in the Introduction to that book, the essential relation between persons which supports self-emancipation is *solidarity* – assisting another party under *their* direction – asking "How can I help?" I will deal with these concepts in the context of social movements and political struggle in more detail presently, but solidarity and participation in emancipatory collaborations are essential in helping young people suffering from exclusion, victimisation, isolation and other social ills. The pre-condition for solidarity is that the person themselves is struggling for their own freedom. Here I will focus on the work of Vianna.

In 2003 Vianna (2022) was appointed to the post of psychologist at a foster home in New York and was introduced to the mostly African-American youths living at the group home as someone to whom they could talk who would "help them with their emotional problems." Vianna had indeed been trained as a clinical psychiatrist. However, he had become convinced that the overwhelming majority of the psychological problems he was being asked to fix did not originate inside people's heads but in the social conditions in which people were living. He had then switched careers and taken up Vygotskian psychology and Activity Theory. "Help them with their emotional problems" was not Vianna's idea about what he was going to be doing in this institution.

This led Vianna into sharp conflict with the administration of the home until one afternoon he arrived at work to find that all the residents had been sent to the park in an effort by the administration to block his work with the youths. So he went to the park to meet the youths, and began the slow work of gaining the trust of a group of utterly alienated youth. It took up to two years before some of them would even look him in the eye. But the youth witnessed the way Vianna made himself vulnerable, the way he advocated for them, the disrespectful way the institution treated him and how he refused to conform to the institution's punishment procedures, and identified that Vianna was on their side, not that of the institution. This was the lynch-pin, Vianna said, to building solidarity with the residents. It is worth noting that in order to trans-form the group home, Vianna had to begin by *transgressing* its norms.

The management had a practice of going home early on Friday afternoons, so Vianna used that time to show movies, especially subversive movies – *One Flew over the Cuckoo's Nest* was a particular favourite – which resonated with the kids' resistance to efforts to control them. Vianna expanded this activity by taking small groups of kids to Manhattan on the weekends. Good behav-iour was necessary to qualify for these enjoyable trips and Vianna did not hes-itate to challenge the boys over abusive behaviour among themselves. He then received a grant to support the progress he was making and used the money to hire a video professional and engaged the youth in a collaborative project to produce a movie. The kids wrote the script and played all roles in the produc-tion, with the assistance of the professional, and used the opportunity to test out their critique of the world around them (as they had seen in the movies Vianna had introduced them to). This participation in a collaborative project, a project which, while remaining at the level of expression, built powerful bonds of trust, introduced them to critical ideas. Vianna spent time in the kids' rooms and introduced them to writers such as Paulo Freire, Erich Fromm and Cornell West – challenging one might have thought for barely literate youngsters – but because the need for these critical ideas had arisen naturally out of their own collaborative efforts to formulate a critique of modern patriarchal, racist capitalist society, they had the motivation to overcome difficulties and made progress. Vianna even introduced them to mathematics, applying the Activity Theory of Davydov and Galperin and made breakthroughs which their school mathematics teachers had failed to achieve. Although it took years to reach some of the older youth, most of the younger ones made considerable social and intellectual development through his program.

After about three years, the whole character of the group home had changed. Now new residents coming into the home from the street, police custody or domestic violence discovered an environment of mutual trust and solidarity; the character of the home had changed permanently, even after Vianna had moved on after four years. Obviously, the same racist, patriarchal, capitalist society was there at the end of the project as at the beginning, but the home was now graduating youth with an understanding of the source of their problems in their social environment, and a determination to overcome them by their own efforts, bringing meaning to their lives. Vianna & Stetsenko (2014) claim that it is not in *adapting* to their situation that people develop, but in *changing* that situation. It is the conviction of activity theorists that solidarity and self-emancipation through participation in collaborative projects can bring a person to a level of personal autonomy which is consistent with human flourishing to the maximum extent possible within the limitations of existing social relations. At the same time, it produces the agents who will be able to contribute to changing that environment.

This kind of approach is widely used (though not always in such an explicitly political sense) in very many schools and institutions. Young people in their mid teens, who are just beginning to form new social bonds outside the home and find a social position for themselves can benefit from such "project learning." Here, science or social studies classes take on projects relevant to their community and groups of students work together in collaboratively searching for solutions to social problems and where possible implementing them and observing the results of their work. Environmental projects are always a favourite with today's youth. The approach rests on the same idea that knowledge is meaningful only in the context of collaborative projects, and *formal* knowledge acquired in the classroom and books may very often never find soil in which to grow. Even advanced academic ideas can be grasped by young people if those ideas answer to a need arising from their own activity. So it was that barely literate youth were reading Erich Fromm in New York and a 16-year-old boy in Delft, Holland, invented a machine to extract plastic waste from the ocean. This type of learning, based on the subject's own activity, is in sharp contrast to the formal learning still dominant in schools to this day.

1.1   *Agency*

In my article, *Agency* (Blunden, 2021a), I pointed out that the current fad among socio-cultural theorists for discussing "agency" obscures the fact that "agency" can be little more than an abstract heading for a range of at least eight different concrete concepts according to the development of a person and their social situation from childhood to adult and from home to the life of a citizen in a democratic socialist sustainable world, each concretised through a distinct unit of analysis. Nick Hopwood (2022) took this observation a step forward by comparing in detail claims by Sannino (2020), Edwards (2017; 2020) and Stetsenko (2019) for a concrete concept of agency anchored in different conceptions.

1.1.1   Vygotsky on Self-control

Vygotsky's (1931a) study of the development of self-control through the appropriation of cultural artefacts (words, tools and signs) is an exemplar for the study of "agency." This study includes a description of the waiting room experiment: a subject is left in a waiting room without any explanation, and is observed to use their watch to determine the moment when they get up and leave.

In this chapter, Vygotsky is focused on understanding the *psychological* basis for voluntary action by a human being subject to the laws of biology. He concludes that voluntary action can only be understood through the combined action of two distinct processes: (1) the formation of a *decision process* using an otherwise neutral stimulus, and (2) *closure* when the selected decision process has produced a new stimulus and the person reacts in the way they themselves determined in advance. "Behaviour," he says, "is determined by situations and reaction is elicited by stimuli; for this reason the key to controlling behaviour lies in controlling stimuli" (p. 201). A little later he expands this formulation a little: "intention is a typical process of controlling one's own behaviour by creating appropriate situations and connections, but executing it is a process that is completely independent of the will and takes place automatically" (p. 211).

Vygotsky has added the *situation*. A person manifests self-control insofar as they have determined the *situation and* the neutral decision procedure. The waiting room experiment tells only half the story, for in this experiment the subjects have had little control over the situation they find themselves in and do not understand its significance. "Human freedom consists specifically of man's ability to think, that is, that man is cognizant of the developing situation" (Vygotsky, p. 209).

Thinking is a psychic process which resolves a problem by resort to already established auxiliary connections in the brain (*op, cit*, p. 207). Vygotsky placed his research subjects in a situation and he so complicated the situation that the subjects were unable to resolve it using their existing psychological resources, and then offered the subjects, directly or indirectly, a die as a new neutral means of resolving the decision. The die was not the first means to which the subjects turned, but a last resort. There was no suggestion by Vygotsky that use of the die was a germ cell or unit, far less a *typical* means of decision making;

indeed it is more likely that a child subject would turn to the adult researcher and *ask* how they should decide. Indeed, the appropriation of a cultural arte-fact often means asking a more experienced other or using a reference book, procedure or other cultural product *intended* for the resolution of problems.

Nonetheless, the appropriation of the use of a die by the subject does suggest a germ cell for the *formation of a new auxiliary stimulus*; the subjects appro-priated a means which was suggested to them directly or indirectly by others evidently more in control of the situation, included it in their activity and incor-porated this means into their ongoing intellectual resources. Throwing dice, looking at a clock, writing a note, finishing one's coffee, hearing an alarm – all these are not only artefacts, but artefacts which have been culturally marked as means of deciding to act.

The characteristic of specifically human activity and human freedom in par-ticular is that it is mediated by *thinking*. Consequently, it is of great interest to know how thinking develops. Vygotsky showed that thinking develops by the appropriation of cultural means. This is a general universal truth but *Thinking and Speech* (1934) is the work where Vygotsky elaborated the most essential process in the development of the mind, appropriation of *spoken words*. The means entailed in the development of the intellect and the personality as a whole are diverse. The appropriation of cultural means is a general feature of the development of the personality, but it is a mistake to lump all such dis-tinct processes of human development together under "artefact mediation" as if they were one and the same process.

Further, Vygotsky states that human freedom consists in both controlling our situation and fixing the connections by means of which we think. Vygotsky does not further elaborate on the significance of controlling our situation. In general, all his psychological work was done by placing subjects in a situation and then observing their actions. If we expand our vision beyond the lab. to include formation of the situation, then it is apparent that while controlling one's situation is challenging, CHAT researchers cannot ignore it. Creating, con-trolling and avoiding situations is the most important element of self-control.

In all discussions of agency it must be kept in mind that agency includes both the means mobilised by a person to achieve their end *and* the capacity of a person to determine their own ends. Put it this way: it is one thing to be able to get food, quite another to overcome the need for food; to be free to go shop-ping means little if you are in the thrall of advertisers; it is one thing to be top dog in the prison but it is better to avoid prison in the first place. As Amartya Sen & Drèze (2002) pointed out, it is not enough to have a voice, one must have a *critical* voice.

Psychologists usually come to the problem of agency in the context of an individual who wants to get their own way in some social situation. This is an extremely limited conception of agency. Activity theorists have gone somewhat further by looking to how an individual can affect the social means of achieving their goals and, most significantly, how a person can reframe a problem so as to gain control of *their own* will and how they can establish collaborative relationships and change the situation rather than simply adapting to it.

1.1.2   Sannino on Collective Decision Making

One of the domains in which "agency" may be manifested is participation in collective decision making under conditions where the norm is for consensus. In this scenario an individual participates in committing an entire group to a shared goal. Annalisa Sannino (2020) made a study of collective decision making by reproducing Lewin's and Vygotsky's famous waiting room experiment with a *group* of her own students, rather than an *individual* research subject. The same paper went on to offer insights into how actions by an individual can open the way to broader emancipatory social change, theorised under the heading of "transformative agency." But before discussing this idea, the misunderstanding of collective decision making which was exhibited in this study must be dealt with.

Sannino told a group of her students to meet her in a room at a given time, but then failed to turn up and videoed their response with a hidden camera. The students were torn between equal and opposite "stimuli": boredom versus the desire to do as they were told by their professor. At one point a student suggested that they wait until they'd finished their coffee and then join their fellows in the cafeteria. This suggestion was not agreed to, but as time dragged on and after several attempts, they took the use of a cultural artefact (writing a note) to determine their joint action. They finished their coffees, and the suggestion was picked up and the students retired to the cafeteria. Sannino used this result to conclude that Vygotsky's original waiting-room experiment worked when applied to a group: in the face of equal and opposite "stimuli," a group would use an external stimulus (finishing their coffee or writing a note) to make a decision. This is reminiscent of the ancient mode of decision making called *necromancy* (outsourcing difficult decisions to the gods), and still used in the form of tossing a coin, for example. Sannino interpreted that a suggestion once voiced can function as a "forward anchor" (kedge) to resolve an impasse, draw consensus towards itself and determine action by a group without having determined a *reason* for acting through deliberation.

But how significant a part does tossing a coin play in present day collective decision making? How many juries decide on their verdict by tossing a coin? How many unions decide whether to strike or not on the basis of the first suggestion offered? This meeting had no object, so what norms governed its deliberations? And is "stimuli" the appropriate category for understanding collective decision making by human beings engaged in collective practices?

All the subjects were attending Sannino's course, and they made a collective decision in *that* cultural context; as students participating in Sannino's course, the relevant norm was that the professor made the decisions. However, in the absence of their professor there was no shared object. But they *were* a group with relatively strong bonds as fellow students in specialised university course in Finland, so it is unsurprising that they defaulted to Consensus to make their decision, albeit using an external stimulus.

The point of the waiting-room experiment for Vygotsky was that a person selected a stimulus from a cultural artefact to control their own will, and the experiment was a germ cell for the acquisition of cultural artefacts in the building of a person's capacity to control their own actions. The same process is involved when people engage in collective deliberation with a shared language – a "neutral decision procedure." The unit of analysis for deliberation would be an utterance.

What if the camera had been set up in a shop and while three or four customers were waiting to be served the shop assistant disappeared into the back of the shop and failed to return? It is unlikely that the shoppers would have made a *collective* decision because their waiting was not in pursuit of a collaborative project. And what if the chairperson in an important and contentious union meeting had inexplicably absented themself? Most likely the meeting would have appointed a deputy and voted on what to do. That is, Sannino attempted and failed to *isolate the research subjects from their cultural situation* and ignored the cultural determinants of collective decision making. As a result, the experiment succeeded in showing that Vygotsky's waiting room experiment worked with that group of people, but it told us nothing about *activity*.

Nonetheless, Sannino's term, "transformative agency," has entered the discourse of Activity Theory on the basis that Sannino's experiment has established a new concept of "agency." Sannino used the terms "kedge" and "warp": throwing out a sea-anchor (kedge) again and again until it draws a sailing ship out of the doldrums (warp) rather than anchor it against the current as a *metaphor*. Sannino describes three actions by means of which a kedge is used to orient an activity: *throwing out* the kedge; *regaining control* when the kedge succeeds; and *breaking out* of the situation.

Throwing out the kedge means a person making a suggestion or taking a tentative action, still unsure if the move can secure a way out. Regaining control means confirming that the mooted action does indeed offer a viable way out. Breaking out means drawing the whole project towards a new object-concept. (See also Hopwood et al., 2022).

Sannino's observation seems to be that putting a suggestion "on the table" can over a period of time draw consensus towards it and resolve a deadlock. The simplest precondition for reaching consensus is indeed that someone put a suggestion "on the table" and could be called the germ cell for making a Yes/ No decision. But this is a poor metaphor for the agency of a *group* of people as it lacks *deliberation*. This unit would not apply under any of the *actual* paradigms of collective decision making: Libertarian "horizontalism," Majority decision making, Consensus decision making as it is actually practised, or Counsel. Customers waiting in a shop for an absent shop assistant do not generally make any collective decision about whether to continue waiting or give up and leave. In a traditional decision making body using Counsel, it would be regarded as offensive to put a suggestion on the table out of turn, and to take control of the decision would be highly transgressive.

Analysis of collective decision making depends on the relevant ethos which is determined culturally and historically, ethically, not on the psychological plane.

Interpreting this metaphor generously, we could say that when Sannino throws out a kedge what is meant is that the agent has *reframed* the problem. Any suggestion which moved the decision point to something which can be resolved Yes/No in the absence of deliberation would effect this reframing, and Hopwood et al. (2022) have given examples which confirm this interpretation. The idea is thus a marginal expansion of Erving Goffman's (1974) idea of framing which is already widely used in the interpretation of social movement strategy. So Sannino has reduced "agency" to the technique of reframing, but this cannot amount to a new *concept* of "agency" even in the context of consensus decision making. There are other ways of resolving consensus, in particular *rational argument*, whose unit is an utterance not just putting something on the table, or, failing that, blocking, standing aside, disrupting or withdrawing from the project.

1.1.3   Gutiérrez on Transgression

Gutiérrez et al. (2019) identified *transgressive acts* as *indexes* for the exercise of agency. Transgression presupposes that the actor is participating in some activity, and is therefore bound by the norms of that activity. They are participating in that activity because directly or indirectly it meets their life-needs. Nonetheless, it often happens that the relevant activity (or institution or organisation) is failing to meet their needs adequately and may be placing unwarranted demands on them.

In a study of a group of youth participating in a video game, Gutiérrez et al. refer to the youth becoming "historical actors" by deliberately transgressing the rules of the game, echoing Hegel's characterisation of a "world historic personage." The high-flown title for such apparently trivial actions can be justified. Any union activist or organiser knows that the successful transformation of the rights and working conditions of employees always begins with transgressing their employment contracts. Likewise, the great Civil Rights Movement in the USA took off when a handful of Black students transgressed the rules of a department store and demanded to be served at a lunch counter. Every great social change begins with a minor transgression. Changing the norms begins by transgressing the norms. Hegel says as much in the *Philosophy of Right* (1821, §94n). We considered an instance of this transgression in Vianna's work in the New York group house mentioned above.

It is the object-concept of an activity or institution which determines the norms of participation in the activity, and Gutiérrez et al. point to how these norms can be changed, even by those excluded by the norms of the project.

Gutiérrez et al. identified four pointers to the emergence of "historical agency." (1) The recognition of a *double bind* (a.k.a. social situation or predicament, a trap, or conflict of motives); (2) a transgression (a breach in the social order, stepping across a line, breaking a norm) is enacted; (3) Cycles of social experimentation by individual(s) occur over time and a person begins to tinker with everyday interactional expectations; and (4) "The object of activity is expanded. This involves a refiguring of purpose and meaning, and a sense of one's historical role and connection to the larger stream of historical events."

Gutiérrez's idea is somewhat less than reframing; it is more like un-framing, in that it breaks the frame in which the object is being framed, thus opening the way to reframing the object. As in Sannino's conception, development takes place by repeated efforts to break the frame. But Gutiérrez et al. do not attempt to determine a unit of analysis from which a concrete concept of agency could be constructed; rather she depends on features of the exercise of agency by which it can be recognised. This is an abstract conception of "agency."

1.1.4   Stetsenko on Agency

Stetsenko calls her conception – the exercise of agency by means of a person committing to transform the social conditions which have hitherto been a barrier to their own self-realisation – the "transformative activist stance." Stetsenko not only points to this stance as an exercise of agency, but like Vianna, looks to the solidaristic actions of those around a person to support the achievement of this emancipatory stance. Nonetheless, it is that act of commitment which is the germ cell out of which a more developed commitment and a transformative project can grow. As we know from Leontyev's and Vygotsky's theory of personality, this transformation of a person's situation and the related commitments (*otnoshiniya*) occurs through a *perezhivanie*, in which the response of others to a person's striving is crucial. This transformation does not simply involve convincing others to follow their lead; more likely it entails joining an existing project in which the subject will *learn* or *be told* how to be an activist.

It could be said that a person begins to see their situation as neither a result of their own shortcomings nor of an all-powerful oppressor, but as a social situation which it lies within their own power to change. Thus, they have *reframed* their situation, both *for themselves* and others. But it is a very specific reframing which posits a new commitment and a new form of activity for the subject. At the psychological level, reframing a personal problem as a social problem and committing to changing it is indeed the primary condition for the further development of agency which still depends on the subject's social situation. Stetsenko has not attempted to determine a unit of analysis for this phase of agency however, and consequently has failed to determine a concrete concept of agency.

1.1.5   Holland and Edwards on Relational Agency
Holland et al. (1998) seem to have been the first to introduce discussion of "agency" into Activity Theory. However, her conception of "figured worlds" corresponds to activities which lack any genuine object, such as the world of romance. For her then, "agency" is "relational" in the sense that there is no object beyond the activity itself. Anne Edwards' (2017; 2020) conception of "relational agency" points to the fact that a person can only do anything thanks to the collaboration of others. Consequently, the *capacity* to secure collaborators is a crucial element of "agency," still conceived of as a personal attribute, and in general this will mean making a commitment to an already existing project. Interventions could therefore be aimed at fostering this capacity for collaboration.

What each of these studies overlooked, however, is this: how did the activity in which the individual who is the focus of the research is participating, with its norms of action and norms of decision making, originate? Where did the *vehicle* which the subject uses to exercise their "agency" come from? In *Origins of Collective Decision Making* (Blunden, 2014), I took as the germ cell for the construction of the entire domain of political life: *a group of people in the same room, deciding what to do together*. (See below for a detailed consideration of the various paradigms of decision making.) Research revealed several distinct ethical modes of collective decision making which have been inherited from the past and determine the ground on which decisions are made today. The absence of any consideration of culturally and historically real modes of collective decision making suggests that Stetsenko's and Gutiérrez's proposals are inadequate as transcultural units.

1.1.6   Horton on Freedom

Over the course of his work at the Highlander Folk School, Tennessee, Horton trained thousands of the most oppressed people in the South of the USA in the skills needed for their self-emancipation. Beginning in 1932, he trained the unskilled workers who would go on to form the CIO (Congress of Industrial Organizations) in Robert's Rules of Order. In the 1940s, he trained subsistence farmers in how to form cooperatives. In the 1950s, he trained African Americans in consensus decision making and launched the literacy program which made it possible for Blacks to register to vote. That is, in each case Horton taught the skill which formed the germ cell of self-emancipation in the relevant social context. Each skill taken separately lacks universal, transcultural, and transhistorical validity, but Horton did determine culturally-specific units for a concrete concept of collective agency.

1.1.7   Discussion

The individual actor must find at least *some* collaborators if an idea is to be objectified and social change is to be achieved, and in that sense one has to agree with Edwards that "agency" is "relational." But I do not believe that the problem of reframing or otherwise resolving the object of an activity can in general be fully solved using such transcultural models. Analysis of collaborative agency has to begin with the relevant culturally determined mode of decision making.

Whenever people live and act together, we have an instance of collective decision making, whether this is explicit or not. The collectively-binding decision is the unit of analysis of political life taken in the most general sense. I can now see that it is the making of a *Yes/No* decision which is the micro-unit of deliberation in most but not all projects. The relevant macro-unit is the process of deliberation which determines and revises the object-concept of a project. We are dealing with mediated self-determination. So the Yes/No decision is not to be taken simply as convincing someone else, but the achievement of a joint commitment, whether or not the subject got their own way or was persuaded otherwise. In Vygotsky's (1931a) study cited above, a subject achieved self-control by using a device (a die) suggested to them by a more experienced person, namely, the researcher.

In each culturally inherited mode of decision making there is an elaborate *procedure* and system for making decisions, in particular, Yes/No decisions. When any concrete decision is made, whether by Majority or Consensus, then it will require a *series* of Yes/No decisions. In that sense, a Yes/No decision is a micro-unit of collective decision making. If we are to seek units for the elaborate procedures governing the deliberation entailed in making each Yes/No decision, then it would be Bakhtin's concept of "utterance" (a single turn in discourse). Sen's concept of "critical voice" is also a candidate for such a unit, but it would require further specification of "critical discourse" before it could function as a unit in Activity Theory.

If an individual act of reframing is to bring about the transformation of an institution, that transformation must be mediated by a group of people who objectify the original act of reframing and transform it into a collective action. Once the issue is reframed, it still has to be resolved, albeit in a frame which is more propitious. Nevertheless, these transgressive or reframing actions not only reframe the problem for others, but for the subject themself, and this act of "turning the will upon itself" (Hegel, 1821) is crucial to the development of genuinely free will, a.k.a., "agency." The problem of agency departs the domain of psychology once (1) the individual has reframed their personal problems as residing in a situation which they have the capacity to change, as suggested by Stetsenko, and (2) the individual is capable and in a position to work collaboratively with others to change the situation, as suggested by Edwards.

Finally, agency can be fulfilled only in and through the achievement of citizenship in a democratic socialist state living sustainably on its land. For that, the key lies not in any single project, but in the relations between one activity and another, specifically in how one activity supports another activity in realising itself. These relations will be dealt with in later sections of this work.

The word "agency" arose in postwar discussions about agency versus structure, and reached a peak of interest in about 1998. Stepping back for a moment, it should be remembered that in the 1930s, Vygotsky placed the development of the *will* and *volition* at the centre of his theory of child development. Will and volition are terms commonly used for agency within the psychological domain. Each of the phases of crisis which mark the transition from one social situation of development to another is characterised by the child effecting a qualitative change in their relation to their situation. These critical phases are marked by a development of the will, during which the child may become "difficult." All these features of the transitional phases of child development are echoed by these theorists' conceptions of "agency": a change in subject's relation to the environment initiated by the subject rather than by adaptation to the environment, the need for the solidarity of others, and the challenging and transgressive stance of the subject.

Vygotsky used the appropriation of some cultural word, sign or tool as the unit of analysis for the process whereby a person appropriates the social practices of the community in which they find themselves and establishes a degree of active participation normal for a member of that community. So Vygotsky's original research traced the development of agency up to that point. Leontyev's theory of the development of the personality outlined earlier completes the process of actively embracing and furthering the motives and goals of a community. It had to be left to later generations of activity theorists to follow the story up to the formation of these goals and the social situations themselves. Over and above the units considered above, the relation between two projects or activities is the unit which is required for a concrete concept of entire social formations. This concept lies entirely outside the domain of psychology.

Beyond these considerations, writers such as Nancy Fraser (2003) and Pierre Bourdieu (1984) have demonstrated that participation in social affairs is determined on *at least* two different axes. On the one side are socio-cultural hierarchies which are the usual focus of psychologists: how do you make your voice heard in institutions which marginalise you? On the other side is political economy in which the right to participate is directly proportional to one's personal wealth. The major part of "agency" is measured in dollars, and no theory of agency which fails to address either the modification or actual overthrow of political economy can be taken seriously outside of the laboratory.

If I could be so bold as to interpret "agency" as *freedom*, then activity theorists who are looking for a germ cell in the actions of single person or group are fooling themselves. A number of qualitatively different social transformations are required for any one of us to be free. My emancipation depends on much more than what *I* do. Self-determination is mediated. If others continue destroying the conditions for human life, if others support the rising to power of authoritarian dictators, if others pursue get rich quick projects at the expense of the public good, then there is no emancipation for me. *In order to be free I must sacrifice my freedom by making binding commitments with others* to projects whose object is human emancipation. With my actions I can promote general human emancipation. Together with others, I must practice the duty of solidarity. Solidarity breeds solidarity, and in time emancipation may be achieved. But if I seek to attain *my* freedom, my way, without regard to general human emancipation, I am delusional.

2   The Germ Cell of a New Practice

As outlined above, the concept of "germ cell" can be used to (i) reveal the logical structure of a theory or social formation by uncovering its germ cell; (ii)
teach a theory to a novice by building it up from germ cells; (iii) orient a practical intervention by focusing on a practice which is the germ cell of a problem
and its solution; (iv) introduce a new practice in the form of a germ cell in the
expectation that it will proliferate and bring about change.

The following eight sections illustrate how Activity Theorists have used the
idea of "germ cell" to either analyse a practice or transform it.

2.1   Marx's Use of the Idea of a Germ Cell or Unit in *Capital*

In *Capital*, Marx appropriated the method worked out by Hegel in his
Encyclopaedia. By focusing on this one topic, with the benefit of a further
40 years of social and economic development, and by giving his method an
explicitly human rather than *logical* character, Marx was able to do a much better job of the analysis of modernity than Hegel. I can make this claim because
Hegel also analysed the value relation. Hegel determined that a commodity
only realised value in exchange, and that a commodity could have value only if
it was a product of human labour, but he held that the magnitude of value was
proportional to its usefulness. He did not see the contradiction between a usefulness measure and a labour-time measure which inevitably followed from
his claim that exchange-value attached only to products of human labour.

Capital was therefore a paradigm for a new type of science, and Vygotsky
(1927) declared that "Psychology is in need of its own *Das Kapital* – its own
concepts of class, base, value etc. – in which it might express, describe and
study its object."

The writing of *Capital* was an intervention in two senses: (1) it provided
socialists with a scientific means of understanding the crisis of capitalism, and
(2) it educated a new leadership in the workers' movement, including the trade
unions, in a scientific understanding of the capitalist economy. Only with such
a leadership could the workers' movement grow and strengthen itself and
eventually prove capable of organising their own labour independently of
the bourgeoisie and potentially transform the entire nation in the direction
of Socialism. Much of Activity Theory has the same character, so before looking at how the concept of "germ cell" can be applied in *interventions* aimed at
bringing about social transformation, I will first examine *Capital* as a paradigm
of science in which the concept of "germ cell" is inseparable from the concept
of "unit of analysis," each term indicating a distinct sense of one and the same
concept.

In the Preface (1867) Marx says that "in bourgeois society, the commodity-form of the product of labour – or value-form of the commodity – is the economic cell-form." And the opening words of *Capital* are: "The wealth of those societies in which the capitalist mode of production prevails, presents itself as 'an immense accumulation of commodities'."

So we see that at the very beginning, Marx has cast the commodity as both a *germ cell* and a *unit of analysis* of bourgeois society. In 1881, further emphasising the "germ cell" idea, Marx further explained: "I did not start out from the "concept of value." What I start out from is the simplest social form in which the product of labour is presented in contemporary society, and this is 'the commodity'" (Marx, 1881). Nowadays, activity theorists prefer to say that this "simplest social form" is the *exchange* of commodities, a special case of an artefact mediated action. But you can't *accumulate* acts of exchange, only products.

In order to understand the dynamics of capitalist society, Marx could not begin head-on with a critical analysis of capital, generally taken to be sufficient value to purchase means of production. He had to clarify the meaning of *value* and the conditions under which capital could become the dominant activity in society, before moving to analysis of the capital form of value.

Hegel had started his critique of the modern state by beginning with possession, the simplest form, or germ cell, of *property*. So in setting about his critique of capital Marx followed the form of Hegel's critique, but started out from a unit which is "the simplest social form" of *value*. This was the commodity relation, and he found within the commodity relation a series of contradictions which could be analysed and developed and began to reveal the internal dynamics and contradictory structure of capitalist economic life.

Capital begins with the "commodity," but the words "purchase" and "sale" do not appear in *Capital* for 124 pages, just before "capital" is introduced. Exchange of commodities as such almost *never happens* in those societies falling under the accumulation of capital; one sees only purchase and sale. That is, exchange of commodities is invariably mediated by money as a "medium of exchange," and a precondition for the accumulation of capital.

The commodity is therefore a germ cell of value which is *logically prior* to value in its later more developed forms – money, capital, profit, credit, shares, etc. which grow out of the germ cell in just the way an organism *grows out of its germ cell* if the germ cell or seed is planted in a propitious environment. That propitious environment is best provided by a situation in which there are workers whose own means of production are the property of another class. The germ cell is also the simplest *social form* of value, in that the properties which make an object a commodity are nothing to do with any of its physical and chemical properties but are entirely social in content and can only be grasped as such. Further, the nature of a commodity can be grasped *viscerally*, without reliance upon any theory, scientific or otherwise, beyond the experience of living in a society in which commodity production predominates. Archetypically taking the form of a material object, the essential nature of a commodity is that it is an artefact: a product and means of *human labour*. (Services can be commodities as well, but in Marx's day, services were almost exclusively personal services subsumed in private consumption, not the production of surplus value.) Thus the commodity provides a *starting point* from which the entirety of bourgeois society can be unfolded and reconstructed in theory. At the same time, the totality of life in capitalist societies can be analysed as nothing more than an immense aggregate of these units, commodity exchanges.

So it is that the commodity is both the unit of analysis *and* germ cell of bourgeois society.

In Chapter 2, Marx introduces the money-form of commodity, and a new unit of analysis: purchase-and-sale, followed by Chapter 3 exploring the different forms of money.

Chapter 4 begins Part II of *Capital*. Here Marx shows that the commodity relation C-M-C,* selling in order to buy, can give rise to M-C-M' – a capitalist firm, buying in order to sell at a profit. This is the unit of analysis and germ cell of a *developed capitalist society*. Chapter 7 begins Part III by introducing *unpaid labour time* as the simplest social form of surplus value. *Capital* continues by generating units for successively higher and more developed formations of capital. *Capital* proceeds in this way, successively introducing new units on the basis of earlier units, step by step reconstructing the features of modern bourgeois society. Hegel had developed all the books of the *Encyclopaedia of the Philosophical Sciences* in just this way.

The writing of *Capital* was a practical intervention in the workers' movement of the time because it debunked theories like the Wages Fund theory which claimed that what workers gained through higher wages they would lose in working hours because there was a fixed "wages fund." He showed how piecework was being used to intensify labour and many other aspects of exploitative capitalist practices. He showed how, to the contrary, workers could increase their wages or reduce their hours within very elastic limits by strike action without a loss of wages. He also pointed to the immanent historical tendency towards crisis in the capitalist economy, giving strength to the growing socialist movement. It was no manual of socialism, but it *was* a manual for

---

*   Commodity-Money-Commodity, and Money-Commodity-Money.

fighting against capitalist exploitation, and it had no reliance on eternal laws of "human nature"; it presented capital as a transitory social-historical formation, and the whole edifice was built on a specific kind of artefact-mediated action and social forms of activity arising on the basis of this specific kind of artefact-mediated action: commodity production.

2.1.1   The Introduction of Trade into a Traditional Society

The British Empire was built not so much by the military conquest of armies, or the spiritual conquest of missionaries, but essentially by trade. Trade was of course backed up by force and ideology. The East India Company, initially a private trading venture, transformed itself into the government of India and only later, when the local people realised that the fabric of their entire way of life had been destroyed and famine stalked the land and they began to revolt, was the British Army sent in to secure the hold of Empire.

The discovery of gold (and other minerals) has been enough to wipe out entire indigenous communities in New Guinea, lay waste to the Amazon and conquer North America. Once upon a time, trade was something that took place on the boundaries between indigenous communities. In Anglo-Saxon England merchants were non-citizens without any rights who lived a perilous existence travelling between the British Isles and Europe, but it was their markets and later towns and ports which eventually destroyed traditional life in the British Isles, more surely than the Viking or Norman conquests. This is the sense in which the commodity relation acted as a *germ cell* in practice. Commodity exchange functions as a norm of practice and can spread like a virus when conditions are right, and the result is bourgeois society.

Understanding the transformative power of the commodity relation is not limited to past history. Neoliberal governments have successfully wielded the power of commodification to break down community norms and institutions and replace them with market relations, especially since the 1980s: privatisation, outsourcing, one-line budgets, franchising, corporatisation, competition, monetisation, consulting, off-shoring, restructuring, change management, downsizing and so on. These are all moments of the transformation of modern (i.e., pre-1975) capitalism into the postmodern, neoliberal capitalism of today: all based on the conviction that when a practice is converted into a commodity it can spread like a virus.

This draws attention to the dual nature of the germ cell concept: in analysing an existing phenomenon, the researcher aims to *discover* the germ cell of the phenomenon. On the other hand, by introducing a new practice into a situation in the form of a germ cell, the researcher is *inventing* the germ cell in the hope that it will grow.

2.2   *Vygotsky Made Word Meaning a Unit of Analysis*

In *Thinking and Speech*, Vygotsky (1934) made word meaning a unit of analysis for a study of the intellect, and both aspects of the concept – unit and germ cell – were utilised.

Vygotsky's underlying conception was that the intellect is thinking in signs (as opposed to practical intellect, which is thinking with tools). The archetypal sign in this context is the spoken word (the archetypal tool is the human hand). However, Vygotsky did not claim that the intellect was simply silent speech, a claim easily demonstrated to be implausible. Nonetheless, the problem of understanding the nature of the intellect could be posed in terms of the relationship between thinking and speech. The key to solving this problem was to trace the *development* of the intellect from its origin in the merging of speaking and thinking in early childhood.

The unit of the intellect is a concept (i.e., the intellect is an aggregate of concepts), but Vygotsky did not begin right away with an analysis of concepts, but rather he began with *word meaning*. This paralleled the way Marx began his book on capital (whose units are capitalist firms) with analysis of the *commodity*, and anticipated the way that Leontyev built his theory of activities on the molecular unit, *artefact mediated actions* with the molar unit being *activities*. Just as capital is an accumulation of commodities which controls commodity production, and an activity is an aggregate of actions which controls all the component actions, a concept is an aggregate of meanings which generates, and gives coherence and stability to those meanings.

Thinking and Speech begins with a short but definitive chapter arguing that *word meaning* is the unit of analysis for the study of the intellect. This short chapter is the authoritative text on the term as it is used in Activity Theory. However, Vygotsky did not invent the idea, which has a long genesis in Herder, Goethe, Hegel and Marx. I have written elsewhere (Blunden, 2021) on this topic and will not repeat myself here other than to say that lack of clarity in the meaning of "unit of analysis" can only be resolved by tracing the origin and history of the concept. It cannot be conceptualised by listing the features demanded of a germ cell.

Word meaning can be described as a type of mediated action. That is, it does not refer to an entry in the dictionary, but rather to a *speech action*, doing something with a spoken word. This is like Marx's use of the commodity rather than the act of exchange as the germ of value. A speech action does not encompass an entire concept; it simply evokes the concept in one specific context – one sense of the concept. A concept is the aggregate of all the word meanings which evoke it.

However, Vygotsky is at pains to distinguish word-mediated action from tool-mediated action which is the unit of practical intelligence, and from sign-mediated action, such as reading and writing, which can generally only be acquired by instruction. Speech arose in close connection with the evolution of labour (i.e., tool-mediated action) in the very origins of Homo sapiens, and arises spontaneously in child development. Sign mediated action such as literacy, by contrast, arose on the back of technical development (i.e., the development and use of tools) and can be acquired by children only later on.

So these three kinds of mediated action arise in the course of human development but each under quite different conditions. This is why Vygotsky was critical of the idea of lumping them all together as "artefact-mediated action" (Blunden, 2021c).

Word meaning is a unity of speech and thinking, that is, of sounding and meaning. A sound without a meaning is not a word and nor is a meaning without sound a word; a word is essentially both. Word meaning is equally a unity of generalisation and social interaction, and of thinking and communication, and the contradictions between these different functions of words manifest themselves in development. "Word" is to be understood in the sense which is immanent in this concept, that is, it is the smallest collection of sounds which has semantic value in the given context. From a formal point of view that could be a single word or a phrase or maybe even a gesture. One and the same word has different meanings and different words can have the same meaning, according to context, but the unit is word meaning.

Vygotsky's subject matter was not discourse, it was the intellect, whose units are concepts. Nonetheless, the intellect arises out of the use of spoken words in communication and collaboration. In line with his consistently developmental approach to all psychological problems, Vygotsky points out that

> just as we can identify a "pre-speech" stage in the development of the child's thinking, we can identify a "pre-intellectual stage" in the development of his speech. Up to a certain point, speech and thinking develop along different lines and independently of one another. At a certain point, the two lines cross: thinking becomes verbal and speech intellectual.
>
> 1934, p. 112

This insight is essential to making sense of the concept of "germ cell" in his analysis. In the early phases of development a child does not have what can properly be called "intellect," but nonetheless they do think. But this thinking lacks the culturally acquired content and direction provided by word meanings. And even as concepts develop as the child begins to use speech, these are not yet concepts properly so called, not "true concepts." The developing child will not acquire truly conceptual thinking until their teens under normal conditions of development. As the child's use of speech develops, word meaning also develops.

Word use develops in the course of child development from *communication* – demanding and obeying commands – to being a means of *self-control*, commanding her/himself (egocentric speech) to silent speech which becomes successively predicative (i.e., sentences lacking a subject) until disappearing into the dark and inaccessible world of *thought* which is non-sequential. Silent speech fades away in the course of developing into thinking, while outwardly speech changes its character and becomes capable of expressing self-conscious thought. Silent speech and even vocal egocentric speech can resurface when a person is having difficulty with a problem (Daneshfar et al., 2022).

In Chapter 5, Vygotsky uses a series of experiments in which children are trying to sort blocks into groups which are in some sense the same. The blocks have marks on them as well as being of various colours, shapes and sizes. During the experiment the researchers gradually draw the children's attention to these signs and observe the different ways children group the blocks as they become more and more able to emulate the groupings reflected in the signs. That is, they observe how pre-intellectual thought forms, grouping things according to contingent attributes, gradually morph into a form of socialised thinking in which things are grouped in accordance with signs acquired from the wider, cultural world: pseudoconcepts.

The action of grouping objects is a form of action which is not yet true concept-use but can be seen as a stage in the development towards concept formation. Vygotsky's (1934) experiments were able to show how combinations of word meanings developed from primitive "potential concepts" reflected in practical intelligence but lacking in conscious awareness, through to more or less random "syncretic concepts" to "chain concepts" to "associative complexes" to "collections" and "diffuse complexes" to pseudoconcepts – which more or less adequately replicate the adult usage of a word but without understanding the sense in which things are united, and "pre-concepts" which form in the context of play, before finally attaining "true concepts" which can be acquired through instruction and then mature into "actual concepts" as theoretical knowledge is grounded in interaction with immediate experience in the wide world of work and public life.

Experiments like the blocks experiment can take the researcher only so far because true concepts are not just a matter of collecting together things of like kind or named with the same word. As true concepts begin to form, the researcher can continue to trace their development by observing the young person's use of words which implicitly indicate *logical* relations, words such as "because" and "despite." The child's ability to distinguish between the temporal relation and the causal relation indicated in these words tracks the child's abil-ity to form true concepts. The child's ability to use concepts which originate in instruction, outside the realm of everyday experience ("scientific concepts," such as the concepts of Marxist theory which are remote from everyday expe-rience) indicates a further development in their intellect. The maturing of the ability to form and use real concepts is exhibited when concepts which orig-inate in instruction are brought to bear on matters of immediate experience. Thus, even though the intellect eventually transcends word use and even inter-nal speech, it is possible to trace the development of the intellect through the development of word meaning.

Thinking does not entail putting one word meaning after another as in speech. It cannot be so, otherwise it would take you as long to grasp when someone is angry as to explain how you know. Vygotsky compares the transi-tion from the realm of thought to speech to "a hovering cloud which gushes a shower of words." Speaking is a qualitatively different activity from conceptual thinking, but conceptual thinking arises from speaking and first appears as intelligent speech. Similarly, writing appears superficially to be just like speak-ing, but this is not so. Speech arises and continues only in the presence of and in connection with the other person present before you (if not actually, then virtually), and arises spontaneously from the dialogic situation. Writing on the other hand means formulating sentences in the absence of a speech partner, autonomously and with conscious awareness. But reading and writing arise *out of* the practice of speaking, in the context of instruction.

This is the sense in which word meaning is a "germ cell."

Word meaning is a "unit of analysis" in the sense that the intellect can be analysed as nothing other than a mass of word meanings which are structured together as concepts. That is, taken as units of the intellect, concepts are aggre-gates of word meanings.

Vygotsky said that word meaning is constituted by *three different contradic-tions* as a unity of sound and meaning, generalisation and social interaction, and of thinking and communication. This is a unique claim to make for a germ cell. Implicit in the coincidence of these three contradictions are some pro-found insights into the human condition.

2.2.1   Concepts and Activities

Concepts do not just exist in your head. Before you acquired a concept, it existed implicitly in the activity of people around you in some cultural forma-tion, actualising the norms of that community. So "Newton's concept of force" does not refer to something inside the head of Isaac Newton; it refers meanings implicit in the speech and sign-mediated actions of those people using the theory of Newtonian Physics. Put simply, a concept is a form of action, specifically *an activity*, be that a symbolic or a practical activity. A concept is thus a unit of a culture: the aggregate of all those forms of social activity which have normative validity within the culture. Activities are not merely forms of *behaviour*, in which the consciousness of the actors is irrelevant, but forms of *activity*, that is, aggregates of actions which are done *for a reason*.

An activity is a concept, and a concept is an activity. The only difference between an activity and a concept is the *connotation* on the one hand of an internal mental formation, and on the other of outward physical actions. But actually, each subsumes the other.

A culture is an aggregate of activities, and a mind is an individual instance of that culture, an aggregate of concepts and the "potential concepts" of practical intelligence. (Here "activities" refers to *norms* of activity, rather than actual instances which may be more or less normative, just as the beliefs of individuals may be more or less rational and normative.)

Now there are aggregates of actions, whether actions by many people in tandem or by the same person in succession, which are not rational in the sense of being done with any coherent and stable purpose. But this is only to say that behaviour and thinking do not always take the form of good, coherent, true concepts. So, equally, activity may be quite unselfconscious (such as a crime wave or a stampede) or may be guided by bad concepts (concepts which are internally incoherent, such as fringe religious activity) or simply done for the sheer pleasure of doing them (after all, not every sex act is done for the purpose of producing children but has social consequences nonetheless).

Consequently, Activity Theory needs to be able to encompass activities which are not archetypal collaborations aimed at an explicit purpose.

Bakhtin (1895–1975) was a contemporary of Vygotsky who took the *utterance* as a unit of discourse, whether spoken or written. An utterance is a *turn* in conversation, so to speak, and could be a single word or an entire novel. This different unit of analysis of apparently the same phenomenon, speech, provides a different view of speech activity and provides different insights into the same phenomenon. In general, utterance and the associated "frame" capture how actors *position* themselves in relation to each other in their communicative action. Utterances give no insight into concept formation or the formation of the intellect.

This phenomenon – two different units of the same phenomenon – is important. The unit is a unit *of analysis*, that is, it is singled out for the purpose of analysing some phenomenon, to answer certain questions and address certain problems, of a certain phenomenon. While units of analysis must have a basis in the material world, they are not an objectively given facet of the object itself, but rather of the *relation* of the researcher to the phenomenon.

Likewise, when Foucault reflected on the nature of modern society he saw not bourgeois society characterised by exploitation of wage labour, but a vast apparatus of social control. The germ cell which informed Foucault's analysis was consequently the prison! Beginning from the germ cell of a prison leads you to a certain view of modern society. Beginning from commodity production leads to another view. It is a matter of judgment as to which unit is more explanatory in relation to the problems and phenomena which concern you and which corresponds poorly or well to the real subject matter.

2.3   *Vasily Davydov's Mathematics Curriculum*

Vasily Davydov's (1990) mathematics curriculum gave definite practical shape to the idea of "germ cell." Rather than taking up mathematical ideas in the form in which they are recognisable as mathematics and asking students to make sense of arithmetical expressions and algebraic equations as they appear in books, Davydov's curriculum begins from the practical origins of mathematics as he saw it, in practical activity.

Mathematical practice particularly lends itself to playful puzzle-solving activity which can offer an effective motive to newcomers, but it is the rigour of mathematical thinking and its ability to abstract from immediately given sense perception which need to be acquired by students as they engage in proto-mathematical activity. Davydov engaged students in the activity of identifying the weight, colour and size of objects and later other properties such as specific weight and so on. Initially, these are practical tasks leading to understanding the meaning of concepts such as length and weight, still without any attempt to *measure* them. The question of measurement arises initially through the practice of *comparison*, which begins with placing things side by side or on a pair of scales, etc.: (1) this one is heavy, this one is light; (2) this one is heavier than that one.

But what if the two objects cannot be brought together for direct comparison? How can you compare the height of the door with the length of the table? The first idea is to use a stick to copy the length of the table and then carry it over to the door. But this is very awkward. You don't want to make a new stick for every comparison, so you use a short stick and *count* how many of them for the table and how many for the door. Asking the question: how much bigger? calls for a *standard* measuring stick. And from there we see the need to divide the ruler into smaller units, centimetres maybe. And so on and so on.

Paul Ernest 2021 argues on similar grounds that mathematics begins from counting rather than measuring. We will come to Ernest's work presently. But Davydov sets out from the idea that if mathematics is the science of pure quantity, then measuring things is the simplest mathematical task. Judging whether something is heavy or light, long or short, presupposes no mathematical knowledge; it can be judged and understood viscerally. That is, we can form a *potential concept* of weight without any mathematical theory. We can expect then to be able to unfold the whole of mathematics, step by step through the germ cell method originated by Hegel.

One argument for the claim that measuring things is the archetypal mathematical activity is to claim that it was the first *historically* and further that the history of mathematics can be traced from that first historical moment. (Note that this idea by no means excludes there being multiple origins and multiple histories of mathematics and multiple germ cells.) The claim is then that mathematics originated in the Middle East with the measurement of land, water and grain as part of the system of agriculture based on a shared irrigation system.

In this way, the practical intelligence which children already have (potential concepts) is utilised to resolve problems the solution for which lie in culturally inherited practices out of which numerical calculations arise naturally: comparison, addition, units, multiplication, etc. It is important that children are *led* to *re*discover the culturally inherited practices and not simply invited to invent their own solution, because the child's own idiosyncratic solution is not a pathway to mastering the existing culturally inherited body of mathematical knowledge. This process of *leading* the child to the culturally-developed means of solving problems (usually by setting the problem up in such a way which makes the cultural solution more likely to be discovered) includes recognising that the child will come to the problem with their own conception of it. The child's mind is not a *tabula rasa*. Acquiring the cultural conception is facilitated by making the child's spontaneous conception explicit and helping the child transform this conception into the cultural conception.

The standardised activities of mathematics and the symbolic means of representing them arise naturally and rationally out of the practices of handling material objects which are graspable with practical intelligence. Marx did much the same thing in his genealogy of money from primitive exchange of commodities in Part 3 of Chapter 1 of *Capital*.

Thus, Davydov used the idea of the determination of quantitative properties of material objects – length, weight, colour, and so on – as the *germ cell* of mathematics. The practical activity entailed in grasping this germ cell is broadly accessible as it presupposes no concept or theory of the world.

A mathematical intelligence can be grown from the germ cell of practical activity with material objects.

Educators in the Soviet Union took up Davydov's idea and applied it across a range of disciplines in education and child development. Remarkable among these endeavours is the work of Alexander Meshcheryakov (1974/2009) in the education of deaf-blind children. Meshcheryakov adopted the "germ cell" method of education under conditions where his pupils had no pre-existing access to the culture of the world they had been born into. Many children brought to his school had no human traits whatsoever: they could not feed or clothe themselves, control their bowels or speak. Staff at his school had to make it possible for the children to acquire an entire culture beginning from the most elementary interactions with the world of human culture. One of these was *eating from a spoon*. The young people did not know what a spoon was and took no action to take the food from the spoon with their lips. However, tiny step by tiny step they learnt to take food off the spoon with their lips, and later to hold the spoon themselves and become familiar with its shape, use it to take food and go on to identify a chair, and a table, etc, etc., and eat at the table at scheduled meal times with the classmates. Many of his students went on to earn PhDs and became active members of the society, having built up all the concepts of being a citizen in a modern society from the earliest germ cells of civilised life like eating from a spoon, sleeping in a bed or using a toilet.

The choice of germ cell requires insight into the activity in question, and not everyone who approaches a topic determines the germ cell in the same way. Ernest is a Professor of the Philosophy of Mathematics and Mathematics Education at Exeter University in the UK. Ernest reconstructed mathematics beginning from the practice of *counting*. Others, such as Anna Sfard at the Department of Mathematics Education at Haifa University in Israel, use a similar approach. The ability to isolate *one* object from its background and to mentally connect that one to *many* others is a basic cognitive ability which human beings seem to acquire with minimal instruction without any pre-existing cultural accomplishment beyond the common acquisitions of childhood. This basic faculty can therefore can be safely taken as a pre-requisite for mathematical activity, beginning with counting. Ernest points to five principles which need to be learnt in order to count things: (i) you must have a stable series of counting numbers which are always uttered in the same order, (ii) you must assign one and only one number to each object, (iii) the last number uttered is how many objects there are (the cardinal number), (iv) any kind of thing at all can be counted and (v) it doesn't matter what order the things are counted in.

This practice of determining "how many" can be the germ cell for much of mathematics by means of *successive* abstractions. The last number for the whole collection of objects becomes a property of the *whole* set and provides a germ cell for the next step in generalisation. Thus, in each level of mathematics, the germ cell for the next level of abstraction arises from repetitions, patterns, gaps, inversions and contradictions in the preceding level. For example, multiplication is repeated addition, division is inverted multiplication and fractions arise from division which does not produce an integer. This works for series of germ cells all the way up to calculus and group theory.

That counting or measuring are activities which can be acquired by novices as potential concepts without calling upon any other mathematical knowledge can be verified empirically. Both theses can be sustained. Ernest agrees that mathematics had its origins in the irrigated communities in the Middle East along with the invention of writing, but believes that, prior to measuring, the *counting of equal things* (such as the number of bags of wheat or the number of gold bars offered in payment) preceded the measurement of mass quantities of water, grain or land. Which thesis is true is a matter for historians, but Ernest's claim makes sense.

Further, Ernest points out that counting using spoken numbers or by indicating parts of the body are known to precede writing by millennia. Likewise, informal proto-mathematical practices long preceded the discipline of mathematics proper which arose on the basis of written mathematical symbolism and the training of specialist scribes in Mesopotamia and Egypt. Ernest cites Bishop (1988) who argued that counting, locating, measuring (c.f. Davydov), designing, playing, and explaining using proto-mathematical practices preceded the emergence of formal mathematical symbolism. Although counting is deemed by Ernest to be an important germ cell from which mathematics grew, he points out that other proto-mathematical practices, not just numbers and counting, contribute to the formation of a mathematical sensibility. Mathematics also uses proto-geometry as a germ cell from which much of mathematics could be unfolded. This is consistent with the observation by Activity Theorists that potential concepts and a practical intellect precede and provide the foundation for the (verbal) intellect in ontogenesis.

I say mathematics can be reconstructed "dialectically" because the process is not one of using syllogisms to construct successively developed theories. The dialectical reconstruction works because the mathematics at any specific level inevitably leads to a contradiction or undecidable question. For example, if you have learnt about addition and then subtraction, you will come across problems like: 5–7? The student has to "invent" negative numbers to answer this problem. That is, negative numbers arise from a contradiction that necessarily arises from arithmetic which includes subtraction, the reverse of addition. Each new type of mathematics arises by *inventing* a solution of problems which arise in another type of mathematics, that is, outside of its own circle. The concept of a negative number arises in mathematics which does not yet have negative numbers. This is the opposite of the formal method of proof in which axioms are introduced at the start without proof or derivation but turn out to contain the whole theory in embryo.

Hegel took a broadly similar approach to building up all the concepts of the mathematics of his time beginning with concepts of One and Many.

Any science can be elaborated in successive steps like this, in which the result of one abstraction (e.g. counting leading to cardinal number) becomes the germ cell for the next cycle (e.g. cardinal numbers lead to addition, addition leads to subtraction and multiplication, ...). And once arithmetic is established, it forms the germ cell for algebra: an abstraction from arithmetic which the student has previously acquired as firmly as if it were common sense, and algebra can in turn form a germ cell for the beginnings of "modern mathematics" and still higher levels of abstraction. The same process can be applied in any of the sciences and different kinds of abstraction are possible at each stage. The organisation of the different topics into a *coherent series of topics* building one upon the other is the essence of this kind of curriculum.

This is the form which an activity takes in the process of its maturation or concretisation: a succession of phases in each of which a core concept develops from its most abstract (undeveloped) germ cell to a mature, concrete form (a concrete abstraction), which in turn becomes the germ cell for a new phase of development. Each generation builds on the work of the previous generation.

Whether you take Davydov's or Ernest's or Hegel's approach, it can be seen that teaching beginning with the germ cell echoes the historical development of mathematics from the times of the ancients up to the present. But it is not a *copy* of that history. The real history was subject to a multiplicity of contingencies most of which in time have passed away. So the germ cell approach to the foundations of mathematics and the teaching of mathematics is a kind of *idealised* historical development which uses contemporary cultural solutions to problems as they arise rather than recapitulating the forgotten byways of historical development.

By contrast, the formal method demonstrated by Bourbaki (1948) attempted to reconstruct the entirety of mathematics on the basis of formal logic, beginning with a set of propositions in symbolic logic These were already mathematical abstractions of the highest imaginable degree, the outcome of centuries of development and utterly incomprehensible to the non-mathematician.

By "abstraction" here I mean formal representations remote from the experience of the non-mathematician, representing non-intuitive properties of mathematical objects, at high levels of abstraction. The visceral actions of comparing the physical properties of objects are by contrast "concrete" in this sense, but are "abstract" in the sense of simply isolating just one property of one object. Mathematical ideas constructed from this beginning reflect *universal properties* of many objects: abstractions which are "concrete" in this specific sense.

The project of Bourbaki's predecessors, Bertrand Russell and Alfred North Whitehead (1913), to construct the whole of mathematics from a small number of axioms using symbolic logic, had failed as it only avoided contradictions by being incomplete. Eventually Turing proved mathematically that it was impossible for any theory to be both complete and consistent (something which Hegel had demonstrated dialectically a century before). The germ cell method by contrast is by its very nature always incomplete, always unfolding and resolving contradictions, and makes no claim to be a finished theory.

In the 1960s, partially under the influence of Bourbaki and Piaget's *Genetic Epistemology* (1950), school children in many parts of the world were subjected to the "New Maths." The New Maths entailed teaching children mathematics by recapitulating a formal derivation of the concepts of arithmetic, algebra and geometry from *logically primitive* beginnings – types of abstraction (such as topology and binary arithmetic) which lay entirely outside the experience, not only of the students, but of their parents and very often of the teachers – very high levels of abstraction. The New Maths was eventually abandoned, but not before having denied a generation of people any grasp of mathematics or even simple arithmetic. In 1999, *Time* magazine placed New Maths fourth on a list of the 100 worst ideas of the 20th century which began with prohibition.

One of the outcomes of Davydov's extremely productive use of "germ cell" was that the concept of "germ cell" took on *a life of its own,* now no longer seen as being connected to the concept of "unit of analysis."

A new idea (i.e., a new practice) has a greater or a lesser potential to grow into a more developed form of practice, a greater or lesser potential to proliferate, and a greater or lesser capacity to transform other forms of practice into forms of itself. If your aim is the transformation of an entire social formation, the idea of a germ cell which can grow to a more developed form and even proliferate will appeal, but only if it can penetrate other institutions and replicate itself in different domains of activity.

A "successful" germ cell, when planted in propitious conditions, can grow and proliferate and colonise all other forms of activity. But a germ cell will grow into a whole science only if the learner is engaged with it in the context of enquiry. The commodity only makes sense as an economic germ cell if you live in a society where people engage products.

CHAPTER 5

Intervening with Activity Theory

1 Transforming Activities with a Germ Cell

The idea of "germ cell" has found many valuable implementations, solving specific problems and giving us insight into different aspects of social life. The single most significant and revolutionary aspect of the concept of "germ cell" is that the process of development it represents happens not only in theory but in reality. A social formation, institution, activity or form of practice can be transformed by injecting a suitable germ cell. In the pages which follow we will consider some fairly modest but successful interventions using the germ cell method and go on to discuss the implications of using the idea for transformation of the world system.

1.1 *The Sit-to-Stand Exercise*

The sit-to-stand exercise used in home care for the aged was identified as the central outcome of a study by Engeström et al. (2012) demonstrating all the aspects of the concept of "germ cell." Engeström's team carried out an extensive observation and analysis of the city's home care service. The outcome was that the exercise was highlighted as the most important basic facet of the practice of aged care.

The study introduced the concept of "sustainable mobility" – mobility which an aged person could reliably be expected to maintain without constant coaching and intervention by support staff – and identified the exercise which constituted a germ cell for sustainable mobility: the sit-to-stand exercise.

Researchers found that the achievement of sustainable mobility by fragile aged people depended on the resolution of the contradiction between safety and independence. In order to be independent a person needed to be able to move about their surroundings without the support of other people. However, being fragile, this was an unsafe activity, risking a fall which would set back their mobility irreversibly. But without the ability to freely move around old people rapidly lost muscle tone and became more fragile, more fearful and more dependent on others.

The resolution of this trap lay in an exercise which was both safe and would be carried out without intervention and repeatedly throughout the day in the course of exercising their independence in self-care. The researchers realised that the simplest possible exercise, and the exercise which necessarily preceded and was included in every one of the old person's actions was simply standing up from their chair. This already well-known exercise could therefore be a germ cell in that it could be practised *safely* – the subject stands without using the support of the arm rests, but in the event of unsteadiness, they can safely sit down again, avoiding the danger of a fall. If practised repeatedly by the subject, the patients' sense of fragility will be moderated, and it opens the door to the next step, maybe crossing the floor to open a door, going to the bathroom, or whatever, and thus expands to self-directed exercise around the house, in the course of their daily life, sufficient to maintain independence and sustainable mobility.

Further, sit-to-stand is a *unit of analysis* in the sense that it is the simplest form of and implicit in *all* those everyday exercises by means of which a person manages self-care in the home, each of them resolving the contradiction between safety and independence in a unique situation. Sustainable mobility is nothing but getting out of your chair and going on to do things for yourself. Sit-to-stand is not only the most elementary of routine exercises, but all the others grow from getting out of your chair.

The persistence of the new concept of sustainable mobility and its germ cell, the sit-to-stand exercise, depended on writing it into the city's Home Care Strategy document and thus the material used in training staff. Otherwise, the concept would most likely be lost. See also Engeström (2020) for a review of a range of applications and the general approach of his DWR work with germ cells.

Sit-to-stand is a germ cell of the concept of sustainable mobility in two senses. On one hand, the mobility of a given subject grows out of their practice of sit-to-stand, and the subjects are instructed so that they understand this crucial role of sit-to-stand and will practice it sufficiently to maintain their mobility. On the other hand, it forms the germ cell of the concept of sustainable mobility which allows anyone, a nurse or administrator or family member, to grasp the concept of sustainable mobility securely, immediately and concretely, rather than as a formal goal without substance. This twin nature of the germ-cell/unit reflects the fact that any concept is a form of action, and is grasped as such through a person's capacity for action.

This insight can be taken so far as to say that *any concept which cannot be grasped through some germ cell is merely a formal concept*, not a concrete concept capable of encapsulating knowledge of the world or of motivating activity.

At a certain point in analysis, however, "unit" is inapplicable and a number of qualitatively different and complementary parts need to be identified. For example, a sustainable mobility lifestyle includes numerous physical actions which all grow out the simplest exercise, the sit-to-stand. On the other hand, when the sit-to-stand exercise itself is analysed distinct and complementary elements are entailed: the use of the leg muscles and joints which are crucial to mobility and the proximity of the chair which offers a safe-fail outcome if the subject fails. But all the exercises an old person does in the course of self-care are exercises just like sit-to-stand.

1.2 *Junior Doctors Using Purple Pen for Prescribing*

Junior doctors using purple pen for prescribing was a simple germ cell idea implemented and evaluated by Hannah Gillespie (Gillespie et al., 2021), herself a junior doctor at the time, but originally devised by Smith et al. (2013) and then Kinston et al. (2019).

The problem was that medical students and junior doctors never have the opportunity to write prescriptions for *real* patients in *real* clinical situations until they are qualified and responsible for writing prescriptions without supervision. The only opportunity for learning is looking over the shoulder of a senior doctor. A disquietingly high level of errors has been found to occur in prescriptions by medical staff in hospitals. Gillespie proposed that junior doctors be given a purple pen and authorised to write prescriptions on patients' records in that purple pen. Nurses knew that this prescription could not be administered until countersigned by a fully qualified doctor. The nurses supported this practice because it relieved them of chasing after doctors for prescriptions, a tiresome task which the junior doctor was only too willing to do instead. And senior doctors supported the practice as it gave them an extra pair of eyes overseeing emergent patient needs.

The practice of pre-prescribing with a purple pen provides an opportunity for "safe fail" practice by junior doctors, rather than the alternative policy of allowing them only *fail-safe* activities which provide no chance for the junior doctor to act a little beyond their existing ability, confident that if they get it wrong, they would receive appropriate advice from a senior doctor and no one will suffer as a result: a zone of proximal development. In a sense, the purple pen allowed the junior doctors to "play" at prescribing, but in such a way that this play could grow over into serious professional prescribing. This modest variation in clinical practice is a germ cell in that it inserted into clinical practice the concept of "safe fail" activities for students and junior doctors. Gillespie wrote:

> in one hospital trust, they have given the students purple scrubs for the duration of the module. This is different to the usual 'medical student' scrubs (which are navy, with the medical school logo). They are a different colour, but also have the hospital name on them (rather than the

university). There have also been small scale spin offs trying to improve students' compliance with the procedural detail, like printing reminder cards etc. These are, on the surface, less exciting, but do show an overall willingness for clinicians to adopt the idea as part of their practice and something they can contribute to!

Private communication, 2022

This innovation demonstrates the capacity of a germ cell practice to *proliferate* and *diversify* and there is every reason to believe it will *persist*.

1.3   *Collaborative Learning Spaces*

Collaborative Learning Spaces (CLS) were first created at the University of Melbourne by this author (See Blunden & Arnold, 2014) in 1999 in collaboration with members of teaching staff and in response to widespread demand by the teachers. I only came into contact with Activity Theory in the course of this project thanks to collaboration with teaching staff. At the time I was responsible for maintenance of the existing lecture theatres which contained a considerable amount of electronic material, installed in line with the conception of didactic teaching centred on lectures to large classes enhanced by visual media. Academic staff complained to me that these spaces were not suitable for the *collaborative learning* which they wanted to do. On the basis of a broadly expressed view among teaching staff I was able to secure funds from the Administration to build one "Collaborative Learning Space" without at the time any conception of what form such a room would take. I selected one academic who was invited to sketch out a utopian model of the kind of teaching space he needed without regard for resources or the opinion of others. He was invited to 'play' with designing a concept, and as a result went beyond the boundaries which he would have spontaneously set himself. He duly provided a sketch on paper showing the flow of information within, into, out of and around a space required for collaborative learning. I then approached engineers who translated this sketch into furniture and electronic equipment designs, which were then revised in discussion with the teacher.

The germ cell thus rapidly evolved from a word to a sketch to a design and finally to an installation which was made available from the Timetable Office for collaborative learning. I oversaw a series of 24 such spaces built before retiring in 2002, each modifying the original design in some way, mostly to meet the specific demands of different disciplines. I revisited the University twelve years later and observed: (i) altogether 65 such spaces had been built, but demand still outstripped supply, (ii) innovations had subsequently been made in the design which improved functionality in several ways, but the overall concept had remained stable (e.g. students *stood* at tables, rather than sitting on swivel chairs. This enhanced the ability of students to move around and collaborate with each other), (iii) while the University's Building Design Standards retain the term, the name "Collaborative Learning Space" has been joined by a *variety* of terms in the University's vocabulary, but the *concept* continued to be used by the Timetable Office in allocating spaces. Further, 27 of Australia's 39 universities had built Collaborative Learning Spaces, although again different words were used to brand each university's innovation.

I later found that independently in the mid-1990s the North Carolina State University had created similar spaces and by 2012 MIT, the University of Iowa and University of Dayton had followed suit.

The concept of "Collaborative Learning Space" grew from a lobbying practice without any image of what was being demanded, to one specialised classroom in the space of a few months and developed slowly and moderately in the years that followed. The concept proved very persistent and proliferated, though investigations showed that in some cases the proliferation had entailed misconceptions. For example, some rooms used electronic whiteboards such as those used in boardrooms. This facilitated sharing students' work on their own computer, and the teacher's work, with the whole class, and real time editing of documents by the whole class. However, some schools and universities, motivated by considerations of prestige, saw only the smart technology and copied the electronic whiteboard without knowing how to use it for collaboration, and this led to teaching which was decisively *less* collaborative than when the teacher used an ordinary whiteboard. Collaborative learning obviously pre-existed CLSs, but its use in universities, as opposed to schools, was limited. The widely available new spaces mediated the growth and development of the practice and produced some novel models of teaching.

Those teachers who had complained of the unsuitability of the existing spaces for collaborative learning had brought into existence a novel concept for the University's administrators: a CLS, and guidelines were written into the University's construction standards. As a result, the practices of collaborative learning that had existed in the University despite lacking suitable spaces blossomed into an array of sophisticated practices mediated by this novel artefact, the CLS, a germ cell of the concept of collaborative learning in the university context. Two new practices emerged from the creation of this germ cell, one in the University's Administration (centralised allocation and maintenance of teaching rooms), and the other among the University's teaching staff (a range of new modes of collaborative learning).

The germ cell is always an *elementary activity*, and therefore *an artefact-mediated action*. Consequently, the kind of *mediating artefact* in which the elementary action is embodied is of crucial importance to its persistence and proliferation. The mediating artefact may function as a sign as well as a tool for the actions it enables.

1.4   The "Root Model" for Teaching Topics in School

The "root model" for the teaching of science topics in school was developed by Hedegaard (2020) in the 1980s, but failed to take root in the Danish education system.

Hedegaard developed for each school subject what she called a "root model." This idea arose directly from Engeström's (1987) "root model" and took the form of a graphic with three text-clouds connected by arrows. Hedegaard's idea was that children should draw a graphic representing their own conception of a subject area, and then the teacher should lead them to move from their personal "root model" to the scientific "root model."

The failure of Hedegaard's project in applying the "root model" approach to devising a germ cell flowed directly from emulating what was *mistaken* rather than from what was insightful in Engeström's seminal book. Hedegaard devised what she took to be a "root model" of various sciences, elements of a school curriculum, in consultation with academic experts in the respective sciences. Concepts explored included evolution of species, human evolution and social history. Each "root model" took the form of a number of concepts each expressed in a definitional form of words, usually in a "speech bubble" connected by arcs to other speech bubbles. These root models were the refined outcome of the development of the given science and took considerable research to devise. These were provided to teachers. The pupils were then invited to construct "their own" root model of the science that they had not yet learnt, usually in the form of a drawing, with or without speech bubbles and arrows. The task of the teacher then is to bring the pupils' own "root model" into line with the historically developed scientific root model. Even the teachers struggled to understand this idea and found the challenge of developing lessons based on it forbidding. Unsurprisingly, the Danish Education Department never adopted Hedegaard's program.

This approach is to be applauded inasmuch as it recognised that children do not come to the study of a science with a *tabula rasa*, but on the contrary have a misconception based on their immediate experience (an insight for which Piaget is largely responsible), and the approach engaged students in *guided exploration*, rather than direction.

The confusion between "germ cell" and "root model" is here shown in sharp relief. However, I hasten to add that this work is just one element of

Hedegaard's work, and she has many achievements in the study of education and child development to her credit aside from this unsuccessful effort to emulate Engeström's work by taking it seriously. Where her "double move" teaching methodology is applied with a germ cell rather than a "root model," then it is an effective approach, because a germ cell can be grasped on the basis of everyday knowledge *prior to* learning the whole theory.

Another instance of an educational program which based itself on the germ cell idea was the Mechanics in Action program devised by Julian Williams and John Cripps Clark at Deakin University in the 1990s (Williams, 2016). The authors developed a series of mechanics experiments for the classroom from which students not only learnt the basic principles of mechanics, but acquired scientific curiosity and an understanding of the practices of experiment, measurement and generalisation used to solve science problems, many of them problems which arose in everyday life. The potential concepts acquired in these simple experiments, together with elementary measurements, provided students with the basic concepts of mechanics which set them on the road to understanding the entire science.

A great virtue of this curriculum was that it recognised that science concepts grow out of science-like activity, exploring phenomena, solving puzzles which arise from observation by careful measurement and observation. A germ cell will only develop into a scientific concept if it is sewn in science-like activity.

The authors prepared course material, engaged manufactures to produce and supply kits to schools, developed lesson plans aligned with school curricula and trained teachers in using the program, all of which absorbed about 20 years of their lives. But nothing of this remains; suppliers have gone out of business, curricula have changed and the teachers have forgotten all about the program. But the program succeeded in breaking the notorious boredom of mathematics and generated interest and even excitement among the students while introducing them to the basics of a science they would never have otherwise had an interest in. But it did not survive.

This experience is reminiscent of Cole's experience (see below), but in that instance Cole chose to set up an after-school program in the community rather than the evidently hopeless task of getting US schools to adopt an effective program which did not turn otherwise normal and intelligent kids into "learning disabled" youth. Williams (2016) reflected that industry asked schools to produce "labour to be able to think critically to a degree, but perhaps not too critically." I prefer to think that the requirements of capital exert their influence over education systems somewhat more indirectly, but the result is much the same. Aydin Bal (see below) found that racism was so embedded in the communities whose schools he dealt with that he spent a year mobilising the local indigenous community behind him before attempting to change the school. Despite what many teachers think, to change the children, you first have to change the adults, not the other way around.

CHAPTER 6

Political Life

One of the contradictions that confront the activity theorist when they try to use Activity Theory for making change in the political life of a country is that the institutions, and in particular the political decision making institutionalised in electoral systems, objectify decidedly undialectical conceptions of the process of deliberation. Further, systems of economic power place political power in the hands of a small class of mostly immature narcissists and social relations are structured by cultural hierarchies entrenching oppressive relationships. It seems that any rational emancipatory movement would have to somehow work around and outside these oppressive structures in order to subvert them.

Nonetheless, this world is not a homogenous structure. It is full of contradictions and as Leonard Cohen said: "There is a crack, a crack in everything / That's how the light gets in." Many other people are also struggling to find a way to open these cracks, and the insights of Activity Theory give us reason to believe that we can make a contribution.

1 A Trade Union Organising Workers in an Enterprise

What is the *object* of the project (activity) in the case of capitalist firms? For the owners of capital, the aim of a firm is maximising the proportion of total social labour subsumed under the project. In the case of public services, governments set up motivations to proxy for the profit motive. But everyone knows that their own aims are met only as a side effect of some market- or regulation-based *object* (selling products, serving clients, etc.).

Archetypically, the employees are motivated by their wage which will contribute to their own private goals. However, it is by no means given that employees in an enterprise are motivated *only* by their wage, other than in the most degrading lines of work. And likewise employers are also members of the community with a public spirit of *some* kind. The *only way* to determine the various motives at work is to examine the *tendencies manifested in the real collaborative actions*, in the light of possible motives. But invariably, *all* have an interest in resolving the object of the collaborative project, its "merely known motive."

Any real enterprise, public or private, is a collaborative project in which a number of distinct projects collaborate. Each gets a side-benefit from the achievement of the merely known motive. This situation entails on-going, rational conflict between the participating projects, and this conflict will be reflected in all the actions of participants in the collaborative project or activity system.

A group of workers in an enterprise, whether unionised or not, has been the focus of Helen Worthen's (2011; 2014) application of Engeström's Activity Theory. Worthen's use of Engeström's triangular model is distinct from the way its inventor uses it, however. Whereas for Engeström, as for Leontyev, an enterprise (such as a medical clinic or a capitalist firm) is a single "system of activity" or simply "an activity," respectively, Worthen sees *two activity systems* engaged in a struggle with one another.

Leontyev allowed that the object of the activity (such as a patient needing to be healthy or a steel supply needing to be topped up) has a different meaning for the director (prestige, profit) than it does for a member of staff (their wages), and thus the object has a different *sense* seen from the two social positions. In Engeström's conception also, different subjects (represented on the left side of the triangle) within the system of activity may have a different sense of the object. However, for both Leontyev and Engeström there is *one* activity, one collaborative (system of) activity in which *individual* subjects may participate with different motives, but differences between different individual subjects in the system are subordinated to their collaboration in a single system of actions motivated by the same object.

Worthen's practice is Labor Education, and she uses a graphic with *two* of the triangular graphics, representing the viewpoint of the employers on one side and the workers on the other side. In Worthen's application, we can make sense of the 'subject' in the famous triangular graphic – it is either the union (or workers collectively) or the employer. In a sense we have two *coupled* systems of activity. This can be compared with how Engeström represents two NGOs dealing with the same social issue via the conception of a "boundary object," but there is no boundary object in Worthen's application. In Worthen's idea, it is the "purpose" of each activity system, what the unionist or the employer is aiming to achieve, which defines their activity system, rather than the "object" which occupies one node on the triangular network.

Worthen's idea brings to the fore a profound truth to which Activity Theorists hitherto had been blind: there are (at least) two different projects at work in any enterprise where people are working for their living. There may be multiple such projects, each with their own motive (their own *sense* of the object). But these are not individuals alone; the government, regulators and interests groups may be active; the social classes at work have collective interests, with shared conceptions of what the enterprise is about and may be organised in a union. And if not formally, nonetheless implicitly.

The assumption that a firm is an "activity system" made of so many individuals all collaborating towards the same object is a partial truth. The representation of the enterprise as two distinct "class projects" is an appropriate representation of an enterprise in those places where employees are represented by a union or, with appropriate modification, by several unions (or at least a workforce with a sense of solidarity among employees). Here the concept of multiple projects each with a stake in an enterprise is institutionalised in the customs and legal framework in which a unionised enterprise works. In other circumstances, where union membership is low and employees do not have an effective collective voice, then we'd have to say that this is an exaggeration of what is happening in the enterprise. The reality is often that the activity (i.e., the enterprise) is a collaboration between many projects, a *collaborative project*, and the projects entailed include the life-projects of individual workers hoping to make a career and raise a family, as well as the projects of different class fractions or departments within the enterprise, and outside projects (unions, funders, regulators, ...) who also collaborate in the enterprise. Worthen's approach is to teach Activity Theory to the worker activists, and then assist the activists in planning their activity by means of the same kind of work that Engeström's people do in Change Laboratories.

• • •

Hitherto I have considered only activities with a more or less finite reach, but analysis by units allows Activity Theory to tackle broad problems affecting the whole of social life in a country or even more widely.

2   Rival Political Parties Competing for Government of the Country

Rival political parties competing for government of the country is a scenario which did not exist in Leontyev's world, and I am not aware of any study of this phenomenon by activity theorists, but it is certainly of interest for life in almost any country nowadays. The object for all the parties is government of the country, itself an activity. Opposition parties are participants in this project as much as the governing party. What differs between the parties is that they have different concepts of government of the country, different object-concepts (or, in Leontyev's terms, the concept of government has a different sense for each of them). That is, they variously diagnose a dissonance between a concept of governance and its present state. Together with the norms and laws of the political system in which they operate, it is this concept which governs their activity and determines the character of the internal life of each party.

All the legal political parties are *collaborating* in forming a government of the country. Collaboration means that parties both cooperate and conflict over every action, but they do so on the basis of shared norms of political activity.

A political party is a particular kind of activity or project. There are three moments to the concept of a political party: the *universal* moment best encapsulated in its name, leaders or icons; the *particular* moment: the rhetorical, policy and organisational means it uses to appeal to various sections of its base and its various organisations; and the *individual* moment, all the people mobilised by the party. All three moments taken together constitute the party and embody the contradictions within it.

Most countries nowadays have universal suffrage with the right to form political parties to compete in elections, even if political systems differ widely in how these rights are realised and the electoral systems are more or less corrupt. A couple of centuries of experience has surely proved that (1) forming government through the electoral system does not in itself give a party sufficient authority to achieve thoroughgoing reforms, such as the socialisation of the social means of production, necessary for the overcoming of poverty, injustice and destruction of the commons. The class which dominates in civil society has extra-parliamentary means at its disposal (control of the means of communication, the most important economic organisations and the armed forces) to thwart the ambitions of the legislature. (2) In order to carry out thoroughgoing reforms a party *also* needs hegemony for their program in civil society (including the economy), sufficient to be able to carry through political decisions in the face of opposition from vested interests in civil society. An electoral party can only do what it needs to do insofar as there is popular support for its program in civil society. Speeches from the floor of Parliament cannot on their own summon up the support needed to overcome the resistance of conservative forces in civil society. That can only be provided by an extra-parliamentary social movement capable of shaping popular opinion, *and* winning elections if they are fair.

If a party achieves hegemony in civil society for a socialist program *and* elects a government on the basis of this program, then the initiative to block reform falls to the armed forces and foreign actors who could intervene. The revolutionary situation which would be created by such a violent counterrevolution against a legitimate and popular government then depends on the readiness of the people to fight. But that situation lies in a hypothetical future in the case of Europe, North America and other "advanced" countries. Here and now the Left has to be able to win elections on a really progressive program, *and* win hegemony in civil society. That is still far out of reach almost everywhere, with union membership in decline, social movements experiencing a period of quietude, and most Left political parties drawing very small votes in elections.

I will deal with the question of Activity Theory in political life under two headings: elections and opinion formation, before going on to consider the position of Activity Theory in social movements.

2.1   *Elections*

Elections in those many countries in which universal suffrage and elections play a central role in selecting a government, are an *institutionalised* abstract general process of social cognition which requires special attention. In the general case, the struggle of a social movement to determine government policies is a phenomenon very suitable for analysis by Activity Theory, and we will deal with this scenario by reflecting on the Women's Liberation Movement in the next section. The problem which confronts us in dealing with elections is that these institutions are reifications of fallacious conceptions of rationality. They are the *institutionalised antithesis of Activity Theory*, in which individuals make multiple-choice decisions passively, alone and in private, and their choices are aggregated in electorates which are largely arbitrary with respect to the voters' social position, their opinion and the manner of their formation. Nonetheless, elections are largely determined by processes which take place outside of the polling booths, in the newspaper and television editorial offices, the corporate boardrooms and other institutions and movements which make it their business to actively shape public opinion and create the conditions of life in which people become accustomed to think of themselves as independent entrepreneurs and consumers rather than as citizens.

But activity theorists cannot avoid consideration of elections, because no universal movement which is unable (or unwilling) to win a (fair) general election (by itself or via proxies) can fundamentally transform power relations within a nation by any other means. At the same time, elections do not provide a means for social transformation without the active support of non-parliamentary action. Where universal suffrage is in place, winning elections must always be *part* of any struggle to transform a nation, however distorted and prejudicial that process may be.

The winning and losing of elections – the shifting of a few undecided votes in a few geographical electorates for a short period of time – is, however, a topic best left to *experts* in that topic, people who can think in tick-boxes and

do the relevant maths. What activity theorists can do is to assist in the formation of a counter-hegemony in civil society and in the formation of progressive
and egalitarian public opinion by whatever means are available.

2.2   The Formation of Public Opinion

The formation of public opinion is in general a topic of immense interest and,
unlike electioneering, is amenable to analysis by Activity Theory, particularly Vygotsky's ideas about the place of instruction in learning. I know of no
research by an activity theorist into this topic, so all I can offer here are some
untested ideas which I believe would be worth exploring.

The vast industry engaged in the study of public opinion focuses on the
one hand on opinion surveys without any attempt to study how opinions are
formed, and on the other, on the production of media aimed at *persuading*
a target audience. At the same time it is widely recognised that opinions are
formed overwhelmingly through interaction with trusted peers, and that people (adults at least) are more or less impervious to persuasion via the broad-
cast media unless already inclined to the view promoted. Investigations have
shown that even face-to-face persuasion by a skilled campaigner demands at
least several hours to change one voter's mind on a controversial topic, if it is
possible at all. The prospect of any activist organisation changing the views of
millions of voters by one-on-one persuasion is remote.

Generally speaking, once a person adopts a stance in respect to matters
of public debate, they are very reluctant to change that stance and the well-
known "confirmation bias" ensures that any new information is interpreted in
the prejudicial light of an already-determined standpoint. Nevertheless, opinions are formed and do change and it is a matter of vital public importance to
know how opinions are changed on a mass scale.

The well-known materialist view that opinions are products of circumstances and upbringing, was refuted by Marx in his famous Thesis on Feuerbach
#3, on the basis that it divides society into two: the educator and the educated,
leaving unanswered the question of who will educate the educators. It will
be the people in a given social situation who will be changing both the situation and people's minds about that situation. But the dichotomy between the
authoritative opinion makers on one side and trusted peers on the other fails
to offer a viable and practical understanding of opinion formation.

I further claim that the idea of opinion formation as a direct response to
a situation (learning from direct experience alone) is fatuous. Thanks to the
philosophical work of Hegel and the psychological work of Vygotsky this
model is now discredited. A person's relation to the world is *mediated* by texts,
and changes in how a person perceives their situation depend on the cultural

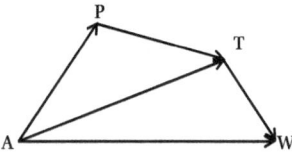

FIGURE 6   Subject
(A) Interprets the
world (W) using a
text (T) but a peer
(P) mediates the
reading of the text

process mediating that perception. The crucial relation is not the relation between a person and the situation itself, but between a person and a *text* interpreting that situation in some way.

I propose that the unit of analysis for the study of opinion formation is a person (A) interpreting a publicly-available text (T) under the advice of (i.e., mediated by) a trusted peer (P, supposed to have expertise in the question at hand) and subsequently interpreting the world (W) in the light of the text.

The contradiction entailed in this unit lies in the notion of "trusted expertise."

The peer P may be trusted by the person A, but may have no relevant expertise in the text, T. On the other hand, P may be a stranger whose trustworthiness is questionable, but on the other hand is an expert in the matter of the text, T. Or the peer may be to some degree trusted and to some degree expert.

Prior to puberty, children may generally be relied upon to share the values and opinions of their parents – for how could they know any better? – but by the time they are of working age or entering tertiary education, they have formed opinions "of their own" chiefly through interaction with their peers, and have taken up the identity of a social position of their own making. Given this, it would seem that "confirmation bias" would be at its weakest during those years, typically years nine to twelve at school, when young adults are working with their peers to carve out a social position of their own. So this cohort would be most suitable to study for how a peer, broadly understood (friend, mentor, teacher, uncle, ...), is able to mediate the interpretation of a culturally sourced text.

Once a young person has entered upon social life as an adult, they may indeed form opinions on this or that matter as they arise in their life, but the social position from which such opinions are formed changes only gradually, and their social milieu in turn changes only gradually as their life unfolds.

I look forward to a researcher in the Activity Theory tradition following up this question. The point is to understand how a person weighs up the reliability of the advice of a trusted friend who knows little of the issue at hand. What factors cause them to seek a second or expert opinion or ask for their friend's source? What factors undermine the perceived trustworthiness of experts? To what extent are people able to judge the expertise of a friend and what weight do they attach to the friend's expertise or lack thereof? How can questions be framed so as to incline people to accept that their friend does not have sufficient expertise?

A study such as the above is far from solving the problem of the formation of public opinion. Crucial is the shape of the expert-trust networks which are built by these relationships. To what extent do they overlap? How extensive are they? How fragmented are they? Are they chiefly one-to-many networks or loose chains? These are big questions amenable to activity theory, but first the basic mechanism of opinion formation must be examined.

CHAPTER 7

Social Movements

By "social movement" I refer to that phase in the life cycle of a project challenging social norms in which people have begun to act in concert with one another towards some ideal, but the activity has not yet been institutionalised as part of the existing social formation. I do not counterpose "social movement" to "revolutionary movement" which is simply one instance of a social movement. The idea that a social revolution could happen in the absence of a supportive social movement is an absurdity. Nor do I counterpose "social movement" to the labour movement, which is an instance of social movement which is in a more or less permanent condition of being institutionalised to one extent or another while to a greater or lesser extent, still remaining a social movement.

As we have seen, activity theorists intervene in institutions even where no social movement for change exists, merely dissatisfaction or malfunction. However, our core mission must be participation in social movements in solidarity with others.

1   The Women's Liberation Movement

The Women's Liberation Movement (WLM) is the social movement which has had the most far-reaching impact both on social life and social theory in the modern era and so could be described as the most fully developed social movement of our times, exhibiting all the phenomena which are of interest to Activity Theory. Activity Theory is exceptionally well placed for the analysis and understanding of social movements. Indeed, Activity Theory is in its element in the study of social movements in general and the Women's Liberation Movement in particular. The general principles which justify this claim will be reviewed presently, but at this point I shall review the development of the WLM in order to illustrate how Activity Theory conceives of a social movement.

First, the Women's Liberation Movement (like any social movement) is *an activity*. It is an activity because it is an aggregate of actions which *binds and identifies itself* by relations of collaboration. Actions which are related merely by common features might give grounds for an outside observer to characterise it as an activity in the first phase of its life cycle, but such a wave of actions is not yet a social movement.

In particular, all the actions making up the WLM are jointly motivated by a shared concept of women's emancipation, despite the fact that this aim has a different *sense* in the eyes of women of different social strata, i.e., different strata of women have a different concept of the place of women in the world and consequently, different motivations. Further, unlike the classical activities considered by Leontyev, the WLM aims not just at the reproduction of an object, but fully justifies characterisation as a "project" because it is explicitly *transformative*. That is, it explicitly aims to transform the entire social formation, not just to fix a problem. And unlike the "systems of activity" considered by Engeström, it has never had a single, even faintly stable or consensual division of labour, internal decision structure or boundary. It has always been a "runaway activity," to use Engeström's (2008) apposite term: self-directed and beyond the control of any other project.

1.1   *The Life Cycle of the WLM*

The life cycle of the project of women's emancipation is of particular interest, both in its own right and as an illustration of the problem of analysing the development of any social movement (See Krinsky & Blunden, in press). The history of the WLM would be a suitable title for a book series not one chapter in one book, but the aim here is just to outline the Activity Theory view of the WLM.

According to Simone de Beauvoir (1949), the WLM dates back to antiquity, but throughout, different strata of women in different lands forced open different doors. The Liberal Feminists of the 18th century were already enquiring into the origins of women's oppression, and demanding education, the vote and access to 'male' roles.

However, the WLM has classically been characterised by "waves," in which the upsurge of street activism by the Suffragettes from around 1900 to around 1930 has been dubbed the "First Wave." This characterisation obliterates the struggles of women of the 19th, 18th and earlier centuries and the activism of the Social Democratic women in the 1890s, probably on the superficial basis of the absence of street protests. The WLM of the 1960s and 1970s is then described as the "Second Wave" and the more critical movement mostly located within the walls of the academy in the 1980s, the "Third Wave." In line with the "wave" approach, various campaigns (such as the #MeToo movement in 2017 and the protests triggered by abuse of women in the Houses of Parliament in Australia in 2021) are then further conceived of as minor waves. However, the historically protracted project of women's liberation was never a single line. It advanced in different registers among different social strata and different cultures at different times, and street protests are a very crude measure of its intensity.

Blindness to the subterranean phases of the life of a movement makes it impossible to understand either its periods of overt activism or its ultimate achievements. The wave conception of social movements is very superficial. It expresses the impression that social movements rise up from nowhere, peak and then fade away again, leaving behind some residue of social change, until the next wave rolls in and the activists can get their banners out of the basement again. Completely overlooked are the molecular changes taking place somewhat out of sight between the waves of public protest and the irreversible changes wrought by most waves of activism and generating the conditions for the next wave. It is superficial because it sees only the public protests and discounts all other modes of activity, giving the impression of quasi-natural processes which allow the enthusiastic activist only to wait for the next wave.

Krinsky & Blunden (in press) argue for the conception of a social movement as one phase in the "life cycle" of a *project*. "Life cycle" was not intended as a metaphor (birth, youth, maturity, old age, etc.), but rather a *logic* of development inspired by Hegel's Logic which sees social movements but *one phase* in the development of projects: cycles of change in a larger social formation which begins with what has been called a "social non-movement" (Bayat, 2009) before manifesting itself as a social movement as commonly so called and then merging with and transforming *other* projects (institutions, movements, organisations, customs, etc.) and eventually becoming one concept or practice alongside others in a changed social formation now manifesting new contradictions and generating new "social non-movements." So we have a continuous cycle of development, each cycle creating conditions for the next cycle.

While there is a definite cyclical nature to this process, as illustrated in Figure 4 above, this does not imply that a cycle begins only when the previous cycle is complete. On the contrary, the changes wrought by one wave of protests are still in the process of being institutionalised as a new movement begins on the basis of contradictions latent in an earlier movement. And one and the same demand in successively more concrete formulations may wash through a society multiple times before its work is done. But every new concept exhibits the same complete cycle in the course of its realisation.

The same approach, embedded in Hegel's Logic, Vygotsky's Cultural Psychology and Activity Theory, was brought to bear to understand in more detail the life-course of the whole project in my book, *Hegel for Social Movements* (Blunden, 2019).

The phases of the life cycle of a project are thus in the first place three-fold.

(i) The social non-movement (Bayat, 2009) is the first phase of any project. Here there are more or less numerous individual or group actions which arise spontaneously from the efforts of people to simply carry on with their normal life. They are not protests or acts of sabotage, but simply collisions of people's actions with the state or dominant norms of behaviour which may result in unasked-for counter-actions by the state or social superiors, and conflict. The social non-movement does not arise as a result of any ideological insight into social mores. On the contrary, the conflicts are not sought after but arise as a result of reactions to a person's everyday activity. Insofar as consciousness of the social non-movement arises, it is by *observation* of these conflicts from both participants themselves and outsiders. It emerges in much the same way as a "crime wave," an uncoordinated spontaneous response to conditions and registered by the frequency and quality of events.

Long before street protests signalled the "Second Wave" of the WLM, large numbers of middle-class women were holding down careers and working-class women were refusing to give up the manufacturing jobs they had cornered during the war. This was *despite* an onslaught of propaganda telling women that they not only *should* but *had* returned to home duties, a myth exposed by Lynn Beaton (1982). The contradiction of women acting outside of norms while simultaneously accepting those same norms is shown in sharp relief by the female separatist anti-war movement, Women Strike for Peace (WSP), which took their anti-war demands to the streets in the early 1960s and not only accepted but *weaponised* their status as "housewives" and mothers. This was echoed somewhat later by Save Our Sons in Australia. Members of WSP (see Swerdlow, 1993) were largely career women, despite their self-identification as "typical American housewives." Their daughters, on the other hand, rejected these norms outright and went on to initiate the "Second Wave." Likewise, women were challenging gender norms and nagging their husbands to do more housework for many years before these issues became topics of debate in the press. The attentive eye observed these molecular changes building up, and it was just such an attentive eye which allowed Beauvoir to write the founding document of the modern women's movement almost 20 years before street protests broke out in the US.

"Sexism" entered the language in the US in 1968 and I take this to mark the initiation of the "Second Wave," although it is clear that it had been building up under the surface for 20 years. "Patriarchy" entered the language closely following on the heels of "sexism," overtaking it in the 1980s. Sexism indexes the immediate experience of exclusion and misrecognition; patriarchy on the other hand indexes a generalised critique that reflects the impact of a social movement with its vision of a better world.

During this period in the development of a project, the developmental task is for the separate actors to become aware of each other and make contact. One of the most important means of doing this in the 1960s was through literature: books and magazines publicising and theorising women's experiences.

In the US, young women also came together because they were participating together in supporting the Civil Rights Movement and in the Student Protest movement and women objected to their treatment at the hands of male comrades in these activities. Spectacular actions like Zelda D'Aprano chaining herself to the doors of the Arbitration Court in Melbourne in 1969 also alerted women to the issue and helped generate the development of the movement among working class women. Consciousness-raising groups played a similar role in the late 1960s. Here the developmental issue is simply making people aware that they are not alone and begin to think about a better world.

(ii) A social movement is the middle phase of the life cycle of a project. This is the phase during which an adequate concept of the movement is constructed with a theory and program for social change. The social movement phase is extremely rich, beginning with the effort to name and identify the conflict which has arisen in social life and draw together all those who are implicated. There is a struggle of form and content as the movement seeks the appropriate vehicle for its demands: should we have members and pay dues? should we form a political party? Then as the movement faces counter-actions by representatives of the status quo, the movement develops a sense of realism. It begins to evaluate the effect of its own actions.

A feature of social movements is the determination of a single symbol or name, often an artefact loaded with social significance (See Engeström & Sannino, 2016; Popovic, 2015), which vividly and succinctly expresses the aspirations of the movement: a flag or symbol like the hammer and sickle, a colour, the face of a leader (think of Che or Mao), or the chakra – the spinning wheel which symbolised the Indian Independence Movement and is shown on the Indian national flag. During this phase, subordinate concepts are developed in the form of new norms of behaviour, belief and meaning. The initially abstract concept becomes much more concrete. Norms of behaviour are interconnected with visions of a better future.

The social movement phase of the WLM began sharply on the heels of the Civil Rights Movement in the United States. Literature played a central role in the development of the WLM, with books mediating "consciousness-raising groups" in which women talked through their situation with other women. This recognition of one's situation and identity through dialogue with others is a crucial feature of the growth of social movements, and books and manifestoes play a central role in these reflections. The word "sexism" argued that women were the subjects of a prejudice just like racism, just as Martin Luther King before them had drawn inspiration from the National Liberation Movements of the 1940s and 1950s. The word "sexism" provided that focus, the idea that women were subject to a particular form of exclusion, the sharp point of which would be used in the next phase of the project in which laws and norms would be transformed.

Typically for the development of a project, the social movement phase of the WLM began with the conviction that all women were in the same situation, facing the same oppression and should therefore stand shoulder to shoulder to fight sexism. From identity comes difference. In the 1980s, the demand to "smash the glass ceiling" was raised, but this was far from the minds of working-class women. The "Third Wave" arose from the discovery that not all women suffered from the same oppression; working class women, women of colour and women in the global south had *other* priorities. Contradictions of this kind are demobilising but are the necessary precursor for the future development of the movement if it is to bring about the necessary transformations. The differentiation is in fact an indicator that the movement has penetrated and merged with diverse social strata.

During this phase, the movement is not yet *recognised*. Other than broad rights to free speech, association, etc., the movement has no special rights. Their demands are not reflected in legislation or social practices generally. Full-time employment in the movement is rare; participation is based on personal commitment. People feel free to criticise the movement and question its right to exist. And it is reversing these features of a social movement which are key to making the transition to the next phase: getting your demands legislated.

(iii) The phase of transformation and development arises when the social movement breaks through and a clear concept of their central demand begins to become established and broadly recognised. As a result, overt street protests and other such manifestations of alienation decrease. Activists often mistake the onset of this victorious phase of development as decline and are disappointed (See Jamison & Eyerman, 1991, for example). In fact, this moment marks the beginning of *real* change as the project begins to penetrate other movements, government and institutions and social norms begin to change. Equal pay, sexual harassment laws, affirmative action, de-gendering of law and finance, no-fault divorce, etc., start to become the law of the land.

Women cannot be liberated from domestic servitude, even at the hands of the most sympathetic husband, without equal pay for work of equal value, which cannot be achieved without breaking down the gender division of labour. This measure in turn depends on equitable division of household responsibilities so that women can compete without the burden of home responsibilities holding them back. Access to traditionally male jobs cannot be achieved without penetrating the male-dominated trade unions which have collaborated with employers in suppressing female wages and blocking the entry of women to male-dominated trades. No progress can be made in breaking though the glass ceiling without the promotion of women at lower ranks which entails changing the law (with the need for female lawyers and judges), changes to the education of girls and the expectations that their own parents have for them. And women cannot command equal pay and achieve career progress without the support of rape crisis centres, domestic violence laws (which entail penetrating the police force) and healthy manufactured food, reliable and effective domestic appliances and access to good quality, free childcare; otherwise women rightly suspect that if they go to work the health of their family will suffer, surviving on manufactured food. And so on. Thus begins *the long march through the institutions*, in which the concept of an "emancipated woman" is given *concrete* form by *merging* the concept of Women's Liberation with every other concept in the culture. In the process, Women's Liberation is transformed from a social movement mobilising women on the basis of their immediate interests to a society whose laws, norms, mythology, education and labor processes, etc., have been feminised.

Leaders of activist groups who were lobbying government or setting up voluntary centres now get jobs in the bureaucracy enforcing anti-discrimination laws and policies, or become lawyers defending women's employment rights or consultants training police on dealing with domestic violence. Instead of criticising trade union leaders, women become union leaders especially those covering feminised trades. From demands inscribed on banners, the demands of women's emancipation become paragraphs in legislation.

Obviously, these transformations are not achieved in a single go. The social formation, an aggregate of projects all at various stages of their life cycle, inevitably gives birth to new waves of conflict and outbreaks of protest. When all openings for minor adjustments in the ruling compromise have been exhausted, a new social movement must break out.

Nostalgia for the old days of street marches and occupations is generally out of place when you have your people on the inside, but there comes a time when the patriarchy really digs its heels in and female insiders prove incapable of fixing things. The developmental issue at this point is to be ready to go back into the streets and mobilise the masses of women to step up. This is what was going on with #MeToo and the upsurge of outrage over violence against women in Australia in 2021.

1.2   The WLM as a Learning Process

The WLM is a learning process, as is any social movement. Activity theorists are not alone in viewing social movements as learning processes (see Jamison

& Eyerman, 1991, for example, with the concept of "cognitive practice"), but as activity theorists we have the entire knowledge and experience in education and personal development accumulated by activity theorists since Vygotsky wrote his first book, *Educational Psychology*, in 1926. Activity theorists, the majority of them employed in Education and Child Development, have *always* regarded learning as a socio-cultural process. Accordingly, activity theorists have developed a number of concepts which can be deployed for the purposes of understanding and intervening in social movements as learning processes.

(i) Instruction leads development. This is a central tenet of Vygotsky's contribution to learning theory. Left to themselves, children will *not* spontaneously rediscover the scientific solutions to problems which have taken many centuries of collaborative labour to discover and which have been formulated and transmitted by cultural means from one generation to the next. They have to be led.

The same truth applies to social movements, not because participants in social movements are uneducated – indeed the participants, taken individually, are more often than not educated people – but rather that the "collective personage," the *project*, is in its infancy. It is breaking new ground, and the knowledge relevant to the ground-breaking work it has to do does not spring spontaneously from the conditions of its own life. It is true that everyone is the expert in their own life (Horton, 2003), but most people are not experts in the broad range of knowledges relevant to the *transformation* of their lives.

In 1902, Lenin made the same point when he cited Kautsky (1902):

> The old ... programme quite rightly stated that the task of Social Democracy is to saturate the proletariat with the consciousness of its position and the consciousness of its task. There would be no need for this if consciousness arose of itself from the class struggle.
>
> LENIN, 1902

and Lenin then commented:

> This does not mean, of course, that the workers have no part in creating such an ideology. They take part, however, not as workers, but as socialist theoreticians, as Proudhons and Weitlings; in other words, they take part only when they are able, and to the extent that they are able, more or less, to acquire the knowledge of their age and develop that knowledge.
>
> LENIN, 1902

Nothing could be more mistaken then than for a leader to "leave it to the members" to decide upon policies and strategies. On the contrary, leaders must study everything relevant to their struggle – politics, law, psychology, whatever – and must become teachers as well as leaders and make every effort to assist as wide as possible a stratum of movement actors to acquire scientific understanding insofar as the need arises from the conditions of their struggle.

Gramsci (1971) was making the same point when he pointed to the crucial roles of "organic intellectuals," those participants in the movement who, thanks to their occupation or upbringing, had access to scientific material, and could bring that knowledge into the activity of the movement. The Mechanics Institutes, many of which still stand today, are monuments to the value the early trade union movement gave to learning.

But the learning of a social movement goes deeper than this. Social movements are breaking entirely new ground, they are experimenting with new norms and customs, and they are challenging longstanding institutions without any historical precedent for alternatives. They are engaged in cutting edge social research, whether or not they are conscious of doing so. At the very least social movements are testing hitherto untested hypotheses. It is the "collective knowledge" which is created by and is the possession of the whole movement which is most essential.

The rich literature of the women's movement is proof that the leaders of WLM understood the need to work over the entirety of available literature and share this knowledge with the movement. The consciousness-raising groups of the 1960s are testament to the fact that the pioneers of this movement knew that they could not overcome the ideological barriers on their own and sought opportunities for collective study. The relationship is mutual. Since the 1950s, the theorists of successive social movements – Socialism, Civil Rights, Women's Liberation, Environment – have stimulated the development of social theory and penetrated deeply into the academy. This must be so because it is social movements which change society, and nothing can be learnt outside of the struggle to change the society.

Who knew what would be the outcome of women leaving their exclusive role as childrearers, cooks and carers, under conditions in which their menfolk were not yet ready to step into the gap? Who knew what would happen when this gap would be filled by the market through manufactured food, takeaways and restaurants, commercial childcare services? Who knew what would happen when all manner of psychologists, counsellors and social workers took over the care work which was formerly borne by women trapped in domestic servitude? Who knows how the strong social fabric which was maintained by the domestic labour of women can be recovered on the basis of an equitable division of labour? This 'research' is the work of social movements.

The move from individual learning to social learning by movements and institutions is not a metaphor. The concepts of Activity Theory used in education and child development are equally relevant (even more so in some respects) when the subject is not a single person but a social practice.

(ii) The Zone of Proximal Development is probably the most well known of Vygotsky's concepts in learning theory and it is of exceptional importance for participants in social movements.

Vygotsky always deployed this concept in the context of a child making a "leap" in development from one stage of development to the next, when the subject is obliged for a moment to "act above themselves." In passing through the Zone of Proximal Development, the child and their carers are managing a critical phase in the child's development. The child must extricate themself from their social situation and establish a new identity, a new level of activity in a new social situation in which they are treated by others in a new way. The critical period through which children pass at this time is characterised by conflict and manifestations of difficult behaviour which pass away once the transition is accomplished (see Blunden, 2011), but play is also an effective means for a child to act above themselves in the zone of proximal development.

From time to time a social movement must also pass through critical periods. Having reached a certain level of activity in which they can easily, for example, mount street protests and public meetings, at a certain point they may be posed with going beyond this level of activity and engaging in new forms of action. For example, they may have to face up to the need to engage in civil disobedience. Or, people who have hitherto engaged in protests must make the transition to taking up positions in institutions and implementing change.

Brecht de Smet (2015; 2020) studied the development of the workers' movement in Egypt during the years leading up to the Arab Spring and used the concepts of social situation of development, interiorisation, neoformation, prolepsis, as well as zone of proximal development from Vygotsky's Cultural Psychology.

Interiorisation refers to the process in which actions in which the subject (here a social movement) engages with *other* subjects, later become a function of the *internal* life of the subject. *Neoformation* refers to a new form of action which appears in a subject in the course of development and the creation of this neoformation is for a time the central problem of the subject. *Prolepsis* refers to the process in which a subject acts in relation to a situation before it is actually in existence and thereby tends to bring the anticipated situation into being.

De Smet points out that so long as a trade union group continues on with gradual expansion at more or less the same level and kind of activity, the group does perfectly well in managing their own activity. However, when the situation demanded a move to a new level of activity, such as when the workers were obliged to move from shop floor organising and on to the streets to participate in protests, new forms of organisation were required and the transition generated crises. De Smet also drew on Gramsci's (1971) ideas of "organic intellectuals" to understand the role of leaders in coping with this change in the social situation workers occupied as they entered the political realm.

Vygotsky taught us a lot about these crucial phases of development. First, they arise when the subject (here taken to be a social movement) begins to find their social situation a limitation rather than a benefit and new forms of activity now fall within their horizons of imagination. The contradiction here is that they *want* to act at the higher level but they do not yet know *how* to act at the higher level. Second, as a result of this contradiction difficult and uncooperative modes of activity may enter their character, but these are transitory and will fade away once the development is successfully completed. If the transition is aborted, then the difficult types of behaviour may continue; the need is to push through and make the development. Third, during this phase the subject can manage activity at the higher level, but only *with assistance*. In de Smet's analysis this idea is understood in terms of hands-on leadership by the "organic intellectuals." If the movement is not ready for the development, then even given the best efforts of the leader they will fail; they are not ready. On the other hand, if the subject manages the higher level of activity (engaging in a street protest for example) albeit under close leadership and at a small scale, then this is a signal that the movement is ready to make the transition.

During its history, the WLM went through a number of important changes in the nature and level of their activity. The first such transition was the move from the molecular activity of the period of "social non-movement" into public protest, and it was during this period that the consciousness-raising groups were most intensely active. Another important change was the transition from protest to the long march through the institutions and again leaders were placed under a great deal of stress during this transition, taking up positions in the establishment and dismantling the structural barriers against which women had been battering. Another transition which required the initiative of intellectuals within the Women's Movement was the moment when the universalist WLM came up against the counterclaims of women of colour and women in the Global South and people with other gender identities. During these periods of change, new forms of activity were adopted and the leaders and intellectuals of the movement were called upon to help the movement find a way through and manage the conflict which accompanies such transitions.

(iii) Germ cells play a crucial role in the development of all social movements. As mentioned above, the germ cell can be constituted in an artefact which gives particularly graphic form to a concept (See Popovic, 2015 for numerous examples), or an image, like a logo, but more frequently the germ cell is embodied simply in a *word*.

"Sexism" was probably the most important word in the history of the WLM, expressing succinctly women's affiliation with other oppressed groups and the universal character of the movement, embracing all women. "Glass Ceiling" was a germ cell for the development of measures to open the higher ranks of work hierarchies to women at the same time as marking off a middle-class women's movement from the women of the working class who rallied behind the idea of "Equal Pay!" In this way, different phases of the movement were initiated and encapsulated by these key words or slogans which over a period of years following their entry into the language expanded into concrete programs and analyses. Hash tags play the same role – #MeToo.

Each new successful slogan or buzzword marks the opening of a new chapter in the life of a movement. A germ cell typically represents a form of activity, and de Smet observes that the strike is the germ cell of the labour movement.

Though this is less so in the WLM, the same role can be played by a *person*. In the women's movement various writers have become *icons* of their movement, standing not just for Women's Liberation in general, but for a specific critique, or simply for a specific issue or instance of injustice. It is particularly important that when a person finds themself being shaped by the media as an icon they have to think very carefully about how they respond. Rosie Batty faced just such a situation. When her ex-husband murdered her son and the press knocked on her door and asked her how she felt, she knew that she had an opportunity to shape the discourse around domestic violence in Australia. Instead of opening the door and playing the role of grieving mother, she stepped up to the camera already adopting her role as a spokesperson for the anti-domestic violence lobby, even though she had never before been an activist.

In the workers' movement, leaders – Marx, Lenin, Bakunin, Lenin, Trotsky, Che, etc. – have more often played the role of symbol and icon as well as index of the movement they led. It was Anja Koski-Jännes (1999) who first hypothesised that if a sign is simultaneously icon, symbol and index for an idea, then it has especially powerful semiotic power (See Colapietro, 1988 for the interpretation of this semiotic terminology). However, the women's movements have deliberately avoided elevating leaders into icons (See Swerdlow, 1993) along with hierarchical structures, so far as possible, because women have seen these features as inconsistent with their object.

(iv) *Perezhivanie* is a key concept in the development of the personality and of development in general. It is key to understanding the development of social movements and projects. This entails the concepts of what I will call "group *perezhivanie*" and "project *perezhivanie*."* The reason for this rather clumsy terminology is that there are at least three different ways in which "collective *perezhivanie*" can be understood, each of them different and important for understanding crises in the development of social movements. All *perezhivaniya* are by their very nature *collective* inasmuch a single person can undergo *perezhivanie* only in and through a trauma in relations with their life-projects, projects which exist independently from them in the world around them in connection with other people. All *perezhivaniya* entail collaboration with others, and sometimes a whole cohort of people experience a *perezhivanie* at the same time in connection with the same or a similar situation, but independently of each other. If all the individuals share some characteristic or are in a similar situation, and are aware of this commonality, then this may create the *potential* for a move to collective striving – something quite different from side-by-side striving, and this can make the transition to the type of *perezhivaniya* mentioned above, where we have the concepts of group and project *perezhivanie*.

A project *perezhivanie* is manifested when a project itself undergoes a profound crisis in its object. The source of the crisis might be the total failure of a campaign, the government moving to suppress the movement, a split of the project into two or more rival projects, a sudden breakthrough demanding a change of identity, an attack by a one-time ally, a loss of interest among activists or some combination of the above. Every participant in the project and every action that is carried out as part of the project will be affected.

A project *perezhivanie* is quite distinct, however, from *perezhivaniya* in the lives of all participants. Everyone may be going through a *perezhivanie* but it is not necessarily a *perezhivanie* of the project, or at least, may not be seen as as such by those experiencing it. For example, all the participants in the women's movement in a country will be traumatised when the country finds itself in a war, but until the war impinges on the activity of the women's movement itself, there is no project *perezhivanie*. And when a movement is going through

---

* I thank Beth Ferholt, Laya, Sohrab and Julian Williams for an extended conversation on this topic through 2021.

a crisis, not every participant will be aware of the crisis, or at least not in the same way.

Finally, a "group *perezhivanie*" is a *perezhivanie* affecting a group of people participating together in the same activity. For example, all the students in a class as they confront and resolve a particularly engaging task set by their teacher. This is a collective *perezhivanie* in the full sense, but it does not necessarily indicate a project in crisis. Anecdotally however, it appears that when a project enters a *perezhivanie*, very often key groups of participants in the project experience the *perezhivanie* immediately and before the same *perezhivanie* grips the whole movement.

For example, as the Equal Pay fight began there were a number of women who found themselves on the front line of this fight and experienced either the crushing weight of betrayal or the exhilaration of victory in the workplace or in the courts. Further, it seems that such key groups play a role in alerting and preparing the entire movement to the coming *perezhivanie*. This is how these early martyrs to the cause become *causes célèbres*. This meso-level of *perezhivanie* is important in the realisation of *perezhivaniya* at the level of entire projects.

(v) The distinction between the merely known motive and effective motive was introduced by Leontyev (see Introduction §6). This distinction is relevant to teaching a child to read or an employer needing employees to work for them. It is also relevant to building social movements. Every organiser will be aware of need to provide motivation for a new delegate or recruit to get active in the movement.

Great social movements like Environmentalism, Socialism and Women's Liberation faced the same problem: how to engage with subjects who had not yet grasped the utopian vision and formed the motivation required to make the sacrifices necessary to build the movement.

The ideal – a sustainable world, a classless society or a society beyond patriarchy – seems very far off, unattainable and frankly difficult to imagine, far less sufficiently real to effectively motivate sacrifice and struggle. Social movements solve this problem at two different levels. In the first place, organisers make their events exciting, enjoyable, social learning events. In the second place, the movements embrace intermediate goals which resonate with the immediate needs of important sections of their base.

In the 1790s, English Jacobins, radical democrats inspired by events in France, hoped to achieve universal suffrage in Britain. They were subject to severe repression and crushed. Later, their radical wing joined their fate to that of the British workers in the Chartist movement, organised under the banner of the National Charter Association. This offered the radical democrats an opportunity to engage with their disenfranchised base.

The National Charter Association, the first working-class political party, founded in Britain in 1840 to win the vote for working-class people, never achieved its aim despite winning to their side most of the 5/6 of adult British population who were denied the vote, and in the face of stubborn refusal from Parliament, went into decline in 1848 after being rebuffed for the third time. But in the meantime, the NCA provided an opportunity for working class men and women to engage in political debate, learn how to run political meetings and branches and build a national organisation despite being all but totally illegal. The NCA printed daily newspapers which were read avidly and held social events. The NCA effectively brought the British working class into existence, and it was the attractions of participation and belonging which drew people to it as much as the hope of political emancipation.

After 1848, Socialism began to grow as a movement whose ideal was public political power in the hands of the organised working class. On the whole, however, its members were self-educated artisans, most of whom looked to organising in the workplace rather than politics to solve their problems. A new generation of socialists in the 1880s encountered a new kind of working-class movement: the unskilled mass of workers in the docks, gasworks and factories. The socialist ideal could be realised by this new agent, the mass trade union movement. Ever since, socialists have joined their trade union and taken up responsible positions and led the day-to-day economic struggles of wage workers. They do not say to the workers: "Expropriate the boss! Overthrow capitalism!," they fight for *marginal improvements* in wages and conditions and welfare, which was exactly what the union members expected and asked of them. These very gains of course, ultimately, undermined the motivation for Socialism. As workers gained more and more control over their lives, the State took over the role of welfare, health and education and workers became more prosperous. This is certainly not intended to suggest that this was a mistaken strategy. Far from it, it is an unavoidable phase of social transformation.

The Women's Liberation Movement faced the same problem and made the same kind of decisions. Women's emancipation is thinkable only on condition that it is achieved by the activity of women themselves, and not at the gift of any other party. The founders of the WLM had visions of a world in which gender had no social or political meaning, significant only in the domain of sex, love and childbirth. But this was a vision beyond the ken of the overwhelming majority of women. So how was the WLM movement to enrol the female masses in the fight against the patriarchy? They set up rape crisis centres, campaigned for free child care, lobbied government and employers for equal pay and forced their way into male jobs, pilloried the police and councils for failing to make the streets safe for women, and so on. It was by such means that women not already committed to the vision of a feminist utopia could be motivated to participate and take those first steps towards demolition of the patriarchy. But few activists actually benefited more than what the struggle cost them in time, money, friendships and peace of mind. The benefits were largely enjoyed by their daughters, who often took for granted the hard-won gains of their mothers and grandmothers and even declared that nothing had been gained after all!

But it is by these means that the world has been changed, and if it is not all destroyed in the approaching environmental catastrophe, we can thank the visionaries who dreamt of the end of capitalism and patriarchy but devoted their time to the little improvements that workers and women asked for, the really effective motives. In general, those who did participate in these movements have remained loyal to those ideals, despite seeing them become largely taken for granted and invisible to new generations.

As MacIntyre has said, it is unlikely that any of the institutions of modern society could be maintained without the little rewards offered to those who participate whether in wages, prestige or whatever. Social movements have learnt the same lesson, paying attention to the immediate needs of participants as well as their long-term goals. The "merely known motive" cannot really be theorised as a *motive*, as a psychological category. People who participate in movements do not do so instrumentally, *in order* to achieve that final goal, but rather for reasons which are best understood in *ethical* terms and in terms of *identity*. To suggest to someone, for example, that they were fighting for Socialism because they would benefit economically from such an arrangement would be taken as a grave insult by any Socialist and quite misunderstands the consciousness with which people participate in great collaborative projects like Socialism and Women's Liberation.

The ideal of a social movement is formally expressed in a representation of a future utopian world. Concretely, however, the movement's ideal is manifested in their norms, especially their practical norms, that is, how people are expected to deal with each other within the movement. It is not uncommon for utopian and ethical ideals to be comically in contradiction with one another, as in the socialist parties which advocate democratic socialism while operating as a little dictatorship internally.

1.3   *Decision Making within Projects*

Decision making within projects is the vital means by which the rationality of projects is realised, and by means of which participants acquire commitments and undergo personal transformation. These processes should not be taken for granted and even where there is no formal process, *all collaboration entails ongoing collective decision making*. Activities are truly collective or collaborative only to the extent that deliberation and some form of collective decision making determines their course, and it is only thanks to such a process that projects are intelligible.

Decision making within projects has been a topic for activity theorists. Most recently, Sannino published a study which was dealt with above in the section on "agency." What all previous studies have ignored is that when people make jointly binding decisions, they do so only in some specific project, which has its own norms, and in specific cultural and historical conditions. It cannot be presumed in the absence of evidence that (1) participants will make decisions by Consensus, or (2) the project (if any) to which the decision contributes has no impact on *how* decisions are made. Before decision making can be analysed, it is necessary to determine the social, cultural and ethical expectations for how decisions are to be made.

I made an extended study of this process in *The Origins of Collective Decision Making* (Blunden, 2016a) utilising the method of analysis by units characteristic of Activity Theory. The unit of analysis I used was a group of people in the same room making a jointly binding decision with respect to a shared project. The results of this study were that three paradigms of decision making have emerged historically and each has their place in present-day projects: (i) Counsel, (ii) Majority and (iii) Consensus. Distinct from collective decision making is (iv) Laissez faire, in which participants do not make mutually binding decisions, and cases where the participants represent distinct projects, in which case the paradigm could be (v) Negotiation, (vi) Colonisation, or (vii) Solidarity.

If we ask what would be a micro-unit, then on one hand we would have to consider, with Sannino's metaphor, that the action which is the pre-condition to any decision would be to 'put something on the table' on a Yes/No basis ("throw out a kedge"). But collective decision making *essentially* entails deliberation, so we must expand this unit to include deliberation of some kind and making a Yes/No decision. The unit of deliberation is an utterance. However, each of the paradigms of decision making I have identified is a *system* of decision making and entail forms of deliberation, which are in general highly structured. No deliberation at all is a limiting case for all paradigms.

As Vygotsky pointed out in his original explanation of the concept of "unit of analysis," the unit is not necessarily the smallest entity. The unit of water is a water molecule, *not* hydrogen and oxygen atoms. The water molecule can in turn be understood in terms of a system of elements. Accordingly, each of the various paradigms of decision making must be studied as a deliberative procedure in its own right.

(i) Counsel originated in traditional society and continued to be the dominant form of decision making in feudal society. Under Counsel, one person – the Chief, the Abbot, the paterfamilias – has the moral responsibility to make decisions but is obliged to listen to the views of everyone else before deciding, after which their decision is binding upon all. Even today, one person may have this role in a one-parent family, as the owner of a small business or in the event of some project on which their personal fate alone depends. The ethic of Counsel is a *virtue* ethics based chiefly on the personality of the leader.

Literature abounds, in Africa for example, about the virtues demanded of a chief in conducting *Lekgotla* or in business studies discourses where we find lists of the virtues of leaders and typologies of leadership style. Ethics, as seen by Activity Theory, is discussed later under the heading of "The Ethics of Collaboration." It will suffice to point out here that further analysis must be an ethical one.

(ii) Majority originated with the birth of voluntary association in the mediaeval guilds, and was further developed by trading companies and the trade unions and from these bases among the ordinary people, implanted itself in parliamentary bodies, displacing Counsel. Over a period of a thousand years, ordinary people fought for the principle of universal suffrage and majority rule which by the middle of the 20th century became the norm for all forms of public political collective decision making.

Deliberation under Majority takes a very specific form regulated by one of several rule books, in the US by *Roberts' Rules of Order*, in the UK by *The ABC of Chairmanship*, written by the trade unionist, Walter Citrine.

The ethic of Majority is an ethic of equality, solidarity and tolerance, reflected in one person one vote and the tolerance which minorities and majorities show for each other in their co-existence. It is a *deontological* ethics, i.e., an ethics based on adherence to and proficiency in specific rules and procedures.

(iii) Consensus originated among the Quakers in the 1650s in response to severe repression resulting from undisciplined activity by their own members which drew the wrath of the state down on them. Consensus became the decision making paradigm of choice for the Peace Movement in the US in 1960, and then the Women's Movement and eventually penetrated all social movements.

Consensus respects dissenting views but does not tolerate them and endeavours to overcome dissent by deliberation or failing consensus, the status quo ante. Generally, if consensus cannot be achieved, then Laissez faire is preferred. In order to avoid such crises, some organisations use qualified consensus, such as 75%, before a decision can be binding. The dominant virtues of Consensus are inclusion and patience. In addition, like Majority, Consensus has a deontological ethics.

In addition to these three paradigms and the libertarian paradigm in which decisions are *not* collective, any real activity is generally structured so as to *subsume* one paradigm of decision making under another. For example, the typical capitalist firm will be structured by Counsel, but Consensus will be subsumed under Counsel with shop-floor workers collaborating with one another in the actual work of producing the product and the Board of Directors using Consensus to guide the policies of the enterprise. Likewise, the typical trade union makes decisions by Majority, but routinely uses Consensus to formulate a decision before putting it to the vote. Or, a medical team supporting a patient facing a critical operation will recognise the patient's decision via Counsel, but then implement the procedures by Consensus. Activity Theorists often presume that Consensus is the default decision making procedure, but this is not the case.

In his Discourse Ethics, Jürgen Habermas (1992) proposed a very stringent set of principles assuring the equal participation of everyone affected by a decision. These principles are applicable to any of the paradigms. They entail requirements for clear communication, participation in good faith, respect for a better argument, openness to any relevant argument and openness to criticism.

The long march of women for emancipation has been closely tied up with the evolution of collective decision making. In general, Counsel marked the exclusion of women from decision making altogether, as it was only widows who ever enjoyed this right. Majority gave women an equal say, but it took centuries before they were able to freely exercise that right. Women were always the fiercest advocates of majority rule, being prominent in the Chartist Movement of the 1830s and then the Suffragettes before World War One, before embracing Consensus in the 1970s.

The earliest Feminist organisations used Majority, as their activists had come from the Labour Movement. But the move to Consensus was begun in 1960 by a female Quaker member of WSP (Women Strike for Peace) and two female members of SNCC (Student Nonviolent Coordinating Committee) who were instrumental in seeding Consensus in the social movements. Very soon, Consensus came to be widely seen as the "feminist method of decision making" although it is now ubiquitous in social movements and other voluntary associations.

However, it is important to recognise that *each* mode of decision making has its place. You cannot operate an *alliance* with Majority since members of the minority party simply leave if they are out-voted. Organisations such as trade unions or governing bodies do not use Consensus where mutually hostile social or political groups do not have the option to go their own way. A comic once suggested that Marie Antoinette could have saved the French monarchy with a single voice if the French Revolution had adopted Consensus decision making.

(iv) *Laissez faire* is the result of a *failure* of Consensus. *Laissez faire* has made a comeback as Consensus-based norms have intersected with ideological fragmentation since the millennium and a virtue has been made of it in celebration of diversity and pluralism. Many anarchistic projects now make little effort to achieve consensus and participants simply go their own way under the banner of "horizontality" (Maeckelbergh, 2009). *Laissez faire* represents the *absence* of collective decision making, the absence of collectivity, and the consequent loss of personal and social development. The ethic of *laissez faire* is individual authenticity.

The question always remains: which ethic and which set of procedures applies in which circumstances.

Counsel is appropriate where one person has moral responsibility for the decision made. But since others in the group will be affected by the decision the Chief is obliged to seek the views of everyone else. This ethic applies not only in hierarchical communities, but one where one person's fate is at stake in the decision. This would be the case where the decision is whether to carry out a difficult medical procedure. Clearly, this is for the patient themself to decide (if they are able), though they must listen to the advice of family and doctors before deciding because the participants all have a stake.

Majority is appropriate where the participants are reliant on solidarity. If "we're all in this together," then different factions simply have to tolerate one another and solidarise around the majority decision. So there is neither reason nor opportunity to patiently wait for consensus. This is obviously the case in the labour movement where solidarity on the picket line is an existential question. But more generally, Majority applies where the project owns some asset – property, income, the support of a membership or the authority of government – which cannot be split up without drastic loss for the participants. It is normal in such projects for participants to hold radically incompatible concepts of the object of the activity, such that consensus is likely to be out of reach in any case.

Consensus applies when the participants' main asset is each other, so a minority always has the capacity to go their own way. Under these conditions, it is necessary to have the patience needed to find a compromise or "third way" with others you disagree with, but if you can't reach consensus you can go your own way. It is often overlooked that parting ways is always on the table when trying to reach consensus. It is not necessary to tolerate others you don't respect, but if you are working with someone then you pay them the respect of trying to reach consensus with them.

Laissez faire is appropriate either where there is no joint project, or where participants believe that the object is best achieved by each party acting according to their own lights, as is likely to be the case in art, science, religion and philosophy, where consensus may be illusive and majority decisions absurd.

As discussed above in the section on agency, I do not believe that any of the three paradigms of collective decision making really lend themselves to analysis by units below the level of the Yes/No decision itself. They are essentially *systems* of decision making with several distinct elements and more importantly specific *procedures* for decision making.

Counsel is a form of collective decision making in which the final decision (to which all must consent) is the decision of one well-informed human being. Consequently, Counsel is capable of making indefinitely concrete decisions. People sometimes doubt whether Counsel is really a *collective* form of decision making. It is, because the Chief takes advice from all participants, and because it is the decision of one well-informed person, it is an exceptionally powerful paradigm of decision making.

Counsel is the typical paradigm of decision making in medical contexts – the patient, whose welfare is on the line, is Chief, and the doctors advise the patient. In some circumstances, a specialist is the Chief who makes the decision which lies within their area of specialism, but with the advice of others in other specialisms. It is also the predominant mode of decision making in civil disputes inasmuch as the judge makes the final decision after listening to the evidence and arguments of opposing counsel.

On the other hand, Majority and Consensus can only make decisions of a Yes/No type. Concrete decisions are made by a series of Yes/No decisions. This is particularly important in Majority. Anyone concerned with enhancing the power of a participant in some project should, like Horton, first of all be training them in making decisions of this kind, – i.e., a series of Yes/No collective decisions. Every concrete decision can be broken down into a series of Yes/No choices. This sounds like a really crude concept of decision making, and indeed it is; that is the price for making collective decisions. On the other hand, it is often the case that a Majority decision mandates an Executive who is responsible for implementing the decision and it may be at this stage that the decision is fully concretised using Consensus.

If there is a unit of collective decision making it would be the collective Yes/ No decision. But concretely, participating in Majority or Consensus demands familiarity and fluency in applying the procedures for each mode.*

Horton made training activists in decision making the focus of the training program at his Highlander Centre in rural Tennessee. In the 1930s, he trained the trade unionists who went on to found the CIO organising low-paid workers in the US in *Robert's Rules of Order*, and in the 1950s he trained the activists who would go on to found the SNCC and the Birmingham Bus Boycott in Consensus Decision Making, and later he trained the Civil Rights workers who ran the literacy program which gave African Americans the chance to use their right to vote.

These procedures have been developed over a long historical period in certain cultures and not others. If these procedures are not present in a culture, then it is essential to the prospects of success of any emancipatory social movement that activists learn one or other means of collective decision making.

• • •

Psychology generally has a poor record in understanding collective decision making. Moscovici & Doise (1994) for example, declared that decisions could appeal to one of three authorities: tradition, science and consensus, and concluded that science produced the best decisions. Insofar as this makes any sense at all it can only be a tautology. Sannino, as outlined earlier, effectively took deliberation as making suggestions until hitting on a consensus view. Generally speaking psychologists have ignored the fact that decision making is governed first of all by *ethical* norms rather than cognitive efficacy, with moral revulsion for decision processes which contradict deeply held cultural norms.

1.4   *Transforming the Object-Concept*

Transforming the object-concept of a project is a means by which individual action can bring about real social change, mediated by participation in the project. Generally speaking, individuals can only change the world in collaboration with others, that is, by joining a collaborative project. Normally, collaborative projects act within fixed cultural norms and individual actions within a project are constrained by norms specific to that project. So the crucial act

---

* For Majority see https://www.marxists.org/glossary/terms/s/t.htm#standing-orders, and for Consensus see https://www.marxists.org/glossary/terms/c/o.htm#consensus-decision -making.

of self-determination that a person does is to make a commitment to a chosen collaborative project.

In projects with equitable conditions for participation, the object-concept can be changed by rational argument. In general, the object concept of a project and the associated norms do develop over time in response to experience and as a result of deliberation. That is why we say that a project is a learning process. So even if there is no project which is pursuing an object perfectly in line with your aims, if you make a commitment to a project then you have the opportunity to change the object of the activity.

Activities (or projects or practices) are meso-level forms of human activity. You cannot change the economy or save the planet, but you can change the aims of an economic venture or environmental project and that project may contribute to changing the economy or saving the planet. Commitment to a project is essential to giving a meaning to "agency" beyond arranging the deck chairs on the planetary Titanic.

Decision making in projects is governed by norms, and these norms may frustrate participants who cannot find a way of contributing or whose suggestions are dismissed out of hand. As Gutiérrez et al. (2019) have suggested, bringing about changes in the object-concept of a project almost inevitably entails *transgressing* the norms of the project. This is because the dominant norms are themselves special determinations of the object-concept.

Sannino's work suggests that changing the object of an activity entails finding a way to *reframe* the object concept, rather than accepting the terms of debate and trying to change the agenda simply by patient deliberation in branch meetings.

Stetsenko's work confirms the experience of many activists that if you want to change the direction of a project then you have to take on the burden of doing the basic work of the movement in its current configuration. The leadership role that flows from taking on the work gives a person greater opportunity to reframe the object-concept.

So now we see how to take hold of the helm on the Titanic, but is that enough? An individual can only change the world by participating in a project, but can *succeed* only to the extent that the project can find support in other projects.

1.5   *Relations between Projects*

Putting the problem of how to change the world very succinctly: people will do what they do; everyone has their commitments and will participate in projects of their choice. But what determines whether this results in any change of direction in the world situation depends on *how projects support one another*.

The relationship between projects is, so far as I know, theorised by activity theorists other than this author only by recourse to the limited notion of "boundary object." The whole point of using a unit of analysis is to deploy an understanding of the unit to understand the larger phenomena resulting from the aggregation of a large number of such units. This can only be done, however, given a conception of how different units (projects or activities or practices) *interact with each other*.

How does knowing that the unit of analysis of water is the H_2O molecule help us understand how water can form clouds, rain, rivers, oceans, icebergs, sleet and steam? Without going into molecular physics, the key is in the shape of the H_2O molecule together with the effect of heat. Molecular physics does not call upon some molecular connecting device to bind water molecules together in various ways: the clue is in the shape of the water molecule itself and the H and O bonds. Likewise, we must look to the activity itself and its object-concept to understand how an activity interacts with other projects.

The method of using a "boundary object" to theorise interaction between two or more activities has been used by Engeström in the scenario that some object (for example, homelessness in Finland) is the object of different "systems of activity," e.g., different NGOs are addressing the problem of homelessness. As it happens, it is not only the *Arbeitsgegenstand* (the object worked upon) which is shared: competing projects also share cultural norms, stakeholders and some resources. The nature of the collaboration will depend on points of agreement and difference in the object-concepts of the competing projects. On top of this we have the boundary object, which is the same for all the participating projects, but is the object-concept of some other activity. When illustrated in a diagram, the boundary object representation of this scenario looks like a bowl of spaghetti. The point of having a unit of analysis of activity is to be able to grasp activity as a whole. A theoretical image which is more complicated than the object it represents defeats the whole purpose of analysis by units.

The original idea of "boundary object" was as infrastructure, either an artefact such as a library, or an activity such as a political system, which is meant to serve the aims of all relevant projects. Analysis always discloses, however, that the supposedly neutral object is a reification of a certain social position and furthers the aims of that social position rather than others. Everyone uses the boundary object, but disabled people may find that the library was never meant for them, and the given political system suits some political projects better than others. A boundary object is more likely a shared means than a shared object.

• • •

As a side benefit of my (Blunden, 2016a) study of collective decision making I theorised the relations and interactions *between* projects in terms of how a project *assists* another project. I identified three different modes of collaboration between different projects based on how a first project lends supports a second project:

(v) Colonisation (or philanthropy) is the first relationship under which one project supports another: the first project simply takes over the second project. This was instanced when, for example, France colonised Algeria and used the land and labour of the local people to further the national aims of France. Algeria was made a Department of France in 1848 but this incorporation brought little benefit to the people of Algeria. Nonetheless, for better or worse, Algerians were drawn into the Francophone cultural world and Algerian culture and national consciousness were suppressed.

This is the same relation as when a charity like the Salvation Army rescues a destitute person off the streets, houses and feeds them and then inducts them into the religious life of the Army. This relation is quite general: large firms take over struggling competitors, and powerful trade unions can come to the rescue of groups of workers whether or not they want to be rescued. Likewise, some left-wing groups seem to be based on a program of colonisation inasmuch as their social base is very limited and yet they aspire to lead the entire country and manifest little interest in building coalitions. Even the best revolutionary governments who take power at the head of a powerful movement, but then lose popularity, can end up as colonisers.

The problem with colonising a project is that their body may be rescued but their soul is lost. In recruiting them to your project you destroy their spirit. So colonisation is the last resort when a project is defunct and the people need to be rescued. But researchers need to take care to avoid the attitude of the philanthropist; helping people out with your own good ideas may do more harm than help.

(vi) Negotiation (or bargaining or exchange) is the normative relation between independent subjects in bourgeois society. Businesses live by buying and selling from each other, bargaining in good faith and dealing with each other fairly. Workers and their trade unions bargain with the employers for the price and conditions of their labour-power. This kind of wheeling and dealing is equally common in international politics, everyday life and politics. It is marked by mutual recognition, respect for the other project and autonomy. Projects make a deal for mutual benefit and then go their own way, or make limited agreements for co-existence which do not interfere with their mission. Social bonds may develop as a side effect of these external relations between projects, however. This is the normal relation between a researcher and a research subject in mainstream positivist science; subjects may be paid for their participation, just like wage workers.

Negotiation should not be confused with Consensus. In Consensus, the parties are committed to a common project throughout. In Negotiation, the parties are happy to walk away if no benefit is on offer, and any agreement made is only pro tem.

(vii) Solidarity is practised when one project goes to the aid of another but instead of colonising the other, offers to work *under the direction of the other*. It asks "How can I help?" Both parties retain their independence but each develops from the engagement, while the weaker party endeavours to regain control of its own activity while the supporting party has the capacity to limit its commitment according to exigencies.

Solidarity is the ethic of the workers' movement, having entered the English language from the French at the Chartist Convention in London in April 1848 and written into the Rules of the International Workingmen's Association in 1864. Solidarity is the ethic which guides activity theorists in their interventions and will be further discussed below.

The three paradigmatic modes of relation between projects – Colonisation, Negotiation and Solidarity – may subsume one another in concrete interactions. For example, in wage labour Colonisation is subsumed under Negotiation because once the workers have sold their labour-power they work under the direction of the employer; Collaboration as such may be subsumed under Solidarity when supporters participate in the other project's activity.

Collaboration as such refers to that situation where independent projects voluntarily give up their independence and merge their membership, assets and activity. When this is achieved, the object-concept of each of the projects must be merged, each modifying and including the other. This is the stage when a social movement completely penetrates an institution and no separate existence seems necessary.

An example of collaboration as such is seen when the WLM in Australian penetrated the ACTU (Australian Council of Trade Unions) leading to the ACTU establishing a Working Women's Centre within its own structure. The WWC became an energetic centre which drafted policy and legislation against sexual harassment, identified the impact of the gender division of labour on the Equal Pay fight and formulated the demand "Equal Pay for Work of Equal Value!" thus projecting the distinctive concept of Socialist Feminism.

Helena Worthen (2021) identified what she called "inside/outside organisation" through her participation in efforts to unionise casual academics in the US. Casual (a.k.a. "contingent" or "sessional") academics are the precariat of academia and up to the present their interests have been poorly represented by the unions representing "faculty" (i.e., academics with permanent positions). Casual academics have networked and met independently of union structures and combined to pressure the unions representing faculty to provide effectively for academics in precarious employment conditions. Essentially the same relation is in play when refugees demand that the union defend them or when women call upon a male-dominated union to do something about equal pay and misogyny in their own ranks and their collaboration in depressing the working conditions of women. This relation is a kind of converse to solidarity in that the weaker party uses its strength to attract the solidarity of a stronger project.

In all these practical relationships, both projects are *changed* even if the *coloniser* incorporates only caricatured versions of the colonised culture. This path may lead to disaster, but most modern nations are built on such conquest. Alternatively, in *Exchange* a mechanical relationship between projects arises in which each adapts whatever elements of the other's culture suit them and co-exist. The result is an "ethnic mozaic" kind of "multiculturalism" which leaves in place the contradictions within and between the projects, often leading to further fragmentation. This is increasingly the dominant relationship of our time.

In the case of solidarity, there is a genuine learning between the parties and the prospect of genuine collaboration as such emerges. Solidarity is the ethos of the future running counter to postmodern fragmentation.

In general then, activity theorists are guided by the ethos of solidarity in their research and intervention work.

1.6   The Urpraxis of a Movement

An Urpraxis is a germ cell form of practice. The Urpraxis of a movement is the most vital concept for understanding its development and fate. This is the simple action, which if universally practised, constitutes the guiding ideal of the movement.

"Urpraxis" is derived from the German: "Ur-" is a prefix meaning archetypal, as in *Urtext* or *Urwir*, or *Urphänomen*, and *Praxis* is the German word for practice. So, Urpraxis means a germ-cell practice, a simple form of practice, easily understood in its own right without calling upon any theoretical frame, which has the potential to grow and develop into an entirely new social formation.

The Urpraxis of a movement is the simplest form of practice which encapsulates the new world to which a movement aspires and expresses its ethos. What the Urpraxis of a movement may be is not immediately obvious, but requires reflection.

Marx showed that doing a deal (exchange) is the Urpraxis of bourgeois society and specifically, buying in order to sell at a profit is the Urpraxis of capitalism. The Urpraxis of Socialism is solidarity (more on this below), but what is the Urpraxis of Women's Emancipation?

This is not me for to determine, but my thought would be that it is the refusal of a woman (or the refusal to expect of a woman) to do "women's work," since it is the gender division of labour which is at the root of the oppression of women. Women can be considered emancipated in a world in which gender has nothing to do with labour. As Beauvoir (1949) points out, there are features of a woman's biology (menstruation and pregnancy, for example) from which women may never be free (other than in exceptional instances). All that can be done is to arrange affairs so that so far as possible the burden of a woman's reproductive functions is shared so she has access to equal participation in the labour process.

I have focused on the gender division of labour because I think that if women were not tied to "women's work," then political and social emancipation follows with necessity. But I may be wrong. Domestic patriarchy makes it impossible for a woman to compete in the labour market on an equal footing with a man. Patriarchy in the workplace makes achievement of equality at home impossible because the woman is always more or less dependent on her husband. But it seems to me that "women's work" is at the heart of this wickedness.

But this was not always clear. Even in the 1970s and 1980s there were women who doubted this ideal and instead proposed that women *celebrate* their femininity, just as at a certain point in the Civil Rights Movement in the US, the slogan of "Black is beautiful!" was raised. But surely this conception which affirms difference is a transitory conception aimed at overcoming negative stereotypes.

But what about "celebrating difference"? There are differences which will remain disabilities, so long as the wider society fails to *adjust itself* so as to open the way to equal participation for those who for this or that reason cannot participate on an equal footing. In her critical discussion of the notion of "recognition," Fraser (2003) advocated "parity of participation" as a criterion upon which emancipation could be measured. Equality of participation in domestic labour, and equality of participation in the world of work. Difference does not contradict emancipation so long equality of participation is achieved.

In reflecting on social movements I have focused half of what I have had to say to consideration of the Women's Liberation Movement because the women's movement is the most fully developed of any kind of project (or activity or social practice) and exhibits *all* the phenomena which it is the business of Activity Theory to understand.

The point is that *any* activity has the potential to exhibit the wide range of features identified in the above paragraphs. Consequently, these concepts abstracted from and mostly illustrated in the Women's Liberation and other movements provide a pallet of ideas for the analysis of more limited, less developed activities which an Activity Theorist may need to analyse.

CHAPTER 8

Incoherent Activities

Not all activities live up to the norm of being a collaborative project like the WLM. I have already considered the limiting case of the social movement "in itself," the "social non-movement" in which the relevant actions are *not yet* collaborative.

And I have considered the case of an individual life-course as a limiting case of a collaborative project in which *one person* alone is the object of every action and the object of all the actions therein is simply to live a good life.

But some activities *fall short* of the ideal altogether because the participants are acting either with no clear conception of what they are aiming at or they are are doing what they are doing *for its own sake* entirely, or their collaborative activity is so wildly misdirected and heterogeneous, their stated aim so implausible, so unstable and incoherent that it cannot be understood as an object-oriented activity, except perhaps that at some point in the future the meaning of their activity may *become clear* to the participants.

In general, it is said that such phenomena are 'not now' projects in the full sense of the word. They may *never* overcome this underdevelopment, but they can be analysed as practices (or activities or projects) which are underdeveloped, degenerated or distorted in some way, or in terms of radically inappropriate mismatch of understood and effective motives.

I consider several such cases below, for if we wish to understand the world and take "activity" as our substance, then we cannot have the luxury of saying: "Well, this is not an activity."

1   *Activities Characterised by a Shared* Motif

The idea of using *motif* I have appropriated from a paper by Morten Nissen (Banks, Neergaard & Nissen, 2021). Nissen's work deals with a group of social workers serving marginalised young drug users in Copenhagen. He points out that the word "*motif*" in Germanic languages translates as "motive" in English as well as "motif" in the sense in which it is used as a concept in aesthetics.

To use a concept of aesthetics in the characterisation of an activity is to take the activity under an aesthetic frame, that is, to view it as a work of art. To take an activity as a work of art, to regard it aesthetically, does not presuppose that the motive of the producer was aesthetic.

Aesthetics differs from a theory of practice precisely because in aesthetics, an activity may be judged to be virtuous and enjoyed without the implication that the practice serves the observer's or anyone else's practical interest or needs. That is, it is judged from the opposite standpoint from that of *object-oriented* activity theory. Virtue is appreciated for its own sake, whatever may have been the intention of the actor. This contradiction lies behind appreciating Leni Riefenstahl's movies or Wagner's operas.

Vygotsky viewed art in terms of its capacity to illicit emotions in the viewer, creatively producing an artefact which gives material form to an inner feeling, reproducing in the reader the experience of the author, and evoking a kindred emotion in the audience. Emotions lie at the root of concepts and are the spring of action. Vygotsky's theory of creativity is a subject of great interest among Vygotsky scholars at the present moment, and the insight that activities can be judged through an aesthetic frame offers new avenues for the development of Vygotsky's ideas.

A motif is an element of a work which invests the whole work with its particular aesthetic (emotional) character. It can be a single element whose content 'spills out' and drives the unfolding of the work (such as a striking event which is echoed in a series of consequent events making up the plot of a novel), or it may be a pattern which repeats itself, perhaps in successive forms, driving the development of the whole (such as is common in musical works). Thus a motif is a simple element which characterises the whole practice, and therefore gives a possible means of *grasping the activity as a whole* and characterising its distinctive character alongside other activities, without *reducing* the work to that one figure. And yet, "motif" falls short of *"object."*

Nissen et al. use the idea of motif somewhat indirectly; a young person is invited to make a short video on any topic that takes their fancy, and the video is analysed aesthetically with the assistance of a professional film-maker, with the aim of determining the motif which is "driving" the action in the video. The suggestion is that this motif has been transferred from their own life experience. By making this motif objective and explicit, the young person shares this inner feeling with the social worker in a way that astonishes and engages them in productive shared reflection.

The first thing this idea provides is the opportunity to mobilise the insights of art criticism for a psychological purpose, to regard a young person's activities not from the point of view of the object they are self-consciously trying to realise, but less developed, embryonic motivations, motivations which have not yet developed to the point of conscious awareness, but are still at the stage of emotion. In a case cited in Neergaard & Nissen's paper, a young drug user had made a movie by placing the camera on his bicycle. The adviser remarked that the motif of the video was "hanging on." This opened the youth to reflecting on this truth about his life at that moment.

We can take emotions as *germ cells of activities*, the germ cells of reasons for acting that have not yet reached conscious awareness (Blunden, 2017), but embodied in a creative artefact and revealed by aesthetic analysis.

We can look at a person's life-project through this aesthetic lens.

What unites the series of actions, archetypically all executed by the same person, is not an object-concept as such. Leontyev would (if he were to be consistent) respond that the activity which lacks an explicit and understood motive must have a "subjectively and objectively hidden motive," and this may indeed be exactly the case. It may be that the motive has not yet come into consciousness, but yet is expressed aesthetically.

But let us suppose that the motive is not hidden from the subject or the observer. For example, a group of youth engage in a football game or a man joins a bushwalking club or a chess club. There is nothing hidden about the motive here. On the other hand, these activities are enjoyed in their own right not as goals serving a more remote motive. It could be claimed that the motives of these activities are social needs like sociability, fitness, rehabilitation, and so on, and so are not problematic and in need of a distinctive analysis. Nevertheless, the activity which is enjoyed for its own sake rather than by bringing some *Arbeitsgegenstand* into conformity with its object-concept is in a sense an archetypal activity precisely because it is not subordinate to some greater project: its object does not lie outside of itself.

But the example of the young drug users belies the claim that such activities are necessarily only enjoyed in themselves and lack social implications and are not in need of theoretical analysis. All creative activities offer insights into the social conditions surrounding the artist and are definitively *social* not merely individual activities.

1.1   *The Solar Punk Youth Movement*

The Solar Punk youth movement is an example of a social movement which cannot be grasped as an object-oriented activity, except in the sense that the object develops from a germ cell which is purely aesthetic.

My niece participates in this social movement. What these young people do is share ideas about technologically wired, sustainable and humane possible future forms of social life. This is *not* a movement *aimed* at *bringing about* such a future. The bitter political struggle which is entailed in *that* project is quite unwelcome within Solar Punk. They are indifferent to accusations of utopianism just as a science fiction reader or writer would be indifferent to that accusation. To cast Solar Punk as an object-oriented activity, and to ask what its object is, would be to misunderstand it. The young people participate for the internal rewards enjoyed in this activity. The movement is collaborative in its ethos and is surely of considerable social and political interest.

1.2 The Anti-vax Campaign against Public Health Measures

The anti-vax campaign against public health measures is past its peak at the time of writing, and by the time this appears in print I hope that there will be a number of books on the shelves of bookshops analysing what this movement was about. At the time of writing, however, I see no satisfactory account.

The anti-vax movement defies analysis if we conceive of it as an object-oriented activity and we take its object at face value. If it is to be judged as an object-oriented activity, its apparent motive is to bring about a libertarian dystopia in which there is no moral or legal restraint on any individual's actions including the right to spread infectious disease. This is apparently the "merely known motive." The effective motive for which individuals join, it seems, is that they want to overthrow some particular legal restraint on their activity such as vaccine or mask mandates or lockdown measures.

But doesn't this belie the *motif* of the movement which expresses a kind of egoistic entitlement and unbounded misanthropy? And if we were to take the explicit motive of freedom from government interference at face value, why is is that white supremacist parties are so prominent in organising anti-vax and anti-mask protests? These are people who, far from professing a libertarian ideal, stand for the most repressive kind of state-enforced communitarianism. The same people who angrily defend their right to *not* wear a mask, condemn others for wearing a mask. The same people who angrily defend their right to spread an infectious disease, in Texas, deny the right of women to abortion. The libertarianism is highly selective!

Does it make sense to say that the motif of the protests is the feeling of entitlement held by those social strata who believe that they are being displaced by other social strata flowing from the changing nature of the labour process and increasing international mobility? That these strata feel a class resentment at the loss of their miserable privileges and express this is an exaggerated display of entitlement? And that this motif is more significant than the ostensible object of the protest?

Is this contradiction between the immediate claims of participants and the dystopian object of the protest encompassed by Leontyev's distinction between the merely known motive (a libertarian dystopia) and really effective motive (assertion of personal entitlement)? It seems that the effective motive for participants in the anti-mandate and anti-vax protests was very diverse. One march in Melbourne included building workers opposing mask mandates so that they could go to work on building sites, Christians claiming that God would protect them, people claiming rights under the 14th Amendment to the US (*sic!*) Constitution and white supremacists carrying Nazi symbols. The march stopped for a few minutes as it crossed the West Gate Bridge, so that the Muslims could have a prayer session! For most participants it seemed that there was an immediate, personal motivation for participation in the movement, but these immediate motivations seamlessly morphed into utopian visions in which everyone's own conception of freedom was realised, however incompatible with everyone else's.

I know of no Activity Theory analysis of this movement, but it needs to be done. In what way do such movements give us any hint of their future evolution? In Australia, the protests gradually exhausted themselves in the face of intransigence on the part of the State governments and paralysis of the Federal government, but in the US we see the anti-health movement capturing government in places like Texas. It would seem that such complex processes need to be analysed through an aesthetic rather than a pragmatic lens.

• • •

Activity Theory is an *active* approach to the world. From its very beginnings, Activity Theory has developed through intervening in the world. Vygotsky, for example, revealed the fundamental character of cognition by offering cultural artefacts to children who were trying to solve some puzzle, and from this germ cell Activity Theorists leant how to teach functionally illiterate children to read by assisting them in using texts to understand the world. Activity Theorists have gone on from education of children to transforming institutions such as schools and hospitals. But Activity Theorists soon discovered that, in general, even the best designed school would not survive without the active support of the community it serves. What ever happened to Dewey's Laboratory School? Why aren't there hundreds of these schools 100 years later? No human problem can be solved in isolation. Thus, Activity Theorists have moved to tackling the sources of problems in the social environment itself.

From here I shall move to consider those research projects in which Activity Theories have subordinated their research aims to the aim of transforming the world, planting the seeds for a future world.

CHAPTER 9

Formative Interventions

1 Construction of Utopian Forms of Activity as Educational Artefacts

The construction of utopian forms of activity for young people excluded by the school system has been used by activity theorists. I shall begin, however, with a couple of heroic counter-examples.

In 1993, the right-wing government in Victoria announced the closure of Richmond Secondary School, a public high school located in an idyllic riverside locale and servicing the working class community of inner city Richmond. The local community objected and with leadership from a Marxist activist, and the support of the Victorian Trade Union movement, and socialist and anarchist groups, the school was occupied using *direct action* and the school remained open thanks to an unemployed teacher who volunteered their labour. "Enrolment" shrank however, as the majority of parents accepted offers to place their children in other nearby schools. The occupation was eventually broken up by a ruthless police attack and a new high school for 180 students now occupies the site.

The occupation is remembered by the Left in Melbourne as an heroic last ditch struggle against the then newly elected right-wing Kennett government, but it would be very difficult to establish that any pupil benefited from the occupation, or that the education provided during the occupation served as any kind of model for progressive education. No one benefited apart from a small group or activists and a handful of youth who for once in their lives found themselves at the centre of everyone's attention.

According to Anarchists, this kind of *direct action* is the best means of mobilising the poor and working class to solve their own problems by their own collective action. In the light of the founding documents of the International Workingmen's Association (Marx, 1864), this seems to be exactly what is required: self-emancipation by the solidarity of the working class itself! But to see in this albeit heroic action the self-emancipation of the working class is to see the world through rose tinted glasses. Only a small group of parents participated for any period of time, the support of the union movement was little more than symbolic and the formerly unemployed teacher struggled to maintain the low standard of education offered in the school before its closure was announced. If the local community learnt anything from the experience, it is unlikely to have been the virtues of direct action in achieving emancipation.

The same comments apply to the *Occupy!* movement which was initiated in Wall Street in 2011. Whatever else may be said about this movement, it focused on *economic inequality* after several decades in which protests against oppression located in the economic structure had been marginalised by the identity movements which had followed in the wake of the great unifying struggles of the Civil Rights and the Women's Liberation movements. This was an important gain which has proved irreversible.

However, the aims of *Occupy!* went beyond making an effective protest and putting inequality back on the agenda. It aimed to plant the seeds of a new kind of popular democracy in which the ideals of "horizontalism" would be fostered as people learnt to participate in making collective decisions in big open air "general assemblies" and delegation and majority voting were eschewed.

In reality, these general assemblies were largely dysfunctional and never had the potential to scale up much further than a voice can carry in the open air. In other words, the protests were tied to an anarchist conception of direct action and "contamination," i.e., witnessing the successful and exhilarating general assemblies people would be inspired to adopt this kind of decision making in other parts of their life. Of course, no such thing ever happened. The last weeks of the protest were marred by drummers who refused to stop their incessant drumming, which made the assemblies intolerable, and no one was willing to stop them, until the police moved in, took it out of their hands and broke the whole thing up. A small core of anarchist activists was trained in these practices and moved around the world to participate in further "convergences" but aside from a welcome and timely increased awareness of economic inequality, there was little impact on the wider population.

Nonetheless, there are some indelible truths in these direct actions. It is true that people learn from direct participation in political processes and such participation is a sine qua non of the achievement of socialism or any degree of social progress. It is true that direct action is meaningless if it does not succeed in engaging the active support of the relevant community. But still, a powerful protest even by a few individuals can make a point, and both the actions mentioned above did that. But above all an action must be successful in what it claims to some degree if it is to have the desired progressive impact. A direct action – housing homeless people in rundown slums for example – which does not meet the original need is good for the activists but worse than useless for the homeless people.

The most significant ideas of direct action are that it aims (1) to mobilise the subjects themselves to (2) successfully solve the problem at issue, rather than focus on government to come to their rescue. Calling on government to solve a problem means not tackling the problem itself but instead focusing on protest, and is not part of direct action. Calling on government to solve a problem is distinct from mobilising to change or overthrow a government which has failed to act, which is ultimately the only way of finding an enduring solution.

Insofar as protesting effectively can be a vehicle for bringing a community together in defence of its own interests, protest can be a very good thing. It is generally going to be the first reflex of an aggrieved community. Failure in that first reflex can provide the impulse to go beyond protest and seek their own solution to a problem. It is possible that a community does not have within its own ranks the expertise required to solve the problem, but they may be moved to *ask* for that assistance, and when a community asks for assistance then this is an opportunity to which Activity Theorists need to respond.

An exemplar of *this* kind of direct action was that given by Horton's Highlander Centre which offered training for workers engaged in struggle, beginning in the 1930s and continuing to this day (Blunden, 2016a). An even more significant educational intervention is the 5th Dimension, an initiative led by Cole and others which continues to proliferate to this day (See Cole et al., 2014).

1.1   Mike Cole et al.'s 5th Dimension

The 5th Dimension was initiated in 1987 in response to a request to investigate the phenomenon of so called "learning disabled" children, a "disability" which only manifested itself in school classrooms. When the researchers endeavoured to videorecord what was happening in the classroom, the teachers politely asked them to take their cameras elsewhere. Rather than abandon the children to a school system which was systematically failing them, they decided to themselves undertake the task of teaching them to read outside of the formal school setting. The school agreed that the researchers could set up an after-school program available to the children who were failing to learn in the classroom.

A prototype called "The 5th Dimension" was set up:

> The 5th Dimension was fashioned loosely on a "Dungeons and Dragons" metaphor, which was popular with children at the time we began this work and has continued to have a life of its own in cyberspace. A large space was arranged with computers scattered about, often near the walls, in such a way as to allow two or three people to use a single screen to work together on solving a puzzle. A physical maze was placed in a prominent position, with a few entrances and exits and many doorways between rooms.

Each room contained a card with the name of two activities on it, at least one of which was likely to be a computer game. The children would each have a physical avatar, a "cruddy creature" they could use until they demonstrated some proficiency in achieving a high level of performance in some minimal number of 5th Dimension-related tasks. There were many artefacts provided to encourage literacy and numeracy: a "task card" specified the performance necessary to move up levels within the 5th Dimension (including, of course, the game itself), a hints book contained tips for people who wanted to succeed quickly, tips that the children wrote to complete task cards. A playful Wizard would sometimes appear on the rickety computer network we had set up to enable chat with the children, and to give an air of mystery to the 5th Dimension itself. And so on. Lots of enticing tasks, lots of choice, undergraduate students present to help out when the going got tough or participants just hang around and chat while waiting for someone to finish using a game you want to play. An afterschool micro-world/club, with its own local cultural norms, favoured practices, standout personalities, and an enormous diversity of children contented to spend their time engaging with the program and each other several times a week.

COLE ET AL., 2014

This prototype succeeded in *attracting* children, who attended voluntarily for the enjoyable activity and social interactions. 5thD provided an environment for collaborative learning, and initial evaluation demonstrated some improvement of participants' performance in school, and parents were positive about the program. Following Wartofsky's schema, Cole refers to the 5thD as a 'tertiary artefact':

which can come to constitute a relatively autonomous 'world', in which rules, conventions and outcomes no longer appear directly practical, or which, indeed, seem to constitute an arena of non-practical, or 'free' play or game activity.

WARTOFSKY, 1973, p. 208

As creative and effective as this idea was, many equally effective models, such as Dewey's Laboratory School back in the 1920s, had come and gone. The point was not so much the model of teaching, but how to *sustain* it! All previous attempts to reform school education along similar lines had disappeared without a trace.

The 5thD model was a collaboration between a *university* with a course in Education and Psychology whose students needed opportunities for field work, and a *community institution*. The community institution could be a youth club, library, hospital, school, church or whatever – some entity which wanted to provide after-school activities for local youth, had premises and could provide at least one staff member to supervise the site. Note that "the community" was not treated by Cole et al. as an abstract phenomenon (c.f. the Richmond Secondary College project mentioned above), but was determined as a specific really-existing project indigenous to the community.

The initial 5thD project was funded by the Mellon Foundation for six years, but after that it would have to survive on its own resources. It turned out that a 5thD would survive on average three years before some problem would emerge: the library needed quiet, problems arose with insurance, the demographics of the suburb changed, the Health and Safety demands became prohibitive, the responsible Dean at the university changed, ... The demands, especially on the community hosting organisation, were often formidable. Even though the organisation, the young people, the parents and the grad. students all loved the project, sooner or later something always went wrong for which there were not resources to fix.

The research team met regularly and all these issues and their work-arounds were recorded and provided data for later research. Although the *average* life span was three years, some lasted much longer and some are still operational today 35 years later. In the meantime 5thD has been replicated in over 120 sites across the US and in countries across the globe. In order for even the best-designed school to be sustainable amidst a constantly changing social environment, it is necessary for it to maintain the active support, not just of the community *in general*, but of institutions which themselves have an enduring place in the community. Research conducted by Cole over the past 35 years, during which some projects have succeeded in living as long as the researchers themselves, has developed a deep knowledge of why good projects fail and how an institution like 5thD can be sustained in a late-capitalist environment like the USA, usually without government support and without the ongoing support of any funding agency.

Cole calls this approach to research "mesogenetic methodology" for the way the project develops over a time span less than historical, more than episodic, approximating the life span of the individual researcher. Mesogenetic methodology allows concrete knowledge of a practice to be developed such that the project *reproduces itself out of its conditions*, and does not fade away when the creator leaves or the funder pulls out. The project thus becomes a genuinely *living* entity, reproducing itself out of its environment. Decades-long commitment is required to achieve this goal. Not only is *lasting change* produced, but a deep understanding is gained of the processes which *undermine* progressive reforms.

Cole now refers to this methodology as "utopian methodology" inasmuch as the method creates a "utopia." It is "utopian" because it is an effective educational institution which attracts the voluntary participation of the young people, and, because it is an imaginary world, in the heart of an environment in which the education system is generally a mere means for sustaining and reproducing the class system. It is not isolated in a lost valley in the Himalayas or forgotten island (normally the required condition for utopias) but exists *in daily interchange* with the normally hostile context of late capitalism. Perhaps the best way to understand the use of "utopia" is as a rhetorical response to demands to "be realistic" and accept the oppressive education system the state provides and beg for minor improvements, as a *rejection* of the capitalist reality.

The capacity of a utopian project to live in constant interchange with a capitalist environment is of exceptional interest for the anti-capitalist struggle, for it is hardly likely that a social arrangement which cannot live within a capitalist environment could overthrow it and/or survive incipient bourgeois relations after an overthrow. Such a living ideal is not only *concrete* (in the sense of actually existing) but is independent of state or charitable support, and can actively survive the pressure of bourgeois habits. A utopia on the other hand is something which can only exist in isolation because it would disintegrate on first contact with the real world.

From the very beginning, 5thD was simultaneously a *research* project (to discover how apparently "learning disabled" youth could learn to read), a *training* program for postgraduate students, *and* a *research* program into the conditions for the achievement of social progress.

The 5thD project is a model for Activity Theory research in Child Development, Psychology and Education.

1.2   *Aydin Bal's Learning Lab*

Aydin Bal's interventions aimed at overcoming barriers to the education of indigenous youth is another exemplary model of an Activity Theory intervention. Bal was active in social movements fighting against inequality, but wanted to use his academic knowledge to *do* something about inequality and racism in schools. Then he learnt about Engeström's DWR, and developed his own variation on the approach, which I outline below (Bal, 2021).

Bal and his colleagues would identify schools where indigenous students were failing to achieve the results which their white fellows were achieving. They would then approach the principal and ask if they would be willing to change that if it meant allowing the school's stakeholders to take control of designing the school's modus operandi. In what follows, "community" refers to the governing structure of the local tribal nation.

If the principal consented, they would then spend a full year meeting with the local indigenous community, encouraging them to take the principal's commitment seriously and work out among themselves what needed to be done; the community also decided *who* was to participate in meetings. Once the community had formulated clear goals, the team approached the school administration and asked them to present to the school's stakeholders (including the teachers) a "map" of the school's system. A "Learning Lab" would be set up composed of administrators (principals, vice principals, and the deans of students), teachers, support staff (e.g., librarians, counsellors, playground attendants) along with family members, students, and community leaders/ members (tribal government's secretary of education). The Lab would then thoroughly critique this map, pooling the knowledge of this wider group, as it invariably turned out that the administration did not in fact know how their own school actually worked!

Throughout this process, the researchers provided food, childcare, translation services, whatever was necessary to achieve full participation by all. Once the *real* structure of the school's activity had been settled, the collective broke into small groups each of which would draft up a "utopian" school system, in which they were told to disregard any limitations of resources, law or resistance by other parties, and simply *imagine* the perfect school system. This direction provided a zone of proximal development in which participants could "play" together to sketch the map a utopian school. By this time, the First Nations people realised that their voice was being heard, that they know as much about the school as the school's administration did and had the confidence to take a lead.

Note that like several of the projects already discussed, this initial phase in which the subject is able to exercise *unrestricted play of the imagination* prior to the introduction of restraints is essential for the creative process and is characteristic of the zone of proximal development when people have to act "above themselves."

In the final phase, the principal joins with a selected group of stakeholders to look over all the utopian proposals and draft out a plan for a reformed school. They present this to the whole group for discussion and seek consensus. Bal's group found that by this stage, their own facilitating role had become redundant; all the stakeholders now trusted the process and were confident that they were being heard, and the school administration has also realised that they have the opportunity to make a better school. The new plan is implemented

and the research group can leave, confident that into the future the indigenous community will be able to see to it that their children are given the best
possible chance to graduate high school without having their own indigenous
culture suppressed.

The remarkable feature of Bal's approach is that he basically uses high level
social movement skills to mobilise the affected group to overthrow their own
system of oppression. But he does so only having already ensured that the
administration is ready to respond to the movement and implement change,
and uses the gravitas of the researcher group to clear the way for a mutually
responsive collaboration. At no point does the research group set a goal or
decide on who should participate, just the various phases as set out above,
which are put before the participants at the outset.

Bal's Learning Lab aims to create a new system of inclusive decision making
which is sustainable and he works with schools for up to three years to achieve
that. Cole demonstrated that a life-long commitment to a project may be necessary both to achieve change and to fully understand the place of a project in
its social environment. The deep roots of the tribal nation in their land guaran-
tees ongoing support for the process.

Bal's approach contrasts with Cole's approach in that Bal sets out to *change
the school*, whereas Cole recognised that the school *could not* be changed sufficiently to overcome the complex problems posed by inner city life in the USA,
and set up the "utopian" school *alongside* the official school. However, both
approaches allowed the participants to design the processes and in both cases
the entire process rested on the active initiative and support of really existing community formations and *not* isolated from the existing conditions. Both
approaches produced outcomes that (all going well) could outlast the support
of the research group. Neither approach entailed any significant involvement
or ongoing support from government or business however, although they did
rely on some level of political support for the reforms being achieved. Both
approaches produced educational results *superior* to the existing mainstream
educational system.

1.3   *Fernanda Liberali's* LACE

Fernanda Liberali's (Liberali & Lemos, 2021) group LACE (Learning in Activities
in the Context of School) in Brazil is as much a social movement as a research
group. It began with a few progressive academics forming a kind of reading
group to explore the various theories of social change, beginning with Paulo
Freire and what they called "critical collaboration." Their idea was to participate
in the struggle of teachers and activists of all kinds, using and enhancing what
they were learning from their reading. Their aim was to form "communities

of change" in which LACE had no particular template they wished to impose, only asking participants to reflect on social change and to think about what is a good life, and learn from their participation.

LACE draws on diverse sources, and these have come to include Russian works on Activity Theory and work by academics around Cole and Engeström, Jean Paul Bronckart's Socio-Discourse Interactionism and Jim Werstch's socio-cultural theory, and over time they developed their own distinctive "Brazilian Activity Theory," a blend of ideas that they referred to as SCHAT: Socio-Cultural Historical Activity Theory. LACE has rarely had a significant amount of funding for any of its projects, which are generally located in the impoverished areas of Brazil. They do not use academic jargon in their fieldwork, but very many members of LACE and their postgraduate students are in fact poor people who have gained their education thanks to interventions by LACE. All their interventions are made in response to demand from communities and remain from the beginning under the control of local actors. By this means, LACE has become a living project, a project which reproduces and renews itself out of its own social environment.

This formation, in which the researchers themselves arise from and serve social movements, with their projects remaining under the control of ongoing associations of the people involved, at the same time, publishing original peer reviewed research of the highest quality for the purpose of learning and building on the funds of experience of fellow activity theorists: this is an ideal to which activity theorists aspire.

2   Postcolonial Projects

Postcolonial projects in the countries which were formerly colonies of the great powers of the 18th and 19th century have a great role to play in the coming period, overcoming the crimes of colonisation and searching for ways of living in this late capitalist world which has brought us to the brink of extinction and plunged billions into poverty and alienation. Activity Theorists have turned their attention to these projects.

Postcolonial project faces some difficult problems. The legacy of colonialism is not homogeneous. The most fundamental ideological characteristics of colonialism originated at the dawn of civilisation, i.e., the emergence of class societies several thousand years ago. The powers which arose in Egypt, Sumeria and the Americas developed practices adapted to the rule of large numbers of people and the management of large concentrations of wealth. These practices include both *literacy*, which is surely an unalloyed good, and *bureaucracy*, which is problematic. Bureaucratic rule ultimately gave us colonial savagery, capitalism and that tick-box mentality which is so dehumanising. Activity Theory arose in the Soviet Union in the struggle against both the oppressive practices of capitalism and the dehumanising positivism which is a variant of that tick-box thinking. But Activity Theory is very much in support of literacy and everything that flows from it.

Teasing apart which components of the colonial inheritance we want to keep and which we want to abolish is a complex question. People in the global North face the same choice actually, though admittedly under very different conditions. Bureaucracy and literacy are not inherently European or North American practices. In fact, both arose outside of Europe and North America, but the way history unfolded meant that it was via Europe that literacy and bureaucracy conquered the world, and did so with unspeakable brutality.

Part of the difficulty is that few in the colonial world want to give up those gains which have been built on the foundation of literacy. They just want their own voices included on an equal footing. Most post-industrial countries have achieved near-universal levels of literacy. Worldwide, 86% of adults are literate and almost all countries have literacy rates over 50%, reflecting the fact that literacy is the foundation of the development of a postcolonial education. But universal literacy will be in conflict with some aspects of life which are indigenous to postcolonial countries.

In general, the elite in *any* society, and the privileged at any *level* in a society, value a critical spirit, provided, as Julian Williams remarked, it is not *too* critical. Traditional societies are not welcoming of collaborative learning for example. Collaborative learning is intended (among other things) to destabilise hierarchical relationships and empower children and the marginalised. Teachers aim to arrange pedagogic situations in which pupils will *discover* the culturally evolved solution to problems by collaborative work amongst themselves, directed by the teacher. This method of education generates children and adolescents who challenge their elders. But in general, traditional societies rely on elders transmitting traditional knowledge based on an ontology which is generally *not* discoverable by experiment, but resides in traditional narratives, strong ethical codes and an immediate connection with the land.

The often-superior knowledge that tradition societies have of their land may offer the opportunity for collaborative learning to meld with traditional knowledge because the land offers the opportunity for experiment to discover traditional knowledge scientifically.

Traditional societies have their own hierarchies, in both tribal structures and family structures. Reproducing the benefits of modernity whilst hanging on to the benefits of traditional cultures presents a challenge to traditional hierarchies, hierarchies which have adapted themselves to colonialism, as it happens.

This is one of the central problems which Activity Theory must deal with.

CHAPTER 10

Ethics

1   The Ethics of Collaboration

I will examine three issues bearing on ethics which are opened up by the use of activities as the substance and unit of analysis for the human sciences.

First, every theory of society is implicitly a theory of ethics, and every ethics is implicitly a theory of society. Social theory cannot succeed in describing and explaining, let alone changing, social life unless it also makes sense as an ethical theory applicable to the society it describes and the methods it uses.

Second, a general ethics must have recourse to both collaboration *between* projects and elaborate relevant ethical principles, as well as the ethics of collaboration *within* projects.

Third, ethical principles can be elaborated by individuals participating together in a collaborative project. Together, these considerations point to a secular general ethics relevant to the modern world based on the notion of collaborative projects.

1.1   *Social Science and Ethics*

In the positivist tradition of science, ethics and science are incommensurable and are kept separate. 'Is' must not be confused with 'Ought'. The only place for ethics in mainstream scientific research is to put boundaries around the activities of scientists to ensure that in their pursuit of knowledge they don't violate the rights of others.

In the tradition of emancipatory science, things are not so clear-cut. Hegel, Marx and Vygotsky did not develop separate ethical and scientific theories; their ideas were simultaneously ethical and scientific. And there are good reasons for this. In general, in any society, people generally *do* act as they *should* act and the practical norms of a community not only reflect what people do, but what they ought to do. So the practical norms of a community correspond to the reasons people give for that they do. And people do act for reasons, not because of inhuman forces acting on them from outside, be they economic pressures, "structural forces" or the pull of desires.

The first problem which arises is that a norm of conduct presumed to apply to the research subject as if it were a simple matter of fact, is in fact the postulate of a theory of ethics which the researcher brings to the subject matter.

The question arises: is that theory of ethics realistic and relevant to the current context?

For example, liberal economic theory bases its science on the presumption of individuals acting as mutually independent, self-interested, rational agents. That is, it proceeds as if this is the *norm* for the behaviour of individuals, and that it is individuals, or groups such as families or corporations acting as if they were individuals, who are the agents in economic life. The fact that agents are neither individual, independent nor self-interested registers as a "distortion" of the market (as "friction" or "rigidity" for example), and as something which needs to be *fixed*. Thus, public service is denigrated and so far as possible replaced with commercial services, public health and welfare sacrificed on the altar of the free market. By making an atomistic society the norm for economics, economists make policy recommendations which have the effect of atomising society and tending to *make* this dystopian libertarianism the norm. Education is deemed to be the personal property of the student, so policy is set so that those who want an education pay for their certificate, get what they paid for, and then expect to be duly remunerated for their outlay. The norm of the independent rational economic agent orients both the science and the ethics. Public education is deemed a cost which needs to be minimised. Policies based on these false assumptions reduce public service to administering contracts, managing funds and prosecuting court cases; public provision of health and education is undermined and the people who provide such services are increasingly isolated and demoralised. Before these ideas came to dominate public policy in the 1980s, one could safely say simply that people do not act in that way. However, after 30 years of neoliberal public policy, increasingly people *do* behave in that way.

Neoliberal public policy tends to *produce* a nation of self-seeking individuals accustomed to the disinterest of the community in their welfare. But it is not the people nor the theory itself which is wrong, but the ethical assumptions on which the social theory and therefore the public policy is based, which is wrong.

Behavioural Psychology is based on the ethical principle that people interact with others with the aim of predicting and controlling their behaviour (as if everyone was an amateur behavioural psychologist). The activity of behavioural psychologists serves to promote and enhance just such strategic action by the marketers, advertisers and political advisers who purchase their services. The result is universal suffrage coexisting with unprecedented levels of economic and political inequality.

A human science which does not make its ethical commitments explicit is deceiving itself and others. Human beings *are* rational and reasonable agents and no study of their activity can be complete without a consideration of *how* individuals decide on what is right, on what they *ought* to do, that is, without an ethical examination which takes seriously the subject's own ethical commitments.

As Anthony Giddens has pointed out, people generally understand the options available to them in their current situation and generally make rational decisions on that basis. It is the distribution of resources and life-chances which is responsible for the different ways people act. That distribution of resources has historical origins, but is reproduced generation after generation thanks to ethical principles embodied in social practice and law. Structural or Functional analysis of a social formation does not reveal anything which compels people to act in one way or another. To understand people we just need to be able to grasp their situation, the specific quandary they are facing, and the ethical principles which are guiding them and generating their motivation, and then generally assume that they act rationally.

Social theorists know that social formations operate according to ethical norms. These norms form part of their data, but they may take the ethics of the scientific project as something separate from the data. All kinds of misunderstanding arise in those circumstances. The ethics applying to participation in a scientific project are more or less widely known in those societies where science has a profile and subjects will easily adapt to the role of being a research subject. But in other social situations subjects may fail to understand the researchers' questions and their own responses may in turn be misconstrued. Care must be taken to ensure that the researcher's ethical assumptions make sense in the ethical domain where they are researching.

1.2   *Modern Ethics*

The idea of 'collaboration' and 'project' (or 'activities') as basic notions for social theory allows us to examine ethical principles that are relevant, not just to participants in an explicitly acknowledged collaborative project, but to interaction with others in general.

1.2.1   Religion and Ethics

The Christian religion has inscribed in its principles the Golden Rule: "Do unto others as you would have them do unto you" (Luke 6:31). In the Muslim *Hadith* (Sayings of the Prophet) we have: "None of you truly believes until he desires for his brother what he desires for himself." This ancient principle transcends all religious boundaries. Versions of the Golden Rule can be found in Bahá'í, Buddhism, Confucianism, Hinduism, Islam, Jainism, Judaism, the Native American and African traditions, Shinto, Sikhism, Taoism and Zaroastrianism at least. The Golden Rule is a gift we have inherited from antiquity, a moral principle shared across all cultures which gives us a basic rule for collaborating with each other.

As part of the Enlightenment project, seeking to place the moral teachings of religion on a rational basis, Kant claimed to prove that as rational beings, we must always treat another person as an *end* and never as mere means (Kant, 1780). From this, he was able to reformulate the Golden Rule as the Principle of Universalisability (hereafter the Categorical Imperative): "Act according to a maxim which can be adopted at the same time as a universal law" (Kant, 1785).

However, even though the Categorical Imperative, whether in Kant's secular formulation or in that of a religious tradition, is indigenous to all cultures, it overlooks the fact that others may not want to have done unto them the same as you want to have done unto you. It fails to take account of the fact that others may have radically different needs and desires. "You wouldn't do that in your own house!" is often not an effective rejoinder to poor behaviour.

Even leaving aside cultural differences and the lack of a shared sacred text, the Categorical Imperative takes no account of the asymmetrical obligations in paternalistic, hierarchical and class social formations. The boss does not expect the employee to do unto him as they do unto the employee. It also violates the basic principle of the market in which *everyone* instrumentalises everyone else. And Kant's commitment to taking others as ends and not means effectively rules out the possibility of acting according to shared ends. There is no "we" in this ethic.

A revival of interest in moral philosophy and secular ethics over the past half-century has led to a number of attempts to rectify the problems in Kant's formulation which takes account of the ethical problems which have arisen as the result of the ethnic diversity of modern states and the rise of the WLM. Foremost amongst the approaches directly drawing on Kant's rationalisation of the Categorical Imperative are Habermas and later Critical Theorists including Agnes Heller and Seyla Benhabib. Also contributing to the approach which I propose here are John Rawls, MacIntyre and Sen.

1.2.2   John Rawls' Political Liberalism

Both Rawls and Habermas approach the lack of a universally respected revealed religion by looking to principles of justice being derived or validated through reasonable and rational dialogue between citizens, whether real or hypothetical. Rawls sees the discourse in which consensus is reached on just social arrangements (1) requiring participants to lay aside any "comprehensive world views" they may hold and (2) basing themselves on mutually accepted *facts*, evidently including taken-for-granted social arrangements, rather than the specific constitutional provisions which are the subject of decision. However, these facts are the product or manifestation of prior social arrangements. Rawls failed to see that only a comprehensive world view can encompass the counterfactual and the consequential, whether or not in a way which is convincing to those not sharing the comprehensive world view in question.

A typical example would be an organisation with all-male leadership which resists affirmative action to increase female participation, claiming that they only appoint on merit. Obviously they do not. Once the paternalistic features of their organisation have been removed they discover that appointment on merit produces 50–50 gender representation. Only a feminist critique could have justified affirmative action, and in the meantime, until systems had been feminised, a lot of men would continue to believe that they had been unjustly passed over in favour of a woman. *Structural injustice cannot be rectified by consensus.* Only a project which succeeds by illiberal means in realising its ideal, changing social arrangements and creating new facts, can create the basis for reaching a new consensus.

Rawls' reasoning from a supposedly "original position" is flawed because the original position is original only in being prior to the constitution and set of laws being legislated and an individual being inserted into a social position. The original position is not original but belated, because it leaves in place comprehensive world views which reflect taken-for-granted social arrangements and consequential "facts" which were supposedly still to be instituted. Only real human beings raised in some definite social situation can engage in the kind of thought experiment which Rawls requires.

However, confronted with the obvious fact that according to his system the entire Civil Rights Movement would have been ruled out (and the same would apply to the Women's Liberation Movement), Rawls introduced an amendment to allow that leaders of a project aiming to change social arrangements would "not go against the ideal of public reason ... if the political forces they led were among the necessary historical conditions to establish political justice" (1993, p. 251). This is a principle of *dynamic justice*, and Rawls is correct insofar as social justice movements change facts crucial to the achievement of the social arrangements they advocate for. But this proviso undermines his whole conception of political liberalism. A certain claim is just, supposedly, if a project exists which is capable of realising the social arrangements in which unforced consensus could subsequently be freely arrived at. So despite Rawls' aim to rule out "comprehensive doctrines," justice can only be determined by making an assessment not of doctrines as such, but of the collaborative projects which realise doctrines.

Whereas Rawls tried and failed to resolve the problem of a multiplicity of world views by limiting the domain of discourse, Habermas looked to a procedural solution.

1.2.3 Habermas's Communicative Ethics

Habermas also responded to the problem of the radical failure of mutual understanding characterising modernity, but rather than attempting to directly prescribe the *kind of discourse* which could justify ethical principles, he opted for a *procedural prescription* in the form of discourse ethics. Empathy has to be transcended with an actual enquiry into the other person's needs.

Taking Kant as his setting off point, he put it this way:

> [Kant] tacitly assumes that in making moral judgments each individual can project himself into the situation of everyone else *through his own imagination*. But when the participants can no longer rely on a transcendental pre-understanding grounded in more or less homogeneous conditions of life and interests, the moral point of view can only be realised under conditions of communication that ensure that *everyone* tests the acceptability of a norm, implemented in a general practice, also from the perspective of his own understanding of himself and of the world ... [I]n this way the categorical imperative receives a discourse-theoretical interpretation in which its place is taken by the discourse principle (D), according to which *only those norms can claim validity that could meet with the agreement of all those concerned in their capacity as participants in a practical discourse.*
>
> 1998, pp. 33–4

Habermas set out the conditions which would allow such a practical discourse to proceed without coercion or exclusion, including, as did Rawls, ruling out dogmatism, performative contradictions, and so forth, so that discourse could expected to produce a rational and reasonable consensus. Continuing to parallel Kant, he derived from the discourse principle the principle of universalisation (U):

> A [moral norm] is valid just in the case that the foreseeable consequences and side-effects of its general observance for the interests and value-orientations of each individual could be jointly accepted by all concerned without coercion.
>
> 1998, p. 42

Although this is framed in terms of justifying moral norms, Habermas went on to make it clear that the principle of universalisation was to apply to real practical discourse, including the making of decisions about real projects, and that it was required not only that each individual affected be *consulted*, but that their reasonable agreement had to be gained.

Thus Habermas made collective decision making the criterion for ethical action.

He granted however, that in the light of the multiplicity of conflicting interests in modernity a "fair bargaining process" would often take the place of actual agreement on the rightness of the relevant action. Continuing along these lines, he formulated the conditions for laws to be regarded as legitimate if they are reasonable products of a sufficiently inclusive deliberative process.

Like Kant, Habermas continued to develop his ethics on the basis of individuals who are taken to be, and take each other to be, ends in themselves, autonomous moral agents, who do things *to* each other but never *with* each other. Despite the move to give procedural form to moral obligations, Habermas's communicative ethics remains, as a number of writers have said, insufficiently concrete. We are left with an indefinite number of atomistic individuals engaged in egalitarian and inclusive practical discourse over some decision with which they claim to be concerned and all are to be treated alike as ends in themselves.

Both Habermas and Rawls fail in their project because they do not take collaboration as the norm for interactions between individuals. Individuals being the author of unmediated actions they take *against* another individual is far from being the typical ethical relation in social life: in the jungle perhaps, but not in a modern social formation. Ethics needs to be based on a form of relationship which can function as the methodological germ cell of a social formation, and one individual acting upon another fails as such a germ cell.

1.2.4   Seyla Benhabib

Seyla Benhabib in particular has pointed out that Habermas's formulation is far too abstract, and in its abstractness it fails to find relevance in real world ethical problems.

> The fiction of a general deliberative assembly in which the united people expressed their will belongs to the early history of democratic theory; today our guiding model has to be that of a medium of loosely associated, multiple foci of opinion formation and dissemination which affect one another in free and spontaneous processes of communication.
>
> BENHABIB, 1996

Benhabib insists that so long as the other is considered abstractly, lacking any determinateness in relation to the subject, the perpetuation of the above fiction has the effect of promoting a destructive kind of liberalism which is blind to the diversity of projects in which people are engaged, and the conflicts between these various projects. Benhabib (2006) illustrated this point with a consideration of the range of quite different definitions of the "citizens" of a nation-state, according to whether kinship, residence, ethnicity, language, work or political participation is at issue. In her opinion, ethical problems arising in the European Union can only be resolved by disentangling these distinct projects, rather than trying to see Europe, for example, as made up of groups of individuals each sharing a unitary nationality.

1.2.5   Amartya Sen

Coming from a study of the measurement and causes inequality, Sen engaged in a life-long internal critique of Utilitarianism. In successive refinements of measures of social welfare and inequality he successively demolished wealth, income, capability, functioning and voice (Sen, 1999) as measures of what it is in a social formation which ought to be more equally distributed. He finally arrived at the concept of "critical voice." It is not enough that some group has an adequate level of functioning and a voice in the making of decisions about social arrangements affecting their welfare: they need a *critical voice* (Sen & Drèze, 2002). This led to his proposal that the foremost measure which was needed to rectify inequality in India was the education of women. It is very significant that critical voice as the substance of justice – not just as a means – arose from a critique of utilitarianism, the ethic underlying modern economic theory.

Sen (2002a) has also made an astute observation on the question of cultural relativism. He observed that, so long as there is some communication with other parts of the world, *every* culture has its own critics and dissenters, and therefore people offering *internal* criticisms of their own culture. Established opinion never offers a reliable measure of what is good in a given social formation, because by definition established opinion is that of the dominant group. There can be no basis for withholding outside criticism of a culture on the basis of deference for cultural relativism, but such criticism can be effective and valid to the extent that it finds effective internal dissenting voices with which it is able to solidarise. So even very broad cultural criticism, to be valid, requires a foundation in real relationships of collaboration. The justice or otherwise of the relevant social arrangements have to be judged by the strength and persuasiveness of the internal dissenting voices.

Sen (2002a) also made an extensive study of majority decision making, drawing largely on the mathematics of complexity theorist Kenneth Arrow. It must be granted that each individual will have a whole array of preferences in respect to some decision domain which cannot be reduced to a Yes/No answer to one arbitrary question, but it can be encompassed by a series of such Yes/No decisions. So even if it is accepted as a principle of justice that a choice between two options ought to be made by majority decision, an elaborate meeting procedure is presupposed in order to reliably and consistently negate the fact that the outcome is determined by the selection of the question to be posed. Sen affirmed that majority voting is in the same position in regard to the question posed as consensus decision making is in regard to the status quo ante, which always acts as a default in the event of a failure of consensus. The only guarantee of a just group decision is a body of individuals educated and motivated to find and collaboratively create a just arrangement, with an effective tradition of collective decision making, an understanding of which is shared among all the participants.

1.2.6 Agnes Heller

Agnes Heller (1986) also found Habermas's approach insufficiently concrete, and among other things she has made an extended study of the Golden Rule, which she reformulated as follows:

> What I do unto you and what I *expect* you to do unto me should be decided by you and me.

I find this formulation unsatisfactory because it still restricts the domain of action to individuals acting *on* one another whereas the far more important domain of activity is what *we do together*, as collaborators, and it is our relationship as collaborators which determines how we consult one another, make decisions and share the blame or credit for the outcome of our collaboration. This Heller never investigated. Undoubtedly individual experiences will always have a privileged position in questions of ethics, but I would contend that individual action can only be approached as a determination of the "we" perspective which must form our starting point, in theory as it does in reality. Taking collaborative projects to be the essential, concrete practical relation between people, I reformulate the Golden Rule in this way:

> *What we do*, is decided by *us*.

That is, by default, I take another person to be a collaborator in a project which is implicated in the moral problem raised between us, and that includes those who are participants by virtue of being or claiming to be affected. Conflict is an essential moment of collaboration. The aim is to seek consensus on what we do, that is, by taking us to be joint participants in a project. If no such shared project is conceivable, then the supposed moral problem is void.

The original Golden Rule specified only what I do unto another, and takes no account of the fact that the impact of my actions on the other may be the result-ant of action which we are taking or ought to take together as collaborators. The Golden Rule modified by the introduction of the we-perspective makes no prescription about what I ought to do in the absence of a we-perspective. However, the we-perspective is to be interpreted generously, including the imputed or prior consent of agents who may be incompetent, highly mediated collaborations or collaborations which are more conflicts than cooperations.

Further, the concept of project collaboration should frame our practical relations even with strangers, not just our immediate collaborators. Universal ethical claims, such as the denunciation of economic inequality, can only be made coherent if they are implicitly addressed to either the state. some social movement, or some agent which can, concretely, mediate between me and those suffering. Such broad claims are coherent only to the extent that a mediating project, and thereby the parties addressed by the claim, are made explicit. You can legitimately ask: what is that to do with me?

Further, a range of different collaborative relations are normative in differ-ent circumstances. What kind of collaborators are we? Whose project is this? These questions have to be answered *concretely*. It is necessary to identify a viable we-perspective. This raises the issue of the various paradigms of deci-sion making which apply to collaborative projects. I will come to these ques-tions presently.

The writer who has come closest to formulating an ethics on this basis is Alasdair MacIntyre.

1.2.7   Alasdair MacIntyre

In 1981, Alasdair MacIntyre published *After Virtue*, which, despite the fact that MacIntyre had recently converted to Catholicism, became a reference point for the secular critique of liberalism. MacIntyre was interested in whether the ethical life of Aristotle's ancient *polis*, where "activities are hierarchi-cally ordered by the *for sake of* relationship" (p. 107), could be recovered in conditions of modernity. MacIntyre looked to the ethical norms operative in "practices" which he understands much as I understand collaborative pro-jects or activities: "Every activity, every enquiry, every practice aims at some good" (1981, p. 139). MacIntyre distinguished between "internal goods" "realized in the course of trying to achieve those standards of excellence which are appropriate to, and partially definitive of, that form of activity" (1981, p. 175) and "external goods" such as prizes, monetary rewards and wages which are used to sustain the practice, and are associated with the transformation of a form of practice into an institution (i.e., effective motives). In this connection, MacIntyre refers to the "corrupting power of institutions" (1981, p. 181), so we see the potential for "fossilised projects," that is, institutions – from organisations such as schools or hospitals to entire political communities, "concerned with the whole of life, not with this or that good, but with man's good as such" (1981, p. 146) – to be both the site for the development of an ethical life or for the corruption of human relationships.

MacIntyre advocates an *ethics of virtue*, rather than the ethics of rights and duties advocated by liberals such as Rawls and Habermas.

1.2.8   Thick and Thin Ethos

One qualification to MacIntyre's ethical project which is important to the task at hand is Heller's (1986, 1988) contrast between the sense of equality and a "loose ethos" which prevails in the marketplace of public intercourse and the "dense ethos" uniting participants in shared commitment to a project. Heller observes that the obligation to treat others as equals is not universal. While we are obliged to treat equals equally, within the practices of an institution "equals should be treated equally and unequals unequally" – the boss gets paid more, managers give orders to subordinates, parents bear the burdens of care for their children, etc. Utopian dreams notwithstanding, there is no real project within which equality is truly the norm. Consequently, Heller points out that the ongoing displacement of the formerly dense ethos of institutional life by the loose ethos of modernity which underlies MacIntyre's concerns is *not simply* a regressive development. The sexual abuse of children that has been taking place, probably forever, in all kinds of hierarchical institutions is a symptom of the dangers of hierarchical institutions insulated from the liberal ethos of outside society. The recent rash of exposés is probably due to the penetration of the dense ethos of these institutions by the loose ethos of modernity. The long-held antipathy to hierarchy in particular and institutionalisation in general which has characterised social change movements demands a response to this problem.

So much for the various approaches to formulating a secular ethics to date, all of which aim to logically invent social norms without regard to the work of real social history. Activity Theory, however, provides us with the opportunity of formulating a new *collaborative ethics*, based on really existing practices of collaboration, which have been a proving ground for ethics for millennia.

1.3   *Collaborative Ethics*

Human freedom can only be attained through mediated self-determination, *i.e.*, participation in projects. The interaction between any two individuals is never unmediated, so the question is always to discern which project mediates the specific relation, and thereby the ethical principles which are relevant to the relation. On the other hand, any stranger is a *person*, and as such is the bearer of inalienable rights, and this is the case irrespective of any concrete relation I have to the other. Whatever relation I have to another person I am constrained by the command that I recognise the other as a person and respect their rights as such. This is the meaning of *human rights*, as opposed to rights indigenous to some specific context.

This situation is reflected where universal suffrage (based on large, arbitrary geographical electorates) coexists with a complex web of civil society organisations and businesses in which concrete person-to-person obligations predominate.

The above review of efforts to devise an ethics appropriate to life in modern, secular nation states, confirms my claim that a secular modern ethics has to be based on the presumption of a relationship of *collaboration* between any two people in some project, rather than on the presumption of atomistic individuals as is presumed in systems of universal suffrage. A duality is necessary, because even while systems of collaboration are the necessary condition for emancipation, they are, unfortunately, also the most common context for oppression, exploitation and marginalisation. Collaborative ethics as such has to be qualified by liberalism. The coexistence of these two contradictory ethics is necessary.

This leads us to a two-step approach to resolving ethical problems. First we must identify the relevant project and the position of the subjects within that project, which specifies the relation between two persons. Failing this, the subjects must be regarded as independent projects with the relation defined as appropriate to a relation between projects. The second step is then to identify the ethical norms indigenous to the given project(s) on the basis of a typology of projects and relations between projects along the lines outlined earlier. For each paradigm there are specific ethical norms. Further, every project has its own ethics, according to its object-concept; however, not in every case can such norms be endorsed as rational and reasonable. The object concept of the project must first be verified as rational before its norms of collaboration can be validated. A wide variety of projects in the world define the ethical relations between participants uniquely. Not all projects are worthy of support however. The validity of a project may be judged in terms of the ethics of relations between projects, i.e., from the standpoint of *other* projects.

The final element of Collaborative Ethics is a consideration of the ethics shaping the paradigmatic norms of collaboration outlined above.

Ethical communities are not constructed by theologians and moral philosophers or even by police and judges. Ethical communities have been constructed by people collaborating in projects, essentially by forms of collective decision making together with the collective implementing of those decisions. Theologians and moral philosophers then subsequently rationalised what they saw before their eyes.

As I have tried to show, the various rights, duties and virtues which are manifested in social life have their basis in the demands of specific modes of collaboration: Counsel, Majority, Consensus and Laissez faire, and forms of collaboration between distinct projects – negotiation, solidarity, colonisation and collaboration-as-such. Each of these modes of collaboration arises in specific social conditions.

The virtues and duties we have mentioned above – honesty, good faith, care and responsibility, solidarity, trust, wisdom, attention, equality, tolerance, inclusion and respect – all originate in specific forms of collaboration.

Collaborative Ethics begins from the proposition that you must adhere to the ethics indigenous to the project in which you are participating, or cease participating. I have already described the demands of these various relations above.

As I demonstrated above, each mode of collaboration fosters certain virtues (Negotiation fosters honesty and good faith, for example, even while presuming self-interest), and each mode of collaboration specifies certain procedures which are obligatory for participants (Majority fosters solidarity and tolerance and demands adherence to meeting procedure, for example). All projects demand ethical dispositions from participants (Counsel demands humility and deference to the Chief among the participants, phronesis and the virtues of leadership in the Chief, for example). Each mode of collaboration is thus a combination of a virtue ethics and a procedural ethics, but specific to the given mode of collaboration.

Any attempt to specify an ethics which takes no account of the collaborative relationship in which subject and other are engaged must be abstract and empty.

In any actual project there will be mores which constitute a kind of idioculture, specific to the object-concept of the project. Awareness of and respect for this idioculture is obligatory for participants. For example, participation in a political party may forbid disclosure of internal information. General rules cannot encompass the infinite variety of such obligations.

In short, the Ethics of Collaboration is the imperative to learn how to collaborate in the concrete circumstances in which you find yourself.

Centuries before the maxim "charity begins at home" was coined, the Prophet Isaiah (58:7) had already said much the same thing. How do we ethically justify that we make great sacrifices for those who are socially close to us but feel no obligation to treat a beggar in India with the same largesse? If we ask what project mediates each relationship, we find that those close to us are by definition those with whom we have a collaborative personal relationship, such as the project of raising a family, for example. But the only project mediating my relation to an Indian beggar is the foreign policy and aid program of the Australian government. As a voter and citizen in Australia, I bear moral responsibility for that policy and my obligation to that beggar flows from my participation in formulating Australian foreign policy (albeit marginal). My duty to the Indian beggar is answered by my duty to promote a more generous foreign aid program, and other measures which moderate global inequality, as a citizen of the Australian national project, *in addition to* the universal duties flowing from liberalism, expressed by Kant as the duty to treat others as ends in themselves. Neither ethic prevents me from jumping on a plane and flying over and giving the beggar something to eat, but I cannot say that I have an obligation to do that. Indeed, my children would rightly complain that I was neglecting my fatherly duty in doing so (if I had children).

If I work at a university, I know that the university operates by a complex mix of collegial committees deciding policy and line management operating from the Vice-Chancellor down. I know I am the moral equal of the v-c but also that if the v-c instructs me to do something, directly or via the management tree, other things being equal, I should comply. As a union delegate of course I may choose to *transgress* that obligation, but it remains a transgression and will be judged by history as such. (What was said above in connection to "agency" remains the case; radical change demands transgression of ethical norms which can only be justified in retrospect). On the other hand, if I am a member of one of those collegial committees, where the Vice-Chancellor sits with academics, admin. staff, deans and such like, I know that these committees use formal meeting procedures as developed by Majority decision making (though always striving to reach consensus). In that forum my only obligation is to adhere to meeting procedure with tolerance and solidarity. The Vice-Chancellor cannot tell me what to say and do and would not try.

And so on and so forth. One's ethical duties and responsibilities in all cases flow from the norms of the relevant project. That is Collaborative Ethics.

1.4   *Participant Researchers*

Activity theorists must be *participant researchers*. That is, they come to theory with a commitment to transform human activity in the interests of social justice and emancipation, and they learn by participating in struggles for social justice and critically reflecting on that experience. They share their insights and open their reflections to criticism by comrades as well as academic collaborators. They are not generally just observers.

The participant researcher does not have a separate, let alone a hidden agenda. Their interest in developing theory is an emancipatory interest and they share that interest with comrades and colleagues alike. Their work is subject to the discipline of the movements in which they participate and they always respect the privacy and autonomy of their comrades. The same goes for participation in "social non-movements" and participation in institutions which are established for the purpose of furthering social justice.

Publication must be subordinate to the successful prosecution of the projects in which activity theorists participate. It can happen that the demands on the researcher to publish and to record conversations and so on conflict with the exigencies of the work the researcher is doing. Unless your comrades can see the value in publishing and understand the need for recording, and so on, the researcher must not hamper the work being done in the interests of publication. If they don't want you to record or they don't want you to interview someone, so be it. These conflicts will not arise if the researcher is fully committed to the shared object of the activity she or he is involved in.

The participant observer is not an anthropologist or ethnologist. It is not our job simply to report how the subjects act. Being equally committed to the object, if the researcher observes a misconception among the subjects, then the researcher is obliged to challenge that misconception, within the demands of the indigenous ethical norms. Trust is gold, and trust is built on collaboration, not just cooperation.

2   Social Class

Very little has been said in the foregoing about social class. The reason for this is that Activity Theory bases itself on *concrete* social formations, class projects, not abstract general demographic categories. The difference may have been academic in the 19th century, but it is crucial in our times. The bourgeoisie no longer confronts a homogeneous industrial working class comprising the majority of the population as it once did. The bourgeoisie remains, however, the "general stumbling block" (*der allgemeinen Anstoß*, Marx, 1843) in the path of social transformation, but the labour process has changed since Marx's death, and with that the working class has changed. The conditions in which a person has been raised – their education, class habitus, social connections, etc. – of course make up the chief elements of a person's situation. But we see classes as *agents* only insofar as there are constituted in forms of activity.

During Marx's lifetime it was an axiom of capitalism that the number of "unproductive workers" in a factory had to be reduced to a minimum. In 1898, Frederick Taylor promoted 25% of the workers at Bethlehem Steel into supervisory positions with a 30% wage increase, and increased productivity by a factor of ten, while splitting the industrial working class itself into numerous strata. The truism that the manufacturer made a profit by keeping hours as long as possible and wages as low as possible was turned on its head in 1914 by Henry Ford, who cut one hour from the working day, doubled wages, and made a mint, while creating a corporatist layer within the industrial working class. Then John Maynard Keynes gave us the economic theory of the welfare state, which in turn gave us what remains to this day the core of the organised working class in the old capitalist countries, in service sectors – health and education, and building and maintaining public infrastructure – allegedly consuming and not creating surplus value, but organised and socialist-minded nonetheless. As macroeconomic reform gave way to microeconomic reform, Toyota turned Frederick Taylor inside out, passing the supervision of labour back to the shop floor and bringing the market inside of the capitalist enterprise itself. Now we have Google and Facebook employing a small crew of software engineers to cream the profits off the unpaid labour of the *users* of their product while Amazon push the productivity of their employees through the roof. At the same time, the most precarious sections of the working class are working 15-minute shifts – falling short even of the conditions which triggered the Dockers' Tanner strike of 1889.

Meanwhile, the flow of people and capital from the great European powers to the colonies was reversed after World War Two. One of the most salient facts of the working class in the old capitalist countries is its ethnic diversity as the flow of people and capital reversed, leaving much of the rest of world in a condition of devastation as the world is wracked by floods, droughts, searing heatwaves, famines and pandemics. Activity theorists have always concentrated their work among the most marginalised and impoverished sections of the population, positioning themselves in opposition to the growing inequality of the late capitalist world. But it does not follow from this that the task of changing this situation rests on the shoulders of the most excluded and oppressed sections of the working class.

One of the features of the class composition of the advanced capitalist countries which has resulted from these changes in the labour process is that the industrial working class has been displaced by a class which, following Guy Rundle, I will call the *knowledge class*. From the late 19th century up until the mid-1950s, the industrial working class was the most *progressive* class in bourgeois society. That is to say, not only the most *exploited* class, not only the class which *alone* was in a position to overthrow the "great stumbling block," but also the most *progressive* class. Because of the fact that its own emancipation was the precondition for the emancipation of *all* the oppressed classes in bourgeois society, Marx called the industrial working class the "universal class."

The industrial working class is no longer the most progressive class in society, but nonetheless remains the class upon whose exploitation the bourgeoisie rests. But most of this class lies outside the borders of the advanced capitalist countries. It is impossible to envisage the emancipation of the precariat and poor in the capitalist heartlands other than in the context of the industrial workers of China, India, etc., raising themselves from sweated labour and poverty. In any case, it is impossible to envisage socialism in the West without or against the white working class in the US or the north of England, or the western suburbs of Sydney and Melbourne, etc.

In former times, the bourgeoisie could rely on the countryside as a counterweight to the industrial working class and its urban allies. The rural masses remain the most conservative sections of the population, but now what remains of the industrial working class and their non-union allies in the distributive and commercial sectors and "small business" – in short the *uneducated* classes – are bases for the *right-wing* in politics. The politics and voting habits of the very wealthy are neither here nor there. They are a small minority, and the continuation of the rule of capital relies on *hegemony*.

Hegemony is the arrangement whereby the capitalist class shares the proceeds of exploitation with other classes – "middle classes" – thereby ensuring that a sufficient social weight has a stake in the existing arrangements. The operation of hegemony presumes that these privileged middle classes are able to play a leadership role in the broader society so as to ensure the conditions for continuation of capitalism. Were the capitalists to keep all the proceeds of exploitation to itself, then the situation which Kautsky anticipated would arise:

> We consider the breakdown of the present social system to be unavoidable, because we know that the economic evolution inevitably brings on conditions that will compel the exploited classes to rise against this system of private ownership. We know that this system multiplies the number and the strength of the exploited, and diminishes the number

and strength of the exploiting, classes, and that it will finally lead to such unbearable conditions for the mass of the population that they will have no choice but to go down into degradation or to overthrow the system of private property.

KAUTSKY, 1892

Beginning in the immediate aftermath of World War Two, on the basis of the historic compromise between the industrial working class and the bourgeoisie and the burgeoning of the welfare state and public enterprises, a new class emerged from the labour process: the knowledge class. With the growth of computer and communications technology and particularly after 2000, this knowledge class displaced the priesthood and the upper sections of the industrial working class and stepped into this hegemonic role, sharing in and distributing the proceeds of capital.

The knowledge class has its base in the media, communications generally, the state and corporate bureaucracy, politics, academia and the broader education sector and subsumes the old middle class in law and medicine. This class deploys what Bourdieu could have called "knowledge capital" and monopolises the superstructure of bourgeois society. It tells us what is morally right and what is scientifically true. It designs and supervises the mechanisms of bourgeois rule, writes the algorithms which control the lives of gig workers, defines our sexuality and gender, tells us how to raise our children, analyses the causes of domestic violence and how to apply for a job. It also mobilises shareholders to push mining companies to adopt emission standards, argues for raising the unemployment benefit, and convinces us that climate change is real and that we really need to wear masks.

The idea that the "ideas of the ruling class are in every epoch the ruling ideas, i.e., the class which is the ruling material force of society, is at the same time its ruling intellectual force" (Marx, 1845) would tend to suggest that this knowledge class – whose ideas certainly are the ruling ideas – is the ruling class in present day capitalism. Whatever else the knowledge class tells us about how to lead our lives, one thing it does *not* tell us is that there is a life after capitalism. The knowledge class write the how-to manual for life in post-industrial capitalism, but they don't own the machine.

The knowledge class is inherently diverse but it is on the whole a progressive class. However, as a class it has no interest in the overthrow of capitalism, a measure which it tends to see as old fashioned and delusional. Its method of thinking is generally that bureaucratic practice of filling out survey forms, putting everything in its appropriate box and adding up the numbers. All that is needed is to adjust the rules of bourgeois society so as to moderate inequality

and eliminate the multifarious forms of discrimination. For this class the working class does not exist but capitalism has existed since antiquity. What an
absurd idea, to "abolish" capitalism!

The knowledge class is neither a ruling class nor a potential ruling class. Its
social role is essentially that of bureaucrats, administrators and managers. But
despite this intermediary social position, there is no doubt that the knowledge
class exert a social influence far beyond the eunuchs of ancient China or the
modern managerial class as such. No arena, no forum is beyond its reach.

The fact remains that there is today no universal class capable of overthrowing capitalism which is both the most politically progressive class *and* the class
whose emancipation constitutes the emancipation of the nation:

> For the *revolution of a nation*, and the *emancipation of a particular class* of
> civil society to coincide, for one estate to be acknowledged as the estate
> of the whole society.
> MARX, 1843

What characterises politics today, as has been obvious ever since the decline of
the great social movements in the 1980s, is that no class and no party *alone* can
achieve *anything*, far less a social revolution. Only through universal solidarity is the overthrow of capitalism possible. Members of the knowledge class,
whose agents and ideas penetrate all classes of society, will play a crucial role in
forming a counter-hegemony. Just as in former times revolutionaries counted
on sections of the army and police changing sides when faced with the final
crisis, today we must look to the knowledge class in much the same way. Such
a development presupposes that the managerial practices of the knowledge
class be supplanted by solidarity, and by this means the precariat and poorest
layers of the working class can take their place in the ranks of the Revolution.

3   The *Urpraxis* of Socialism

The *Urpraxis* of Socialism is Solidarity.

People will participate in projects and give it their best shot. The only problem is that we have to *learn* how to collaborate with *other* projects. Above all
we have to learn the meaning of solidarity and we have to help other people
understand what solidarity means. It is on this alone that the future of socialism depends.

As explained above, the working class is no longer the vast homogeneous
industrial working class of the past. Successive changes in the labour process

have fragmented the mass of wage-workers into innumerable strata such that it is hardly feasible any longer to talk of "a working class." Certainly not in the same way as in the past. But I use the term "working class" now in the sense of a movement which is again merely "in itself" but can return to the stage of world history if it learns how to bind itself together into a single anti-capitalist project, single in its object: a peaceful, sustainable world free of exploitation while diverse in its ways of life. It is in this sense that I talk of the "working class."

As the Rules of the International Workingmen's Association declared in 1864:

> That all efforts aiming at the great end hitherto failed from the want of solidarity between the manifold divisions of labor in each country, and from the absence of a fraternal bond of union between the working classes of different countries.
>
> IWMA, 1864, p. 288

The French workers had invented the word *solidarité* on the barricades of Paris in the first working class uprisings against the bourgeoisie. The French had learnt the hard way that without solidarity the army could defeat them one barricade at a time, as they had in 1830. By 1848, the Chartist movement, which had united the majority of the population of Britain against the ruling capitalist class had also learnt their lesson the hard way.

"Solidarity" entered the English language from the French at the Chartist Convention in London in April 1848, popularised by *The People's Paper* of Ernest Jones and Julian Harney, leaders of the left-wing of the Chartists and founders of the Communist League, for whom Marx and Engels wrote the *Manifesto of the Communist Party*.

The Rules of the International Workingmen's Association began with the maxim: "the emancipation of the working classes must be conquered by the working classes themselves." These two principles: Self-emancipation and Solidarity, together make the irreducible and inseparable foundations of the workers' movement and is the chief legacy that the workers' movement gives to all the oppressed.

That self-emancipation is necessary is almost self-evident; if the working class is to take public political power it can learn and equip itself for that task only through the work of freeing itself and abolishing the conditions of its own exploitation. No one can do that on its behalf. Self-emancipation is self-creation, the way in which working class self-consciousness, in effect, the working class itself, is constructed. Without self-emancipation there can be no working class, only billions of individual wage-workers, socially and politically controlled by capital.

The opposite of self-emancipation is attaining freedom as the gift of another party. Such a thing is actually impossible; a class which is freed by the action of another class or group is only thereby subordinated to their liberators, even if these be well-meaning. How then is the social justice activist to foster the liberation of the working class if the liberation of the working class is to be *their own* achievement? The answer to this conundrum lies in the principle of *solidarity*.

The need for solidarity arises from the fact that the working class does not come into the world readymade as a single, homogeneous, organised stratum of society. It comes into the world divided into strata, trades, national, religious and ethnic groups, and spread across the globe in numerous cultural and linguistic communities, and has become more not less diversified since. Energies are dissipated in numerous projects, very many of which contribute in some way to the socialist project, but independently and often in conflict with each other.

The modern working class can realise its own emancipation only by the *collaboration* of these disparate projects. The aims and methods of projects will differ, but the autonomy of every project within a broad movement remains until at some future time, when, maybe, they voluntarily create and submit themselves to a shared discipline.

When one group finds themself under attack, *provided they fight back*, then others have a duty to come to their aid. This duty and its practice is called "solidarity." The results of solidarity are three-fold. In the first place, as a result of the aid received from others the struggling group may survive. Secondly, they learn who their friends are, and coming at their hour of need, they will not ever forget this.

But most importantly, through their struggle, whether successful or not, their collective self-consciousness, agency and self-confidence is enhanced.

However, this is not automatically the case; sometimes "helping" someone is a violation of solidarity. If another group comes along and "saves" them, then the "rescued" group may be grateful, but their working class self-consciousness is not enhanced but at best subsumed under that of the rescuing party, who in any case, as often as not, do more harm than help.

The principle of solidarity, which guides how different sections of the workers' movement come to each others' aid, avoids such dangers and ensures that the self-consciousness of both the struggling party and the party offering solidarity is enhanced in the very process of bringing them closer together.

It is a simple rule:

when coming to the aid of another party, do so under *their* direction.

You do it their way, not your way. If your own beliefs are such that you cannot place yourself under their direction, if you believe that they are so misguided, then solidarity is impossible. But if they can contribute in some way to socialism then ensuring that they are not defeated is important, and you will surely be able to find *some* way of supporting them according to their own practices. This may be by donating to their fighting fund or sending a message of solidarity or whatever. But if you are going to participate in the struggle of another section of the workers' movement, then the principle of solidarity demands that you do so *under their direction*. The working class is unified by voluntary association, not by conquest or persuasion.

To be clear, this is not a call for unity on the Left. This is neither possible, nor actually desirable. Preparing and building a movement which can overthrow capitalism and make something *better* is the most complex task imaginable, and it is not planned or directed. It is diverse, with many centres. Neither is it a libertarian, anarchist call for self-expression and multiplicity.

We have to learn and teach people how to collaborate; we have to learn and teach people how to practice solidarity. People will do what they will. If people are not struggling for social justice, then there is nothing we can do to make them. We cannot accelerate the *Zeitgeist*. The job of activity theorists is to show people how the practice of solidarity builds a movement for self-emancipation, out of whatever activity is taking place.

A world in which solidarity is universal is already Socialism.

To be clear, again, this is not an argument for a loose movement of diverse projects. That is what *already exists*. This is not an argument against building a party to win seats in Parliament – though this is necessary also; this is not an argument against building a monthly journal of Marxist theory, or an academic journal for sharing research experience – we need all kind of journals and ezines, or a direct action group opposing evictions or an antifascist group to defend communities against racism, or building a cadre of professional revolutionaries, by all means. All these are part of the struggle for socialism. It is not a question of one or the other, but of how to *bind them together* in bonds of solidarity. And at the moment, young people do not even know the meaning of the word.

But it is *solidarity* which is the *Urpraxis*, the *germ cell*, of the socialist project.

3.1   *The Worldwide Anti-capitalist Struggle*

The worldwide anti-capitalist struggle is a problematic concept because hardly any two people in the world share a concept of if and how capitalism could be overthrown and ties between anti-capitalist organisations and movements across the world are generally none at all or worse. We could say that on a global scale there is a "social non-movement" inasmuch as the many movements that exist all act towards a conception of the same object – a world in which social justice, not capital, determines what happens – all act independently, but in sight of one another.

There *is*, however, a global movement to arrest human-induced climate change and large masses mobilised in the fight against political-economic inequality. However, at this moment both these projects face the same stumbling block: political power resides not in legislative bodies but with capital, the main driver of inequality and vandalisation of Nature. So the task of addressing climate change and poverty will eventually bring us to the point of terminating the domination of capital as a necessary means of succeeding in preventing global catastrophe. These are *human* problems.

Further, few of the movements which are fighting against one or another feature of capitalism in their part of the world are fighting for the actual *overthrow* of capitalism at this point.

Erosion of representative, let alone participatory democracy continues apace, war has again returned to the European powder keg, inequality, hunger and disease spread, and above all the global ecosystem edges closer to collapse. The global ecosystem may already be in the process of collapsing: the permafrost in Siberia is melting, the North Atlantic Oscillation which regulates the temperatures of Europe and North America is in danger of inverting, bees are dying and may not be there to pollinate crops in future, the world is drowning in plastic waste, pandemics sweep across the world closely followed by floods, droughts, freezing winters, blistering summers and wildfires. Is it too late?

"Necessity is the mother of invention" it is wisely said, but *what* do we have to invent? At this point it seems equally likely that the authoritarian buffoonery of Putin, Xi, Modi and Netanyahu or the next Donald Trump or Boris Johnson – all of them nuclear powers – will prevail, before the marginalised masses learn to exercise their collective will in the cause of social justice and a sustainable life.

But nothing of this crisis arises from "human nature," except insofar as human nature has given us freedom, a choice. The crisis arises from specific forms of activity which can be changed. The malleability of human nature has been proven time and again. The dominant forms of activity which are leading us to disaster arose from foregoing forms of activity, not from human nature. Activity theory has the most valuable resources for understanding and transforming this activity because it rests, not on "human needs" or "genes" or "social psychology" or any such fantasy, but on an understanding and self-transformation of human activity alone.

The archetypal activities tabulated in Table 2 below are not mutually exclusive categories, but exemplars of the variety of forms which activities can take. Any given activity may exhibit features of one or more of these archetypes. *All* are "activities," "collaborative projects" or "practices."

Any given activity will exhibit features of one or several of the above archetypes.

TABLE 2   Archetypes of activities

An institution	Object-concept is maintenance or restoration of an existing norm. An effective motive is needed for participation.
A capitalist firm	Object-concept is an effective demand. Wages and profit generally function as effective motives.
A practice	Object-concept and effective motive are provided by societal norms, the situation or internal rewards.
A concept	A practice which has become so integrated into the existing culture that is seen merely as one concept alongside others.
A project	Object-concept is an ideal generally challenging existing norms, and may be a really effective motive for all participants.
A social non-movement	Activity which is as yet unselfconscious but consists of separate actions in which actors are responding to the same situation but not collaborating.
A social movement	The middle phase in the life-cycle of a project after actions begin to be collaborative but before it is institutionalised.
An incoherent activity	Object is incoherent, but manifested in a motif, people participate for mixture of effective motives.
An objectless activity	Activity enjoyed for its own internal rewards which are effective motives.
An individual life-project	Object is emergent and becomes clear only in rear vision mirror.
An episode	Object is to resolve a *perezhivanie* which initiates the episode and restores meaning to life.

Conclusion

In the mid-19th century, newspapers and the postal services, and then telegraph and radio, entered people's lives, and ultimately satellite communication and the internet made events on the world stage part of everyday life. From the 1980s in particular, people became intensely aware of the vast social forces determining events around them, originating from beyond the horizons of the world in which people make choices and control their own fate, intruding into their own lives irresistibly and unpredictably. The idea of "structure versus agency," reflecting this contradiction, originated in the late 19th century, but in the first decades of the present century anxiety about this duality has became manic.

Originally, "agency" referred to the capacity of individuals exercising their free will to control events within their own field of activity and in the wider world, while "structure" referred to necessity arising from social structures which thwarted the intentions of individuals trying to make a difference. Structure limits the choices available to any individual, and produces unintended consequences such that the status quo continuously reasserts itself despite your best efforts. Structures also determine the knowledge, imagination and desires of actors such that they act only as is to be expected of someone in their social position, and the system remains fundamentally secure, merely evolving as if by natural law. This leads to the everyday experience of a small domain within whose borders a person may exercise their "agency," learn how to play the game and get their own way, but only so long as forces outside of this domain do not intrude.

In recent decades social theorists and psychologists have tried to overcome this dichotomy. Giddens (1984) with his theory of structuration has debunked the idea of people being prisoners, so to speak, of ideology arising from the structure. On the whole people are experts on their own situation and make rational choices on that basis. However, people's choices *are* limited by the resources which their social situation provides them. Nonetheless, nowadays people are to a greater or lesser extent also aficionados of the social sciences, and no structure can exert itself with necessity unless it can be assumed that the actors are "sociological dopes." The problem with Giddens' contribution is that to understand the motivations of actors he had recourse only to Freud, Erikson and Goffman. This is quite inadequate. Ole Deier (1999), for example, is one who uses Critical Psychology to overcome the dichotomy of structure and agency, but his work remains on the plane of psychotherapy. Max Horkheimer said long ago:

the question today is to organise investigations stimulated by contemporary philosophical problems in which philosophers, sociologists, economists, historians, and psychologists are brought together in permanent
collaboration to undertake in common that which can be carried out
individually in the laboratory in other fields.

HORKHEIMER 1932, p. 9

Activity Theory already provides the theoretical framework in which such
interdisciplinary work can be carried out, with a substantial community of
researchers engaged in interventions which routinely cross the boundaries
between psychology, sociology and social philosophy. Activity Theory is itself
already a collaborative project.

The efforts of activity theorists we examined earlier to theorise "agency"
resolved themselves into the problem of how a person can change their situation rather than adapt to it. We learnt that it is necessary first of all to reframe
one's suffering as the result of social circumstances which it lies within the
power of a person to change by taking up an activist stance. We learnt that in
order to change the situation it will be necessary to transgress the norms and
rules to which a person is subject. We learnt that a person must have the capacity to work collaboratively with others. However, all these observations remain
within the domain of an individual trying to assert their own free will to obtain
the object of their desire.

The idea of freedom contains within it a trap, a contradiction. In order to be
free you must sacrifice your autonomy to make a binding commitment, with
others, to collaborative projects. *To be free you must give up your individual free
will* so that your will can be *mediated* by a collaborative project. Participation
in a collaborative project entails *critical* activity, not merely uncritical cooperation, so the individual will is not *extinguished* in the object-concept of a
project, but is mediated by it.

Self-evidently, such a commitment contains a danger. More often one is
oppressed by one's comrades and friends than by a stranger or enemy. Making
a commitment to a project, a practice, some institution or activity or social
movement, means that you are vulnerable. This is unavoidable. This is why
I have emphasised collaboration as *critical* participation and why in the section on the ethics of collaboration I have insisted that the liberal character of
the loose ethos prevailing in relations outside every particular project needs to
be defended alongside the imperative for projects to collaborate and solidarise
with one another.

Speaking in terms of "levels," we could say there is a micro-level of interactions between individuals which is the subject matter of psychology and a

macro-level of societal life which is the domain of social theory, economics and so forth, in which individuals are mere straws in the wind. Projects constitute the *meso-level* of human interaction. Anyone participating in a collaborative project, an activity of any kind in fact, has the capacity to strengthen or weaken that project, and amend its object or practical norms. Not alone of course, but actions by individuals bound together in some activity or project *do* make a difference to the work of that project. Meanwhile, a successful project has an impact in the big wide world, and all going well it will outlive any individual participant and the errors and limitations of any individual participant are moderated by the collaboration of many others.

Yes, there is structure on one hand and agency on the other, but activities *mediate* between the two. Structures are nothing other than aggregates of activities and activities are nothing but aggregates of individual actions.

It is not a question of which predominates: agency or structure, but how are structure and agency mediated, and the answer is: by activities.

Social theorists like Bourdieu, Foucault, Althusser and many others aim to *expose* the ideological character of the existing social arrangements, to show how appearances mask underlying and persistent relations of power and domination, how at other times in history things have been quite other than they are now and that the claim that existing arrangements are natural and inevitable are false. People are, it is presumed, prisoners of ideologies which make them believe that this is the way things must be.

But so what? An historical consciousness is necessary for creative and critical activity, but *many* people nowadays believe that an oppressive reality lies behind the appearance of democracy, that the universities as much as the news media are pumping out lies. People are largely, nowadays, already thoroughly disillusioned. Giving them critical theories to expose ideology is no more emancipatory than the American practice of allowing everyone to own a gun. It does not lead to emancipation any more than the assertion of individual liberty leads to human emancipation.

Activity Theory is a powerful theory for the transformation of human life in the interests of social justice and emancipation because it seeks not just to *expose* the truth and *disillusion* people, but to develop effective techniques by means of which people change their own situation and transform the institutions and practices in which they are participating.

Activity theorists see that human beings are what they are in the context of the activities they participate in and are committed to. Human beings isolated from the activities that animate and sustain them are not fully human beings at all. Activity Theory sees subjectivity as located *between* people rather than inside them. Because of this, we see "human nature" as almost infinitely

malleable, and that malleability can be exploited to create dystopian ani-
mal farm worlds, Mad Max worlds of failed states or we can build a world
of democratic socialist sustainable communities. These are open questions
at the moment, and the current conjuncture of geo-politics is increasingly
indeterminate.

Human culture, carried forward in the artefacts we have created and passed
on to later generations via the activities we have invented using them, has a
pervasive influence on everything we are. To be a human being is to acquire
this culture, use it, *modify it* and pass it on to the next generation, by modifying the practices we live by and inventing new projects. The artefacts include
spoken words, signs, tools, the land on which we live and the air we breathe.
Regrettably, our natural inheritance is in danger of being unable to continue
providing the conditions for human life. It has become a matter of urgency to
modify human activities so as to guarantee not only social justice but the very
conditions for human life. We know enough about Nature already to know how
to avoid catastrophe; but what is not yet well understood is how to change
human activity. This is our problem.

We understand that it is the experiences, *perezhivaniya,* through which people pass in the course of following through on their commitments that their
personalities are formed. *Perezhivaniya* reshape a person's life as they confront
situations and deal with them. We understand that in general, if someone is
suffering or engaged in unsustainable practices, then the best thing we can
do is to help them change their situation, rather than medicating them or just
persuading them to act otherwise. The crisis of humanity will not be solved by
persuasion, pharmacology or surgery.

The most important insight that Activity Theory brings to those who want
to change their situation is the concept of "germ cell." Identification of the contradiction or trap or situation or predicament or conflict of motives (all terms
used by activity theorists) is the often the first step in finding a way out of the
situation. For example, the notion of safe-fail exercises that allow a person to
learn by making mistakes without doing damage when they fail expresses the
problem of someone entering a practice without the necessary skill to practice
safely. A safe-fail exercise is a germ cell from which a whole practice can be
reconstructed. The task then is to find that little *aperçu* which encapsulates
and transcends the trap. Having defined the germ cell, we still have to discover
its shape, name it, and elaborate its internal contradictions. The concept of
"water molecule" was known long before the shape of the H_2O molecule was
determined.

Sometimes this trap is not immediately obvious but can only be revealed
by extensive analysis. It may be enough to identify the simplest instance of

the problematic phenomenon you are facing, an instance which does not arise from the application of some theory of the phenomenon, but is given to natural cognition. Marx's identification of the commodity as the unit of value in a market economy is the well-known example here. A great deal of dialectical reconstruction was still needed once the germ cell had been identified for the contradictions of capitalist production to be fully revealed through the disclosure of a *series* of germ cells.

Sometimes the phenomenon can be grasped not as a simple action, as such, but in terms of a paradigmatic artefact or tool which is mediating the activity. For example, Marx took unpaid labour as the germ cell of surplus value, reframing the problem of the origins of profit to figuring out how the capitalist expropriated unpaid labour.

Many a time has a problem arising in the labour process been resolved by the introduction of a new tool which forces the operation of a new norm of labour, overcoming difficult problems. Equally, an inappropriate tool or norm or division of labour has proved to be the site of problematic contradictions.

The problem of identifying the unit or germ cell is not one which can be solved by any recipe. It requires analysis. It was possible for Vygotsky to determine word meaning as the germ cell of the intellect only by close examination of the interlocking development of speech in young children – the observation of pre-intellectual speech and pre-verbal intelligence, and their subsequent merging in intellectual speech.

In analysing a problematic phenomenon, the germ cell is something *discovered* by analysis, not invented. Nonetheless, different people will determine different germ cells from the same phenomenon. For example, for Marx the germ cell of bourgeois society is commodity exchange, for Foucault it is a prison cell. The germ cell reflects both how each writer saw bourgeois society and the ultimately the kind of activity they proposed to respond to the oppressive relations it produces. So looking from different standpoints, different germ cells are discovered.

But *solutions* to problems can also be *given* the form of germ cells. "Sustainable mobility" was not something Engeström's team found in the home care system in Finland, it expressed the *object* of the system which was as yet not satisfactorily conceptualised. But the object-concept clearly expressed the task: to find the simplest possible safe-fail exercise which could be the basis for achieving sustainable mobility. In this case, Engeström found that this exercise *already existed*. Once the problem was clearly posed, the staff themselves could identify it. In other cases, a brand new practice might be introduced, as was the case with the purple prescribing pen given to junior doctors in Gillespie's project.

Sometimes, it is not just a question of *improving* a practice through identifying the germ cell of its object concept, but of identifying points of failure, contradictions, and here again germ cells can be discovered by analysis, the predicaments or situations which generate failures. The conflicting processes which are generating conflict can then be disassembled and new arrangements made.

Sometimes, however, the problem is to transform a harmful activity and the issue is the introduction of a new germ cell which has the capacity to grow and proliferate in the activity and transform it by displacing a former practice. For a germ cell to grow it must be planted in activity which is appropriate to the object of activity; solidarity is meaningful only in the struggle for justice.

Again, in any concrete activity, if there is a need for the activity to be transformed, this germ cell probably already exists. It needs to be discovered and fostered. Sometimes, a problem can only be solved by building an entirely new practice from its germ cell up, as has been the case with the 5th Dimension after-school programs.

Foremost in my mind here though is *solidarity*. This is not a new concept or a new practice. The word itself entered the English language, as I have said, with the founding of the first working class political party, the National Charter Association, and was written into the rules of the International Workingmen's Association in 1864. It remains to this day the most pressing need for everyone active in the struggle for social justice, human emancipation and a sustainable society. On the Left in the US the term "intersectionality" has come into usage. This somewhat misunderstands the situation because its premise is defining people by their contingent attributes, taking it for granted that it is on this basis, so-called identity, that people are mobilised. This is not productive. Whoever is active, if their cause is just, must be offered solidarity. The important aspect of solidarity is not that I see someone else, or even that I help them, but that I help them in the way that they ask me to, not according to my own opinion. As I said above, the contradiction entailed in human emancipation is that in order gain freedom one must give up one's autonomy by making commitments to others in the cause of social justice. The endless pursuit of individual autonomy is fruitless. It is the same with our relation to Nature: we must act according to Nature's demands in order to benefit from Nature.

In general, activity theorists do not seek to impose new systems or design processes with sweeping reforms. I find that activity theorists generally look for the small changes that ideally have a kind of viral capability. But I don't believe that activity theorists are "reformists" for this; the right tweaks can be utterly transformative. And the big changes will not be made by activity theorists, they will be made by other people, masses of people, and it is our business to be there with them, making these changes.

I have devoted a substantial portion, one-sixth, of this book to collaborative ethics. For all the talk about "agency" no activity theorist other than this author has ever written a line on this topic so far as I know. And yet, if attaining freedom means giving up one's autonomy by entering into commitments to collaborate with others, what could be more important than the obligations of acting in collaboration with others?

References

Bal, A. (2021). Video interview: https://www.youtube.com/watch?v=DEh3s7u3Xo8.

Banks, M., de Neergaard, E. & Nissen, M. (2021). *Aesthetic Motifs and the Materiality of Motives.*

Bayat, A. (2009). *Life as Politics, How Ordinary People Change the Middle East.* Amsterdam, Amsterdam University Press.

Beaton, L. (1982). The importance of women's paid labour: Women at work in World War II, in *Worth Her Salt*, ed. M. Bevege, M. James, C. Shute, Hale & Ironmonger.

Beauvoir, S. de (1949/1953). *The Second Sex.* Penguin.

Benhabib, S. (1996). 'Towards a Deliberative Model of Democratic Legitimacy', in *Democracy and Difference. Contesting the Boundaries of the Political.* Princeton NJ: Princeton University Press.

Benhabib, S. (2006). *Another Cosmopolitanism.* New York NY: Oxford University Press.

Bishop, A.J. (1988). The Interactions of Mathematics Education with Culture, *Cultural Dynamics v. 1*, Sage.

Blunden, A. (2010). *An Interdisciplinary Theory of Activity*, Brill.

Blunden, A. (2011). *Vygotsky's Theory of Child Development*, lecture delivered at Witwatersrand University, Johannesburg. ethicalpolitics.org.

Blunden, A. (2012). *Concepts. A critical Approach.* Brill.

Blunden, A. and Arnold, M. (2014). The Formation of the Concept of "Collaborative Learning Space" in *Collaborative Projects. An Interdisciplinary Study.* Brill.

Blunden, A. (2014). (Ed.) *Collaborative Projects. An Interdisciplinary Study.* Brill.

Blunden, A. (2015). *Leontyev's Activity Theory and Social Theory.* ethicalpolitics.org.

Blunden, A. (2016a). *The Origins of Collective Decision Making*, Brill.

Blunden, A. (2016b). Translating *perezhivanie* into English, *Mind, Culture and Activity, 23*(4).

Blunden, A. (2017). Spinoza in the history of Cultural Psychology and Activity Theory. *Mind Culture and Activity 25*(4).

Blunden, A. (2019). *Hegel for Social Movements.* Brill.

Blunden, A. (2021). The unit of analysis in Hegel, Marx and Vygotsky, in *Hegel, Marx and Vygotsky. Essays in Social Philosophy.* Brill.

Blunden, A. (2021a). *Agency, in Hegel, Marx and Vygotsky. Essays in Social Philosophy.* Brill.

Blunden, A. (2021b). Fedor Vasilyuk's Psychology of Life-projects. *Hegel, Marx & Vygotsky. Essay on Social Philosophy*, Brill.

Blunden, A. (2021c). Tool and Sign in Vygotsky's Development. *Hegel, Marx & Vygotsky. Essay on Social Philosophy*, Brill.

Blunden, A. & Arnold, M.V. (2014). Formation of the Concept of "Collaborative Learning Space." In *Collaborative Projects. An Interdisciplinary Study*, Brill.

Bourdieu, P. (1984). *Distinctions. A Social Critique of the Judgment of Taste*. translated by Richard Nice. Harvard University Press.

Bourbaki, N. (1948/1950). "The Architecture of Mathematics." *American Mathematical Monthly*. *57* (4): 221–32.

Bruner, J. (1990). *Acts of Meaning*, Cambridge MA: Harvard University Press.

Colapietro, V.M. (1988). *Peirce's Approach to the Self: A Semiotic Perspective on Human Subjectivity*, SUNY Press.

Cole, M., V. Gordon & Blanton, W. (2014). Seeking to combat educational inequality: The 5th Dimension, in *Collaborative Projects An Interdisciplinary Study*, ed. Andy Blunden. Brill.

Daiute, C. & Lightfoot, C. (2004). *Narrative Analysis. Studying the Development of Individuals in Society*. Sage.

Daneshfar, S., Veresov, N, Turner, M. (2022). Private Speech of Multilingual English Learners: A Genetical/Developmental Approach, Chapter 3 in *Inner Speech, Culture & Education*, P. Fossa (ed.). Springer.

Davydov, V.V. (1990). Soviet Studies in Mathematics Education Volume 2. Types of Generalisation in Instruction: Logical and Psychological Problems in the Structuring of School Curricula, trans. Joan Teller. National Council of Teachers of Mathematics, Reston Virginia.

De Smet, B. (2015). *A Dialectical Pedagogy of Revolt*. Gramsci, Vygotsky, and the Egyptian Revolution, Brill.

De Smet, B. (2020). Interview https://www.youtube.com/watch?v=TJCX6d4Uoik.

Dornan, T. (2021). *On the history of medical education told through his own lived experience*. Video interview, https://www.youtube.com/watch?v=6fEoZpO2nE.

Dreier, O. (1999). Personal Trajectories of Participation across Contexts of Social Practice. Outlines. *Critical Practice Studies* 1(1).

Edwards, A. (2017). Revealing relational work. In A. Edwards (Ed.), *Working Relationally in and across Practices: Cultural-Historical Approaches to Collaboration* (pp. 1–21). Cambridge University Press.

Edwards, A. (2020). Agency, common knowledge and motive orientation: Working with insights from Hedegaard in research on provision for vulnerable children and young people. *Learning, Culture and Social Interaction, 26*.

Engels, F. (1883/1987). Dialectics. *MECW, vol. 25*. p. 356. New York, NY: International Publishers.

Engeström, Y. (1987/2015). *Learning by Expanding. Second Edition*. Cambridge University Press.

Engeström, Y. (2008). *The future of Activity Theory. A rough draft*. Keynote Lecture at the ISCAR Conference, Sept. 8–13, 2008.

Engeström, Y., Nummijoki, J. & Sannino, A. (2012). Embodied Germ Cell at Work: Building an Expansive Concept of Physical Mobility in Home Care. *Mind, Culture, and Activity.*

Engeström, Y. (n.d.). *The Activity System.* http://www.edu.helsinki.fi/activity/pages /CHATANDDWR/activitysystem/ .

Engeström, Y. (2020). Ascending from the Abstract to the Concrete as a Principle of Expansive Learning, *Psychological Science and Education 25*(5).

Engeström & Sannino, A. (2016). Expansive learning on the move: insights from ongoing research, in *Journal for the Study of Education and Development,* 39(3). Taylor & Francis.

Engeström & Sannino, A. (2021). From mediated actions to heterogeneous coalitions: four generations of activity-theoretical studies of work and learning, in *Mind, Culture, and Activity,* 28(1). Taylor & Francis.

Fraser, N. and Honneth, A. (2003). Redistribution or Recognition? A political-philosophical exchange, Verso.

Gajdamaschko, N. (2020). https://www.youtube.com/watch?v=76JjZJMRDzE.

Giddens, A. (1984). *The Constitution of Society.* The University of California Press.

Gillespie, H., McCrystal, E., Reid, Conn, R., Kennedy N. & Dornan, T. (2021). The pen is mightier than the sword. Reinstating patient care as the object of prescribing education, *Medical Teacher,* v. 43.

Goffman, E. (1974). *Frame analysis: An Essay on the Organisation of Experience.*

Gramsci, A. (1971). *Selections from the Prison Notebooks,* trans. Hoare, Q. & G.N. Smith. New York, 1 International Publishers.

Gutiérrez, K.D., Becker, B.L.C., Espinoza, M.L., Cortes, K.L., Cortez, A., Lizárraga, J.R., Rivero, E., Villegas, K., & Yin, P. (2019). Youth as historical actors in the production of possible futures. *Mind, Culture, and Activity, 26*(4), 291–308.

Habermas, J., (1992). *Moral Consciousness and Communicative Action,* Cambridge, MA: M.I.T. Press.

Habermas, J., (2001). The Inclusion of the Other. Studies in Political Theory, Cambridge MA: M.I.T. Press.

Hedegaard, M. (2009). Children's Development from a Cultural–Historical Approach: Children's Activity in Everyday Local Settings as Foundation for Their Development. *Mind, Culture and Activity (16).*

Hedegaard M. (2020). Ascending from the Abstract to the Concrete in School Teaching – the double Move between Theoretical Concepts and Children's Concepts, *Psychological Science and Education 25*(5),. 44–57.

Hegel, G.W.F. (1821). *The Philosophy of Right.*

Heller, A. (1986). *Beyond Justice,* Oxford: Blackwell.

Heller, A. (1988). *General Ethics,* Oxford: Blackwell.

Holland, D., Skinner. D., Lachicotte, W. & Cain, C. (1998). *Identity and Agency in Cultural Worlds*. London, UK: Harvard University Press.

Hopwood, N. (2022). Agency in cultural-historical activity theory: strengthening commitment to social transformation. *Mind, Culture and Activity*.

Hopwood, N., Pointon, K., Dadich, A., Moraby, K. & Elliot, C. (2022). Forward anchoring in transformative agency: How parents of children with complex feeding difficulties transcend the status quo. *Learning, Culture and Social Interaction 33*. Elsevier.

Horkheimer, M. (1932). *History and Psychology, in Between Philosophy and Social Science*, ed., G F Hunter.

Horton, M. (2003). *The Myles Horton Reader. Education for Social Change*. Ed. Dale Jacobs. Knoxville, TE: University of Tennessee Press.

IWMA (1864). Provisional Rules of the Association. *The General Council of the First International 1864–1868. The London Conference 1865. Minutes.*

Jamison, A. & Eyerman, R. (1991). *Social Movements. A Cognitive Approach*, University Park, Pennsylvania, Pennsylvania State University Press.

Kant, I. (1780). The Metaphysic of Elements of Ethics, marxists.org.

Kant, I. (1785). General Introduction to the Metaphysic of Morals, marxists.org.

Kautsky, K. (1892). *The Class Struggle*. (Erfurt Program).

Kautsky, K. (1902). Draft of the Programme of the Austrian Social Democratic Party, *Neue Zeit, XX*, I, No. 3.

King, C.A., Griffin, P., Diaz, S. & Cole, A. (1989). A Model Systems Approach to Reading Instruction and the Diagnosis of Reading Disabilities, *LCHC Bulletin*.

Kinston R., McCarville N., & Hassell A. (2019). The role of purple pens in learning to prescribe. *Clin. Teach. 16*(6).

Koski-Jännes, A. (1999). From addiction to self-governance. In *Perspectives on Activity Theory*. Engeström, Y., Miettinen, R., & Punamäki, R. (Eds.) New York: Cambridge University Press, 1999, pp. 435–443.

Kozulin, A. (1991). The Psychology of Experiencing: A Russian view, *Journal of Humanistic Psychology*, Vol., 31 No. 3, 1991, 14–19.

Krinsky, J. & Blunden, A. (in press). Social Movements as Phases in the Life cycle of Collaborative Projects: A Cultural-Historical Approach, *Social Movement Studies*.

Lenin, V.I. (1902). What is to be Done? Burning questions of our movement. *LCW, v. 5*. Progress Publishers.

Leontyev, A.A. (2006). "'Units' and Levels of Activity," *Journal of Russian and East European Psychology*, vol. 44, no. 3: 30–46, M.E. Sharpe.

Leontyev, A.N. (1978). *Activity, Consciousness, and Personality*. Prentice Hall.

Liang, R., Dornan, T. & Nestel, D. (2019). Why do women leave surgical training? A qualitative and feminist study. *The Lancet*, vol 393.

Liberali, F. & Lemos, M. (2021). Video interview: https://www.youtube.com/watch?v=CqjIWX85YGM.

Lingard, L., McDougall, A., Levstik, M., Chandok, N., M. Spafford & Shryer. C., (2012). Representing complexity well: a story about teamwork, with implications for how we teach collaboration. *Medical Education* v. 46.

Luria, A.R. (1932). *The Nature of Human Conflicts: Or Emotion, Conflict and Will*. New York: Liveright.

Luria, A.R. (1968). *The Mind of a Mnemonist. A Little Book about a Vast Memory*. Foreword by Jerome Bruner. Harvard University Press.

Luria, A.R. (1972). *The Man with a Shattered World. The History of a Brain Wound* Foreword by Oliver Sacks. Harvard University Press.

MacIntyre, A. (1981). *After Virtue*. University of Notre Dame Press.

Maeckelbergh, M. (2009). *The Will and the Many. How the Alterglobalisation Movement Is Changing the Face of Democracy*. London, UK: Pluto Press.

Manidis, M. & Scheeres, H. (2012). Towards Understanding Workplace Learning Through Theorising Practice: At Work in Hospital Emergency Departments, in *Practice, Learning and Change*, Springer.

Marx, K. (1843). *Critique of Hegel's Philosophy of Right. Introduction*. Ed. Joseph O'Malley. Cambridge, uk: Cambridge University Press.

Marx, K. (1845). The German Ideology. *MECW vol. 5*. New York: International Publishers.

Marx, K. (1858/1973). *Grundrisse*. Penguin.

Marx, K. (1864). General Rules of the International Workingmen's Association. *MECW, v. 20*, p. 14ff.

Marx, K. (1867). Capital. *MECW, v. 35*. New York: International Publishers.

Marx, K. (1881/1989). Marginal Notes on Adolph Wagner, in *MECW vol. 24*, 531–559. New York: International Publishers.

Meshcheryakov, A. (1974/2009). *Awakening to Life. On the Education of Deaf-Blind Children in the Soviet Union*. MIA Press.

Moscovici, S. & Doise, W. (1994). *Conflict and Consensus: a General Theory of Collective Decisions*. Sage.

Piaget, J. (1950). *Genetic Epistemology*.

Polkinghorne, D. (1988). *Narrative Knowing and the Human Sciences*. Albany: State University of New York Press.

Popovic, S. (2015). *Blueprint for Revolution. How to Use Rice Pudding, Lego Men, and other Non-violent Techniques to Galvanise Communities, Overthrow Dictators, or Simply Change the World*. Spiegel & Grau.

Rezvani, S. (2022). *Solidarity in Critical Situation: The Case Study of "Green Research in Education Group" (GRiEG)*. MSc Thesis at the University of Manchester.

Rawls, J. (1993). *Political Liberalism*, New York: Columbia University Press.

Russell, B. & Whitehead, R.N. (1913/1963). *Principia Mathematica*. Cambridge University Press.

Ricœur, P. (1984). *Time and Narrative. Vol. 1*. Chicago: University of Chicago Press.

Sannino, A. (2020). Transformative agency as warping: how collectives accomplish change amidst uncertainty, *Pedagogy, Culture & Society*, Routledge, *30*(1), 9–33.

Sannino, A. (2020). Enacting the utopia of eradicating homelessness: Toward a new generation of activity-theoretical studies of learning. *Studies in Continuing Education, 42*(2), 163–179.

Sen, A. (1999). *Development as Freedom*, Oxford University Press.

Sen, A. & Drèze, J. (2002). *Development and Participation*. Oxford Uni. Press.

Sen, A. (2002a). *Rationality and Freedom*, Harvard University Press.

Smith S.E., Tallentire V.R., Cameron H.S., Wood S.M. (2013). The effects of contributing to patient care on medical students' workplace learning. *Med Educ.* 47(12):1184–1196.

Stetsenko, A. (2019). Radical-transformative agency: Continuities and contrasts with relational agency and implications for education. *Frontiers in Education, 4*.

Swerdlow, A. (1993). Women Strike for Peace: Traditional Motherhood and Radical Politics in the 1960s.

Vasilyuk, F. (1984). *The Psychology of* Perezhivanie. Progress Publishers.

Vianna, E. (2022). Video interview https://www.youtube.com/watch?v=1-b_zImE3Uo.

Vianna, E., & Stetsenko, A. (2014). Research with a transformative activist agenda: Creating the future through education for social change. *Teachers College Record, 116*(14), 575–602.

Vygotsky, L.S., (1927/1997) 'The Historical Meaning of the Crisis in Psychology: A Methodological Investigation', *Collected Works*, Volume 3, New York: Plenum Press, p. 233–343.

Vygotsky, L.S. (1930). The Instrumental Method in Psychology, *LSV CW, v. 3*, pp. 85–90.

Vygotsky, L.S. (1930a). Mind, Consciousness. the Unconscious, *LSV CW, v. 3*, pp. 109–122.

Vygotsky, L.S. (1931a). Self-control, *LSV CW, v. 4*, pp. 207–220.

Vygotsky, L.S. (1934). Thinking and Speech, *LSV CW, v. 1* .

Vygotsky, L.S. (1934a/1994). The problem of the environment. In *The Vygotsky Reader*, 338–354, ed. Rene van der Veer and Jaan Valsiner, Blackwell.

Wartofsky, M.W. (1973). *Models*. Dodrecht: D. Reidel.

Williams, J. (2016). Becoming un-Disciplined with Science and Mathematics. Keynote speech, *Proceedings of the Deakin STEM Education Conference 2016*.

Worthen, H. (2011). CHAT Learning Theory for Labor Educators: Work Process Knowledge, Activity Theory, and Communities of Practice, *Labor Studies Journal XX* (X) 1–7, Sage.

Worthen, H. (2014). *What Did You Learn at Work Today: Forbidden Lessons of Labor Education*, Hardball Press: Brooklyn, NY.

Worthen, H. & Berry, J. (2021). *Power Despite Precarity. Strategies for the Contingent Faculty Movement in Higher Education*, Pluto 2021.

Index

www.ingramcontent.com/pod-product-compliance
Lightning Source LLC
Chambersburg PA
CBHW070103030426
42335CB00016B/1993